First World War

and Army of Occupation

War Diary

France, Belgium and Germany

58 DIVISION
174 Infantry Brigade
London Regiment
2/6 Battalion
1 October 1915 - 31 January 1918

WO95/3005/5

The Naval & Military Press Ltd
www.nmarchive.com
Published in association with The National Archives

Published by

The Naval & Military Press Ltd

Unit 10 Ridgewood Industrial Park,

Uckfield, East Sussex,

TN22 5QE England

Tel: +44 (0) 1825 749494

www.naval-military-press.com

www.nmarchive.com

This diary has been reprinted in facsimile from the original. Any imperfections are inevitably reproduced and the quality may fall short of modern type and cartographic standards.

Contents

Document type	Place/Title	Date From	Date To
Heading	WO95/3005/5		
Heading	2/6 London May 1917		
Miscellaneous	Subject		
Miscellaneous	Bovis		
War Diary	Sutton Veny	25/01/1917	25/01/1917
War Diary	Havre	26/01/1917	27/01/1917
War Diary	Buire-Au-Bois	28/01/1917	29/01/1917
War Diary	Trenches	01/02/1917	01/02/1917
War Diary	St. Amand	03/02/1917	06/02/1917
War Diary	Trenches Y1 Sector	07/02/1917	07/02/1917
War Diary	Bienvillers	08/02/1917	08/02/1917
War Diary	Trenches Y.1	10/02/1917	10/02/1917
War Diary	Souastre	14/02/1917	15/02/1917
War Diary	Humbercamps	21/02/1917	24/02/1917
War Diary	Bailleulmont	28/02/1917	28/02/1917
War Diary	Trenches	04/03/1917	25/03/1917
War Diary	Boiry-St-Rictrude	27/03/1917	27/03/1917
War Diary	Bienvillers-Au-Bois	28/03/1917	28/03/1917
War Diary	Lucheux	29/03/1917	29/03/1917
War Diary	Fortel	01/04/1917	01/04/1917
War Diary	Caumont	02/04/1917	02/04/1917
War Diary	Mailly-Maillet	04/04/1917	04/04/1917
War Diary	Bihucourt	07/04/1917	07/04/1917
Heading	War Diary of 2/6th Bn Lan. Regt. May		
War Diary	S Of Mory	15/05/1917	15/05/1917
War Diary	W Of Vraucourt	16/05/1917	16/05/1917
War Diary	Bullecourt	18/05/1917	21/05/1917
War Diary	Ecoust	21/05/1917	21/05/1917
War Diary	Mory	22/05/1917	24/05/1917
Miscellaneous	174th Inf. Brigade	13/05/1917	13/05/1917
Miscellaneous	V Corps (1)	14/05/1917	14/05/1917
Miscellaneous	5th. London Regt.	15/05/1917	15/05/1917
Operation(al) Order(s)	174th Infantry Brigade Order No.18	15/05/1917	15/05/1917
Operation(al) Order(s)	174th. Inf. Brigade Order No.19	17/05/1917	17/05/1917
Miscellaneous			
Operation(al) Order(s)	174th. Inf. Brigade Order No.20	18/05/1917	18/05/1917
Miscellaneous	O/c 2/6 Bn London Regt.	19/05/1917	19/05/1917
Miscellaneous	O/c 2/6 London	19/05/1917	19/05/1917
Miscellaneous	O/c 2/6 Bn London Regt	19/05/1917	19/05/1917
Miscellaneous	C Form Messages And Signals		
Miscellaneous			
Miscellaneous	C Form Messages And Signals		
Miscellaneous			
Miscellaneous	C Form Messages And Signals		
Miscellaneous			
Miscellaneous	174th Infantry Brigade-Instructions No.1 For Forthcoming Enterprise	19/05/1917	19/05/1917
Miscellaneous	To C.O.B.		
Miscellaneous	A Form Messages And Signals		
Operation(al) Order(s)	174th Inf Bde. Order No. 22		

Miscellaneous	A Form Messages And Signals		
Heading	O.C.2/6th Bn.		
Miscellaneous	A Form Messages And Signals		
Miscellaneous	C.O.B		
Miscellaneous	A Form Messages And Signals		
Miscellaneous	Patrol Report	20/05/1917	20/05/1917
Miscellaneous	O.C.B Coy	20/05/1917	20/05/1917
Miscellaneous	C Form Messages And Signals		
Miscellaneous			
Miscellaneous	C Form Messages And Signals		
Miscellaneous	Awaiting Disposal		
Miscellaneous	C Form Messages And Signals		
Miscellaneous	Messages And Signals		
Miscellaneous	COB		
Miscellaneous	C Form Messages And Signals		
Operation(al) Order(s)	174th. Infantry Brigade Order No.21	20/05/1917	20/05/1917
Miscellaneous	Amendment No.1 To 174th Inf. Brigade Order No.21	20/05/1917	20/05/1917
Miscellaneous	A Form Messages And Signals		
Miscellaneous	B Form Messages And Signals		
Miscellaneous	A Form Messages And Signals		
Miscellaneous	To O.C 2/6 L.R.	21/05/1917	21/05/1917
Miscellaneous		19/05/1917	19/05/1917
Miscellaneous	Prove. Order Stand Food		
Miscellaneous	To C.O.B.	21/05/1917	21/05/1917
Miscellaneous	C Form Messages And Signals		
Miscellaneous	Messages And Signals		
Miscellaneous	174th Infantry Brigade	21/05/1917	21/05/1917
Diagram etc			
Miscellaneous	Report On The Attack Made On Bovis Trench By The 2/6th Battn. London Regt. On The 21st May 1917	27/03/1917	27/03/1917
Operation(al) Order(s)	2/6th London Regt. Order No.1	29/05/1917	29/05/1917
Miscellaneous	Right Front Company		
Miscellaneous	Left Front Company		
Miscellaneous	Right Support Company		
Miscellaneous	Left Support Company		
Map	Bullecourt Defences		
Map	Map		
Miscellaneous	O.C. D Coys		
Miscellaneous	To Cob Maps		
Map	Bullecourt		
Miscellaneous	O.C. Coy	21/05/1917	21/05/1917
Map	Map		
Heading	2/6th London Regt June 1917		
Miscellaneous	Subject		
Heading	War Diary of 2/6th London Regt From 290517 To 300617		
War Diary		29/05/1917	28/06/1917
Map	Map		
Operation(al) Order(s)	2/6th Bn. London Regt. Order No.2	03/06/1917	03/06/1917
Miscellaneous	Headquarters 174th Infantry Brigade	04/06/1917	04/06/1917
Operation(al) Order(s)	Curl Operation Order No.11	13/06/1917	13/06/1917
Operation(al) Order(s)	2/7th Bn Operation Order No.24	13/06/1917	13/06/1917
Miscellaneous	A Form Messages And Signals		
Operation(al) Order(s)	2/6th London Regt.-Order No.3	14/06/1917	14/06/1917
Miscellaneous			
Miscellaneous	A Form Messages And Signals		

Miscellaneous	Messages And Signals		
Miscellaneous	A Form Messages And Signals		
Operation(al) Order(s)	2/6th Bn. London Regt. Order No.4	22/06/1917	22/06/1917
Miscellaneous	March Table To Accompany 2/6th London Regt Order No.4		
Map	Map		
Miscellaneous	T-U 1/10,000		
Map	Map		
Miscellaneous	Administrative Instructions Issued In Conjunction With 21st Battalion Manchester Regiment Operation Orders No. 62&63	21/06/1917	21/06/1917
Operation(al) Order(s)	Operation Orders No.63 By Lieut Colonel C.E.N. Lomax, M.C.	21/06/1917	21/06/1917
Operation(al) Order(s)	Operation Orders No.62 By Lieut Col. C.E.N. Lomax, M.C.	21/06/1917	21/06/1917
Miscellaneous	O.C. 2/6th London Regt.	22/06/1917	22/06/1917
Heading	2/6th London Regt July 1917		
Miscellaneous	Subject		
Heading	War Diary of 2/6th London Regt 1/7/17 To 31/7/17		
War Diary	Courcelles	01/07/1917	30/07/1917
Operation(al) Order(s)	2/6th London Regt. Order No.5	06/07/1917	06/07/1917
Operation(al) Order(s)	Order No.6 2/6th Bn. The London Regt.	06/07/1917	06/07/1917
Operation(al) Order(s)	Order No.7 2/6th Bn. The London Regt.	07/07/1917	07/07/1917
Map	Map		
Operation(al) Order(s)	Operation Order No.8 2/6th Bn. London Regiment	08/07/1917	08/07/1917
Map	Map		
Diagram etc	Sketch Showing Position Of "A" Coy		
Diagram etc	Sketch Of C. Coys Frontage		
Operation(al) Order(s)	Order No.9 (Ref. Map Sheet 57c Trenches Map)	09/07/1917	09/07/1917
Map	Map		
Diagram etc	Rough Plan Of Trench Occupied By B Coy 2/6		
Miscellaneous	Messages And Signals		
Operation(al) Order(s)	Order No.10 (Ref Map Sheet 57c SE Trenches Map)	14/07/1917	14/07/1917
Operation(al) Order(s)	Order No.11 2/6 London Regt.	16/07/1917	16/07/1917
Operation(al) Order(s)	Order No.12 2/6th Bn. The London Regt Ref. Map. 57 C SE And Trenches Map	18/07/1917	18/07/1917
Operation(al) Order(s)	Order No.13 (ref. 57c SE And Trench Map)	20/07/1917	20/07/1917
Miscellaneous			
Operation(al) Order(s)	Order No.14 (Ref. 57c SE And Trench Map)	21/07/1917	21/07/1917
Operation(al) Order(s)	Order No.15 (Ref. 57c SE & Trench Map.)	22/07/1917	22/07/1917
Operation(al) Order(s)	Operation Order No.16 2/6th Bn The London Regt.	27/07/1917	27/07/1917
Miscellaneous	3rd Division	25/07/1917	25/07/1917
Operation(al) Order(s)	Operation Order No. 17 2/6th Bn. The London Regt.	28/07/1917	28/07/1917
Map	Map		
Heading	2/6th London Regt August 1917		
Miscellaneous	Subject		
War Diary	Berneville	10/08/1917	31/08/1917
Operation(al) Order(s)	Operation Order No. 19 2/6th Battalion. London Regiment	23/08/1917	23/08/1917
Miscellaneous	Operation Order No. 19 2/6th Battalion. London Regiment	23/08/1917	23/08/1917
Miscellaneous	5th London Regt.	24/08/1917	24/08/1917
Miscellaneous	C Form (Original) Messages And Signals		
Operation(al) Order(s)	Administrative Instructions In Connection With 174th Infantry Brigade Operation Order No.39	27/08/1917	27/08/1917

Miscellaneous	Movement Table To Accompany 174th Inf. Brigade Order No.39		
Miscellaneous	A Form Messages And Signals		
Miscellaneous	Messages And Signals		
Operation(al) Order(s)	174th Inf. Brigade Operation Order No.39	27/08/1917	27/08/1917
Miscellaneous	Amendments to 174th Inf. Bde Order No.39	28/08/1917	28/08/1917
Heading	2/6 London Rgt September 1917		
Miscellaneous	Subject		
War Diary	Yser Canal Bank	01/09/1917	01/09/1917
War Diary	Alberta	02/09/1917	05/09/1917
War Diary	Canal Bank	06/09/1917	06/09/1917
War Diary	Reigersburg	08/09/1917	11/09/1917
War Diary	Dambre	12/09/1917	18/09/1917
War Diary	Reigersburg	19/09/1917	20/09/1917
War Diary	HQ. Alberta Springfield Hibou Alberta	20/09/1917	21/09/1917
War Diary	Reigersburg	22/09/1917	23/09/1917
War Diary	Brake Camp	24/09/1917	27/09/1917
War Diary	Audenfort	28/09/1917	30/09/1917
Operation(al) Order(s)	Order No.21		
Miscellaneous	Warning Order	05/09/1917	05/09/1917
Miscellaneous	O.C. All Coys	05/09/1917	05/09/1917
Miscellaneous	6th London Regt Raid	06/09/1917	06/09/1917
Miscellaneous	Headquarters 174th Infantry Brigade	08/09/1917	08/09/1917
Miscellaneous	6th London Regt.	17/09/1917	17/09/1917
Miscellaneous	A Form Messages And Signals		
Miscellaneous	Headquarters 174th Inf Bde	17/09/1917	17/09/1917
Miscellaneous			
Map	Map		
Miscellaneous		18/09/1917	18/09/1917
Operation(al) Order(s)	13 Company E Battalion Tank Corps Order No.3	18/09/1917	18/09/1917
Operation(al) Order(s)	Order No.22 2/6th Bn. London Regt.	18/09/1917	18/09/1917
Miscellaneous	Administrative Instructions In Connection With Order No. A		
Miscellaneous	Administrative Instructions No. 2 In Connection With Operation Order No. A	19/09/1917	19/09/1917
Miscellaneous	Instructions for operations Appendix 10	19/09/1917	19/09/1917
Miscellaneous	Notes As To Tanks		
Miscellaneous	Operation Report	22/09/1917	22/09/1917
Miscellaneous	Report Of Operations 20th To 22nd Sept "B" Company	24/09/1917	24/09/1917
Miscellaneous	Report On Recent Operations		
Miscellaneous	Report Of Attack On And Occupation Of Blue Line 20/21st Sept		
Operation(al) Order(s)	Operation Order No.23 2/6th Bn. The London Regiment	26/09/1917	26/09/1917
Miscellaneous	Report On Operations Of The 20th, 31st & 22nd September 1917		
Miscellaneous	Report No.2 On Raid On Blunt Salient		
Map	Map		
Heading	2/6 London October 1917		
Miscellaneous	7th Inf Bde, 2nd Battn The S. Lancashire Rt War Diary Jan-Sept, 1915		
War Diary	Audenfort	01/10/1915	20/10/1915
War Diary	Poperinghe	20/10/1915	23/10/1915
War Diary	Siege Camp	24/10/1915	24/10/1915
War Diary	Canal Bank	25/10/1915	25/10/1915
War Diary	Kempton Park	26/10/1915	27/10/1915

War Diary	Kempton Park and Line	28/10/1915	30/10/1915
War Diary	Siege Camp	31/10/1915	31/10/1915
Miscellaneous	Questions To Ask Divisions Engaged In Recent Battles	12/10/1917	12/10/1917
Miscellaneous	58th Divn. G.S. 1149	12/10/1917	12/10/1917
Miscellaneous	Headquarters 174th Infantry Brigade	14/10/1917	14/10/1917
Miscellaneous	G.S.1149	14/10/1914	14/10/1914
Operation(al) Order(s)	2/6th Bn. London Regt. Order No.24	23/10/1917	23/10/1917
Map	Map		
Miscellaneous	Message Form		
Map	Map		
Miscellaneous	Message Form		
Operation(al) Order(s)	Order No.25 2/6th Bn London Regt	25/10/1917	25/10/1917
Miscellaneous	O.C. Details 2/6th Bn.	26/10/1917	26/10/1917
Miscellaneous	Reference Operation Order	28/10/1917	28/10/1917
Operation(al) Order(s)	Operation Order No.27 By Lt Col CB D.S.O.	28/10/1917	28/10/1917
Miscellaneous	O.C. A Coy		
Operation(al) Order(s)	Operation Order	30/10/1917	30/10/1917
War Diary	Siege Camp	01/11/1917	06/11/1917
War Diary	Kempton Park	06/11/1917	10/11/1917
War Diary	In The Line	10/11/1917	12/11/1917
War Diary	Canal Bank	12/11/1917	13/11/1917
War Diary	Canal Bank Brake Camp	14/11/1917	14/11/1917
War Diary	Proven Area	15/11/1917	17/11/1917
War Diary	Wylder	17/11/1917	25/11/1917
War Diary	Proven Area	25/11/1917	25/11/1917
War Diary	Coulemby	26/11/1917	26/11/1917
War Diary	Quesques	27/11/1917	30/11/1917
Operation(al) Order(s)	Order No.29 2/6th Bn. The London Regt	06/11/1917	06/11/1917
Operation(al) Order(s)	A Coy Move To Pheasant Trench 2/6th Battn London Regt Operation Order No.30	07/11/1917	07/11/1917
Operation(al) Order(s)	Relief Of 2/7th Coy 2/6th Unbolt Order No.1	09/11/1917	09/11/1917
Operation(al) Order(s)	Relief Of 2/6th By 2/7th Battalion The Line Order No.4		
Miscellaneous	Move From Canal Bank To Brake Camp Order No.5 2/6th London Regt.	13/11/1917	13/11/1917
Operation(al) Order(s)	Order No.30 2/6th Bn. The London Regt.	14/11/1917	14/11/1917
Miscellaneous	2/6th Bn. The London Regt. Order By Officers Report		
Operation(al) Order(s)	Movement Order No.31 2/6th Bn. The London Regiment	16/11/1917	16/11/1917
Operation(al) Order(s)	Order No.33 2/6th Bn. London Regt	25/11/1917	25/11/1917
Operation(al) Order(s)	Order No.34 2/6th Bn London Regt	26/11/1917	26/11/1917
War Diary	Quesques	01/12/1917	07/12/1917
War Diary	Senninghem	07/12/1917	07/12/1917
War Diary	Dirty Bucket Camp	08/12/1917	11/12/1917
War Diary	Turco Huts	11/12/1917	31/12/1917
Operation(al) Order(s)	Order No.37 2/6th Bn. The London Regt	11/12/1917	11/12/1917
Operation(al) Order(s)	Order No.35 2/6th Bn. The London Regt.	06/12/1917	06/12/1917
Operation(al) Order(s)	Order No.36 2/6th Bn. London Regt	11/12/1917	11/12/1917
War Diary	Turco Huts	01/01/1918	08/01/1918
War Diary	Proven Area	08/01/1918	19/01/1918
War Diary	Demuin	19/01/1918	31/01/1918
Operation(al) Order(s)	Operation Order No.38 By Lieut-Colonel C.B. Benson, D.S.O. Comdg 2/6th Bn London Regiment	18/01/1918	18/01/1918
Miscellaneous	Addenda to Operation Orders No.38 By Lieut-Colonel C.B. Benson , D.S.O. Comdg 2/6th Bn London Regiment	18/01/1918	18/01/1918
Map	Map		

Diagram etc	174 Barrage
Map	Map

2/6 London

May 1917

Index..............................

SUBJECT.

3RD DIV.

No.	Contents.	Date.
	7TH INF. BDE., 2ND BATTN. THE ROYAL IRISH RIFLES. WAR-DIARY JAN.-SEPT. 1915	

(56,425). Wt.24,741—161. 2000. 11/20. Gp.164. A.&E.W.

BOVIS

Instructions regarding War Diaries and Intelligence Summaries are contained in F. S. Regs., Part II. and the Staff Manual respectively. Title pages will be prepared in manuscript.

WAR DIARY
or
~~INTELLIGENCE~~ SUMMARY.
(Erase heading not required.)

Army Form C. 2118.

2/6 Bn. London Regt.

Place	Date	Hour	Summary of Events and Information	Remarks and references to Appendices
SUTTON VENY	25/1/17		Entrained at ~~Warminster~~ WARMINSTER, detrained at SOUTHAMPTON & embarked: Unit in 2 parties.	RHC
HAVRE	26/1/17	4am	Disembarked at HAVRE and marched to No2 CAMP - SANVIC -	RHC
			Casualties 1 Sgt and 2 Rfn. admitted to hospital.	
HAVRE	27/1/17		Unit entrained in 3 parties at 12 noon 1pm and 5.30 pm.	RHC
BUIRE-AU-BOIS	28/1/17	10.30pm	1st party detrained at AUXI-LE-CHATEAU and went into billets at BUIRE-AU-BOIS	RHC
do.	29/1/17	3 am	3rd " " " " " " " "	RHC
		7am	2nd " " " FRÉVENT " " " " " "	RHC
Trenches	1/2/17	RHC	Transport trekked to ~~[illegible]~~ HÉNU. Battalion taken by motor lorries to SOUASTRE and attached for instruction to two battalions in brigade sector (138th Bde) at FONQUEVILLERS and HANNESCAMPS (2 Coys to each battalion).	RHC.
ST. AMAND	3/2/17	RHC	One platoon from each Coy took over platoon frontage, remaining 3 platoons from each Coy withdrawn to huts at ST. AMAND.	RHC

RHCollins Capt & Adjt.

T2134. Wt. W708–776. 500000. 4/15. Sir J. C. & S.

Army Form C. 2118.

Instructions regarding War Diaries and Intelligence Summaries are contained in F. S. Regs., Part II. and the Staff Manual respectively. Title pages will be prepared in manuscript.

WAR DIARY
or
INTELLIGENCE SUMMARY.
(*Erase heading not required.*)

2/6 Bn London Regt.

Place	Date	Hour	Summary of Events and Information	Remarks and references to Appendices
			2/2/17 one man killed, two wounded } T.M. 3/2/17 2/Lt F.W. Hubback seriously wounded. He died from wounds 12/2/17	77 (shell)
ST. AMAND	4/2/17		Nos. 1, 5, 9 & 13 platoons relieved by Nos 2, 6, 10 & 14 platoons	RHC
"	5/2/17		Nos. 2, 6, 10 & 14 " " " Nos 3, 7, 11 & 15 "	RHC
"	6/2/17		Nos 3, 7, 11 & 15 " " " Nos 4, 8, 12 & 16 "	RHC
Trenches Y1 Sector	7/2/17		A Coy. occupied right subsector, right sector of trenches, attached to 1/4 Bn LINCOLNS B " " " " left " " " " " " 1/5 " LEICESTERS	RHC
BIENVILLERS	8/2/17		Battn. moved to BIENVILLERS, transport &c at ST AMAND	RHC
Trenches Y.1.	10/2/17		Battn relieved 1/4 LINCOLNS in right battalion sector trenches with H.Q at HANNESCAMPS.	RHC.
SOUASTRE	14/2/17		Battn relieved by 1/4 LINCOLNS and proceeded to SOUASTRE.	RHC.
"	15/2/17		2/Lt LEWIS and 2/Lt A.C. COLTMAN both wounded whilst in Y.M.C.A hut at SOUASTRE	RHC
"			An unexploded anti aircraft shell fell through the roof and wounded the former in the	
"			leg. The latter was wounded in the back of the head by splinters from the roof	
HUMBERCAMPS	21/2/17		Battn moved from SOUASTRE to HUMBERCAMPS, transport at LA CAUCHIE	RHC
	24/2/17		Battn relieved 2/8 LONDONS in sector C2.	RHC

RH Collins Capt. Adjt.

T2134. Wt. W708—776. 500000. 4/15. Sir J. C. & S.

Instructions regarding War Diaries and Intelligence Summaries are contained in F. S. Regs., Part II. and the Staff Manual respectively. Title pages will be prepared in manuscript.

WAR DIARY ~~or~~ ~~INTELLIGENCE~~ SUMMARY.

(*Erase heading not required.*)

2/6 London Regt

Vol 3

Army Form C. 2118.

Place	Date	Hour	Summary of Events and Information	Remarks and references to Appendices
BAILLEULMONT	28/2		Bn relieved by 2/8 Bn. and proceeded to BAILLEULMONT - Casualties in last 4 days 3 men wounded.	RHG
Trenches	4/3		Bn less 1½ Coys relieved 2½ Coys of 2/8 in trenches remainder of battalion on working parties. Casualties sustained by ~~working~~ men of the battalion working as pioneers under R.E. on C2 sector - 2 Killed 4 wounded by T.M. bomb	RHG
	6/3		Enemy bombing raid W 7 a 6.9 covered by heavy bombardment - Casualties 5 killed 7 wounded 2 missing Time 3.0 am to 3.30 am	RHG.
	7/3		Lateral patrol attacked by enemy W12 b 25.30. Patrol consisted of 1 Cpl + 1 man Casualties - Cpl died of wounds, man missing. Time 8.45 pm	RHG
			Also casualties caused by intermittent shelling during day 1 killed 1 wounded	RHG
			Total casualties for week ending 12 noon 8/3/17	
			KILLED 9, WOUNDED 12, MISSING 3 } O.R.	RHG

T2134. Wt. W708—776. 500000. 4/15. Sir J. C. & S.

Instructions regarding War Diaries and Intelligence Summaries are contained in F. S. Regs., Part II. and the Staff Manual respectively. Title pages will be prepared in manuscript.

WAR DIARY
or
INTELLIGENCE SUMMARY.
(Erase heading not required.)

Army Form C. 2118.

Place	Date	Hour	Summary of Events and Information	Remarks and references to Appendices
	8/3		Casualties 1 killed 1 missing on latrine patrol, surprised by enemy patrol	RAG
	10/3		do 2 killed by T.M. fire when on covering party to wiring party	RAG
	16/3		1 Killed 2 wounded shell fire	RAG
	17/3		Patrol went over at 5 P.M. + found enemys trenches vacated by Ransart. Two platoons established posts in Enemys front line system, one on BELLACOURT RANSART road + the other on L'ALOUETTE RANSART road.	a.H.
	18/3		Two companies established outpost position E + SE of RANSART relieving 2/8 BATTN. P.O.R.	a.H.
	19/3		Relieved by 173RD Brigade + Battalion returned to BASSEUX	a.H.
	21/3		Bn. moved to BIENVILLERS. Transport to HUMBERCAMP	a.H.
	24/3		Bn. relieved 2/4 London Reg: in reserve at BOIRY ST. MARTIN	a.H.
	25/3		Bn. relieved 2/3 do + took up outpost position between BOYELLES + ST. LEGER. Transport moved up to HAMELINCOURT	a.H.

[illegible signature]
2nd Lt A/Adj

T2134. Wt. W708—776. 500000. 4/15. Sir J. C. & S.

Instructions regarding War Diaries and Intelligence Summaries are contained in F. S. Regs., Part II. and the Staff Manual respectively. Title pages will be prepared in manuscript.

WAR DIARY

~~or~~

~~INTELLIGENCE SUMMARY.~~

(Erase heading not required.)

Army Form C. 2118.

2/6th Bn London Rgt.

Vol 4

Place	Date	Hour	Summary of Events and Information	Remarks and references to Appendices
BOIRY-ST-RICTRUDE	27/3		Bn. were relieved by 13 Northumberland Fusiliers + went into Reserve at BOIRY-ST-RICTRUDE + transport moved from HAMELINCOURT to same place.	aH.
BIENVILLERS-AU-BOIS	28/3		Bn. were relieved by 1st Lincolns + Bn. + Transport moved to BIENVILLERS-AU-BOIS	aH.
LUCHEUX	29/3		Bn. + Transport moved to LUCHEUX	aH.
FORTEL	1/4		Bn. + Transport moved to FORTEL	aH.
CAUMONT	2/4		Bn. + Transport moved, B+C Coys to TOLLENT, AD HQ + Transport to CAUMONT	aH.
MAILLY-MAILLET	4/4		Bn. was moved in motor buses to MAILLY-MAILLET + transport moved to AUTHIEULE en route for MAILLY-MAILLET	aH.
BIHUCOURT	7/4		Bn + Transport moved to Camp under canvas at BIHUCOURT	aH.

[illegible]
2nd Lt A/Adj.

Vol 5

CONFIDENTIAL
****

W A R   D I A R Y

OF

2/6th Bn Lan Regt

From 20/4/17...........

To..24/5/17..........

May

Instructions regarding War Diaries and Intelligence Summaries are contained in F. S. Regs., Part II. and the Staff Manual respectively. Title pages will be prepared in manuscript.

WAR DIARY

~~or~~

~~INTELLIGENCE SUMMARY.~~

(*Erase heading not required.*)

Army Form C. 2118.

Place	Date	Hour	Summary of Events and Information	Remarks and references to Appendices
S of MORY	15/5		Bn. moved to camp S of MORY in Reserve. Transport moved to SAPIGNIES & took over lines of unit of 91st Bde	[illegible]
W of VRAUCOURT	16/5		2 Coys. moved into position just north of VRAUCOURT Sugar Refinery on VRAUCOURT ST. LEGER Road	[illegible]
BULLECOURT	18/5		Bn. relieved the 2/5th Battn LONDON REGT. in BULLECOURT	[illegible]
	19/5		Transport moved to MORY and occupied ~~took up~~ lines S of town.	[illegible]
	20/5		Heavy enemy barrage caused some casualties	[illegible]
	21/5		Attack made on BOVIS trench early in morning. Our Troops gained objective but were forced to withdraw by a hostile counter attack. Battalion relieved by 2/7th LONDON REGT at night	[illegible]
ECOUST			Casualties during tour of trenches 13 officers & 226 O/R. Battn moved to ECOUST with one Company on Vaulx-Vraucourt road	
MORY	22/5		Battn relieved by 2/10th LONDONS & moved into camp North of MORY.	[illegible]
	24/5		Camp moved to South of MORY into new lines	[illegible]

[illegible signature]
A/Adjt

T2134. Wt W703—776. 500000. 4/15. Sir J. C. & S.

S E C R E T.   G.S.561/3.

174th. Inf. Brigade.

Reference this office wire G.108 of today. :-

1. The front of the Brigade of the 7th Division which will be relieved by your Brigade extends from approximately U.22.c.8.2. - cross-roads U.27.b.1.9. The right boundary is approximately the line U.22.c.8.2. - U.28.a.8.2. - U.28.a.5.0 - U.28.c.0.0. - U.3.central - cross-roads U.3.c.2025. Left boundary is the ECOUST - BULLECOURT Road (inclusive).

2. The situation in BULLECOURT is, at the present moment, somewhat obscure. Our front line posts apparently run along the road from U.22.c.8.2. where touch is maintained with the 173rd Inf. Brigade to about U.27.b.4095. Then comes a gap which it is believed is held by the enemy. The right of the 62nd Division is about U.27.b.0.8. A pocket of the enemy ~~xx~~ apparently is still holding out in the trench S. of BULLECOURT about U.27.b.3.4. It is hoped that the situation in BULLECOURT will be cleared up by the 7th Division before the relief takes place.

3. The front system of defence consists of posts, etc., in BULLECOURT and the main defensive line along the railway embankment U.27.c. and d. There are also some defences on the N.E. side of ECOUST - LONGATTE road.

4. The dispositions of your Brigade on taking over from the 7th Division will be left to your judgment, but it is suggested for the present that two battalions hold the front system. One battalion is placed in support with 2 companies at ECOUST and 2 companies in the second line about C.18.c., the remaining battalion to be in reserve in camp near MORY, B.28.a.

5. The relief will probably take place on the night 15/16th May, and on the morning of 15th May, your Brigade will move as follows :-

2 Battalions to camp at MORY, B.28.a.
2 " to BEHAGNIES and SAPIGNIES.

Bde. Headquarters to L'HOMME MORT.

A halt will be made in these positions till dusk when the relief will be carried out.

6. The advanced headquarters of the Brigade you are relieving are in ECOUST, C.2.a.6.1.
Rear Headquarters are at L'HOMME MORT.
Both battalion headquarters of battalions in the line are near each other about U.28.a.3.1.
A C.T. from LONGATTE leads up to this latter point.

7. The above is merely for your guidance. Definite orders will be issued when received from V Corps.

(sd) J.E.TURNER,
Lieut.-Colonel,

General Staff, 58th (London) Divn.

13th May,1917.

C O N F I D E N T I A L.

Fifth Army (1)
E.P. 102.

14/5/1917.

V Corps (1).

Further information from captured machine gunner of 9th Grenadier Regt. (3rd Guard Division) is as follows :-

He states that on the night of the 11th/12th a section of Infantry Pioneers came up to repair the steps of the dugouts in the BULLECOURT sector. He heard the Officer to whom they reported say that only temporary repairs need be done,as unless the British attacked they were going to withdraw from the line on the 15th.

The prisoner also had a conversation with the same pioneers,who said the DROCOURT-QUEANT Line was now fit for occupation, that a system of telephonic communication has been installed,and preparations made generally for the occupation of the position.

The above is confirmed to some extent by the O.C. 2nd Company 9th Grenadier Regt., who states that although he personally had received no orders as to withdrawal, he knew that the Artillery were ordered to hold themselves in readiness for immediate withdrawal.

Although too much reliance must not be attached to the above statements, there is undoubtedly an impression among the prisoners that a withdrawal to the DROCOURT-QUEANT Line(WOTAN STELLUNG) is probable in the near future, and a very careful watch should be kept for further indications.

sd. H.D. GOLDSMITH,
Lieutenant Colonel.
General Staff.

Fifth Army.
14/5/1917.

-2-

V Corps (1)
IGX.2/2.
14/5/1917.

G.S.566.
58th.Div.

SECRET.

B.M./63.

5th. London Regt.
8th. London Regt.
6th. London Regt.)
7th. London Regt.)
7th. Division.) For information.
58th. Division.)
173rd Inf. Bde.)
185th. Inf. Bde.)

---

1. Reference last para. of Fifth Army No. E.P.102 attached, the closest possible watch will be kept on the movements of the enemy.

2. O.C. 8th London Regt. and O.C. 5th London Regt. will arrange to push forward strong patrols, as soon as their respective reliefs are complete, to keep touch with the enemy and report.

One patrol from right company in the line of the 8th London Regt., will reconnoitre towards the HINDENBURG LINE N. of BULLECOURT in U.22.c. with object of gaining information as to the strength in which the enemy is holding his line.

Patrols from the centre and left Coys. of the 8th London Regt. will push forward into the Western portion of BULLECOURT with the same object.

Patrols from the company of the 5th London Regt. in the Railway Embankment will cooperate with the above patrols by testing similarly the enemy's line South of BULLECOURT West of the BULLECOURT - LONCATTE Road.

3. Patrols pushing ~~xxxxxxx~~ into BULLECOURT will seize any opportunity of establishing posts in front of our present line.

4. Frequent reports will be rendered giving information obtained. Negative information will be useful.

5. Any evidence of beginning of an enemy withdrawal will be communicated at once by battalions to the Artillery, with whom closest liaison in this matter will be maintained.

6. Should the enemy begin to withdrew it will be the immediate duty of battalion commanders to get in touch with battalions on right and left. The enemy must be followed closely, posts being pushed forward progressively as he retires. Cross-roads will be avoided by troops altogether. Should we advance ~~xxxx~~ men will again be warned against hostile "booby traps" particulars of which have been circulated recently from time to time.

7. 5th and 8th Battalions London Regt. will acknowledge.

R. Barrington Ward
Captain,
Brigade Major,
174th. Infantry Brigade.

15th May, 1917.

Copy No. 3

F.T.

174th. INFANTRY BRIGADE ORDER NO. 13.

Reference Map - sheets 57c N.W. and 51b S.W. 1/20,000
Trench Map - ECOUST-ST-MEIN 1/10,000

1. The 58th Division will relieve the 7th Division in the line on the night May 15/16. Command of the front from U.23.c.8.0. to approximately the LONGATTE - BULLECOURT Road running through the centre of BULLECOURT will pass to the G.O.C. 58th Division at 10 a.m. May 16th.

2. The 174th. Inf. Brigade will relieve the 91st Inf. Brigade (7th Division) in the BULLECOURT Sector on the night May 15/16. The relief will be completed by 5 a.m. May 16th, except for the M.G.Coy. of the 91st Inf. Brigade, which will remain in the line until the night May 16/17 when it will be relieved by the 198th M.G.Coy.
Command of the front from U.22.d.0020 to left Divisional Boundary passes to G.O.C. 174th Inf. Brigade on completion of the Infantry reliefs.

3. The 173rd Inf. Brigade will be on the right of the Brigade and the 186th Inf. Brigade (62nd Div.) on the left.

4. The situation in BULLECOURT has been altered since reconnaissance took place yesterday, by a German counter-attack which was delivered during the past night and drove our troops from that part of BULLECOURT lying west of the LONGATTE - BULLECOURT Road.
Our line now runs approximately as follows :- U.22.d.3010 - along road to BULLECOURT CHURCH - cross-roads U.27.b.7548 - U.27.b.8.2.
Unless situation materially changes during the day it is probable that the Brigade will take over the front with one Battalion in line, one in support and two in reserve.
In this case 8th London Regt. will hold the line with 3 Coys. in line and one in support. H.Q. either at S.E. corner of BULLECOURT or in the old Brigade Advanced H.Q. on LONGATTE - BULLECOURT Road.
5th. London Regt. will be in support, with H.Q. and 2 Coys. in ECOUST, and 2 Coys. either along the line of railway in U.26.d. and 27.c or along the ST LEGER - VAULX VRAUCOURT Road in B.24. ~~xxxxxxxxxxxxxx~~ 6th London Regt. will be in reserve at camp in B.28.a. vacated today by 8th London Regt. possibly less 2 Coys. on ST LEGER - VAULX VRAUCOURT Road.
7th London Regt. will be in reserve at camp in B.28.a. vacated by 5th London Regt. today.
Further orders will be issued regarding the above distribution of units and arrangements for guides notified.

5. 174th. L.T.M.Batty. will relieve 91st L.T.M.Batty., under arrangements made between Battery Commanders direct, on the night May 15/16.
198th M.G.Coy. will relieve 22nd M.G.Coy. under arrangements to be made between O's C. Coys. direct, on the night May 16/17. O.C. 198th M.G.Coy. will attach the following personnel to 22nd M.G.Coy. from the night May 15/16 - one officer per section and one N.C.O. per gun.

6. 6th and 7th Battalions The London Regt., 198th M.G.Coy., 174th L.T.M.Batty., and Bde. H.Q. will march from present camps today.
Bde. H.Q. will march to L'HOMME MORT and 174th. L.T.M.Batty., to camp of 91st L.T.M.Batty., at B.21.c. central, which they will take over.
6th and 7th Battalions The London Regt and 198th M.G.Coy. will march to a convenient halting-place near the camps now occupied by 5th and 8th Battalions The London Regt in B.28.a. Halting-places will be selected by Commanding Officers and will be clear of all traffic-routes.
On arrival at the halting-place O.C. 7th London Regt. will get in touch with O.C. 5th London Regt. and arrange to take over camp occupied by the latter as soon as it is vacated.
O.C. 6th London Regt. will make similar arrangements to take over camp of 8th London Regt.

O.C. 198th M.G.Coy. will move on into M.G.Coy. camp in B.28.a. on discovering that it is vacant.

7. All moves in connection with the relief will take place in accordance with the attached March Table. Distances of 200 yards between Coys. and 500 yards between Battalions will be kept.
All moves E. of MORY will be by platoons at 50 yards distance.

8. The following proportion of Officers and N.C.O's etc., of the 91st Inf. Brigade will remain with the 174th. Inf. Brigade for 24 hours after completion of relief.
1 Officer per Coy.
1 N.C.O. per Platoon.
1 Other rank per Lewis Gun Section.

9. All reliefs will be reported to Bde. H.Q. by wiring the word "BLOTTO". All units, except the battalions in reserve, will forward a sketch showing dispositions to Bde. H.Q. as soon as possible after relief.

10. Bde. Report Centre will close at present camp G.11.d.6.5. at 2 p.m. and reopen at L'HOMME MORT at the same hour.
Bde. H.Q. will be at L'HOMME MORT. Bde. Advanced Report Centre to which all reports will be sent will be established at 9 p.m. today in cellars under the Church, ECOUST at about C.2.a.6.1.

11. Administrative Arrangements for the relief are issued separately.

12. PLEASE ACKNOWLEDGE.

R.M.BARRINGTON WARD,
Captain,
Brigade Major,
174th. Infantry Brigade.

15th May,1917.

Issued to Signals at........p.m.

Copy to:-
1. G.O.C.
2. 5th London Regt.
3. 6th. London Regt.
4. 7th London Regt.
5. 8th London Regt.
6. 198th M.G.Coy.
7. 174th. L.T.M.By.
8. Staff Captain.
9. Bde. Signal Officer.
10. 58th Divn "G".
11. 58th Divn. "Q"
12. 511th Coy.A.S.C.
13. 91st. Inf. Bde.
14. 173rd. do.
15. 175th. do.
16. 186th. do.
17. War Diary.
18. File.
19. Spare.
20. do.

SECRET. Copy No........ 3

174th. INF. BRIGADE ORDER NO:19.

Reference sheet, Trench Map, ECOUST ST MEIN, 1/10,000
57c. N.W. 1/20,000.

1. An inter-battalion relief will be carried out tonight.

2. 5th London Regt. will relieve 8th London Regt. in the front line and will form the garrison of BULLECOURT. The approximate dispositions of 5th London Regt. will be as follows :-
(a) 1 Company. Cross-roads U.22.c.9520 to Cross-roads U.27.b.9590.
(b) 1 Company: 3 platoons Cross-roads U.27.b.9590 - Road junction U.27.b.3575, and 1 platoon from Cross-roads U.27.b.1885 along HENDECOURT Road northwards facing West and forming defensive flank.
(c) 1 Company: 3 platoons Cross-roads U 27.b.7547 to Cross-roads U.27.b.1885 and 1 platoon in HENDECOURT Road S. of latter point facing West and forming defensive flank.
(d) 1 Company: 3 platoons in trenches and dugouts in U.27.b. West of the ECOUST - FACTORY Road and 1 platoon either side of Cross-roads U.27.a.8020. facing West.
(e) Posts at present established in front of the front line will be taken over from 8th London Regt.
Posts will also be established in C.T. about 150 yards North of Cross-roads U.27.b.1590 and in Sunken Road at U.21.c.0580.
(f) O.C. 5th and 8th Battalions London Regt will exchange present Headquarters. All details in connection with relief to be arranged direct between Commanding Officers concerned.

3. 8th London Regt. on relief by 5th London Regt. will withdraw to positions as follows :-
(a) 1 Company in line of Railway from about U.27.d.2040 to U.27.c.0030.
(b) H.Q. and 1 Company ECOUST.
(c) 2 Companies in dugouts in VAULX -VRAUCOURT - St LEGER Road N. of SUCRERIE in B.24.a. and b.

4. 2 Companies 6th London Regt at present in VAULX-VRAUCOURT - St LEGER Road will withdraw to camp in B.28.a. on arrival of their relief.

5. All reliefs will be carried out over the top. BULLECOURT AVENUE will not be used by any troops after 9 p.m.

6. Completion of reliefs to be notified to this office by wiring the time and the code word "VICIMUS".

7. O.C. 5th London Regt will continue active patrolling towards BOVIS Trench (HINDENBURG Line N. of BULLECOURT)
All patrols to be in by 10 p.m. Patrolling will start again at 3 a.m. and patrols will be in again by 5 a.m. From 10 p.m. - 3 a.m and after 5 a.m. Heavy Artillery will be firing.

8. Weather permitting, a contact aeroplane (two streamers in rear of one plane) will fly over our positions tomorrow. Infantry in front line, when contact aeroplane signals with Very lights or KLAXON Horn will at once signal to it by flares or any other means such as flashing pieces of tin or glass, waving pieces of paper, shrapnel helmet etc.

9. ACKNOWLEDGE BY WIRE.

R.M.BARRINGTON WARD, Capt.,
Brigade Major,
174th. Infantry Brigade.

17th May, 1917.

Copies to:-
1 G.O.C.
2 5th London Regt.
3 6th London Regt.
4 7th London Regt.
5 8th London Regt.
6 198th. M.Gun Coy.
7 174th. L.T.M.B.
8 Staff Captain.
9 Bde. Sig. Officer.
10 511th Coy.A.S.C.
11 58th Divn "G"
12 58th Divn "Q"
13 173rd I.Bde.
14 186th I.Bde.
15 War Diary
16 File.

.....

Prefix............Code............ Words. Charge.

Office of Origin and Service Instructions.

SECRET.

S.D.M.

Sent

At..................m.

To..................

By..................

This message is on a/c of:

.... *Service.*

(Signature of "Franking Officer.")

Recd. at ....m.

Date..................

From ....

By..................

TO { 173rd. Inf. Bde.) Case. Copies to:- 6th London Regt.) Staff Captain.) Field Artillery Grp

Sender's Number.	Day of Month.	In reply to Number.	AAA
* BMT 159.	18/5.		

1. Boundary between 174th and 173rd Inf. Bdes. will be altered as follows aaa Cross-roads junction C.3.c.1.2. c.3 ~~xxxxx~~ central - Road junction U.27.d.7.0. - Road junction U.22.c.9525 - FACTORY (inclusive to CLAUD)
2. 174th Inf. Bde. will relieve all 173rd Inf. Bde. posts ~~xx~~ West of this line tonight (May 18/19)
3. O.C. 5th London Regt will arrange relief direct with O.C. Left Battn. 173rd Inf. Bde. 173rd Inf. Bde. have instructed O.C. their left Battn. to visit O.C. 5th London Regt. this morning to make arrangements.
4. Relief will take place before relief of 5th by 6th London Regt tonight. If considered necessary by O.C. 5th London Regt. O.C. Right Battn. 173rd Inf. Bde. will leave behind a N.C.O. or man in each post to remain for 24 hours. Liaison posts will be arranged on inter-Brigade boundary by C.O's direct.
5. Number of posts of 173rd Inf. Bde. taken over, details arranged and completion of relief to be repeated by O.C. 5th London Regt to this office. 6. Acknowledge.

From CLAUD.

Place

Time 11.15 a.m.

The above may be forwarded as now corrected. (Z)

(sd.) R.M.BARRINGTON WARD, Captain.

Censor. Signature of Addressor or person authorised to telegraph in his name.

* This line should be erased if not required.

(3198.) Wt. W 1295?/M1294. 375,000 Pads. 1/17. H.W.&V.,Ld. (E. 818.)

S E C R E T. Copy No. 3

174th. INF. BRIGADE ORDER NO: 20.

Reference Sheet, Map 57c N.W. 1/20,000
Trench Map, ECOUST ST MEIN, 1/10,000

1. Inter-battalion reliefs will take place tonight as follows:-

2. (a) 6th London Regt will relieve 5th London Regt in BULLECOURT.

(b) 7th London Regt will relieve 8th London Regt with dispositions as follows :-
1 Coy. Railway Embankment.
H.Q. and 2 Coys. ECOUST.
1 Coy. VAULX VRAUCOURT Road.

(c) 5th and 8th Battalions The London Regt will withdraw on relief to camps at B.28.a.5.8. and B.28.a.1570 respectively.

3. All details of reliefs will be arranged between O.C. Battalions concerned.

4. Completion of reliefs to be reported to this office by wiring the word BLANKETS and the time.

5. ACKNOWLEDGE.

R.M.BARRINGTON WARD,
Captain,
Brigade Major,
174th. Infantry Brigade.

18th May,1917.

Copies to :-
1. G.O.C.
2. 5th. London Regt.
3. 6th. London Regt.
4. 7th. London Regt.
5. 8th. London Regt.
6. 198th. M.Gun Coy.
7. 174th. L.T.M.Bty.
8. Staff Captain.
9. Bde. Signal Officer.
10. 511th Coy. A.S.C.
11. 58th Div. "G".
12. 58th Divn. "Q".
13. 173rd Inf. Bde.
14. 186th. Inf. Bde.
15. War Diary.
16. File.
17. Field Artillery Group.

A

O/C 2/6 Bn London Regt

1.19/5/17

1.19/20

Sir,

I have to report that an Officers reconnoitring patrol 1 Of. 4 OR. left at 3.45 and proceeded up sunken road towards BOVIS trench.

Owing to the daylight the patrol was not able to get to the trench but about 50 yards from it owing to M.G. fire. The patrol was sniped from left of road but was unable to locate the Sniper.

Patrol returned 4.30 am

Casualty One man wounded

R H Collins
Major

R A Coy

Patrol

(1) O/C 2/6. London A 19/5/17

Patrol from Strong Point U 22 C 60.40
Strength 1 Off 1 NCO + 2 men proceeded along BOVIS trench at 2.30 am returned at 4.0 am.

Report At about U22.C.45.40 BOVIS trench is held by a German post. Officer saw 3 men on duty and presumes from this that post is of about 9 men. The flank was protected by concertina wire and in front the barbed wire is not altogether destroyed.

Patrol returned without incident

4.40 am

RH Collins
Major
O/C A Coy

Patrol

O/C 1/2 Bn London Regt. 19/5/17

All posts of A Coy intact, no attack being made on my post.
Shelling caused 3 casualties up to present one killed two wounded.

8.0 am.

R H Collins
Major

O/C A Coy.

Bosche barrage
dawn 19/5/17

"C" Form

Army Form C. 2123.
(In books of 100.)

MESSAGES AND SIGNALS.

No. of Message........................

Prefix................ Code................ Words..........

Received From B By DD

Sent, or sent out At..........m. To.......... By..........

Office Stamp. H.Q. SIGNALS 19 MAY 1917

£ s. d.

/ Charges to collect

Service Instructions. Patrol

Handed in at.................. Office..........m. Received 3.42 a.m.

C

TO C O B

*Sender's Number	Day of Month	In reply to Number	AAA
Rph 3	19		

Party under Lt Clarke just returned 2.30 AM. They found a Lewis Gun & 1 bombing post at about U21d 13.12. They then proceeded up the trench ~~to~~ for about 400 yds to U21d 01.78. No sign of any Boche was to be found but trench practically unrecognisable. The bombing post referred to above was held by the 2/7 Wellingtons ~~whose~~ who had a platoon in the sunken road. A patrol gone out to find [illegible] platoon [illegible]

FROM

PLACE & TIME

* This line should be erased if not required.

(B 3070) Wt. w. 7196—M857 250,000 Pads 10/16 H & S (E436.) Forms/C.2123/3.

1/ 2 section (17 men) 2 Corps. & Sergt Fennel
under 2/Lt Clarke

2. To examine trenches N from
Cuinchy

3/ 12.40 from Cuinchy

4. Followed. Trench 6 [illegible] not marked
Met officer of 7th [illegible] between road
& trench at 20.10. Reported post 800
from Cuinchy up trench.
Trench practically obliterated. Range from
front & right. [illegible]
[illegible] M.G. [illegible] fired [illegible]
[illegible]
Came back same route

5. 2.30 am /

Shrapnel this morning 3.30
quickly and [illegible] /

"C" Form

Army Form C. 2123.
(In books of 100.)

MESSAGES AND SIGNALS.

No. of Message........................

Prefix............Code..............Words..........

£ s. d.

Charges to collect*

Service Instructions.

Received
From..........................
By..........................

Sent, or sent out.
At..........................m.
To..........................
By..........................

Office Stamp.
H. Q. SIGNALS
19 MAY 1917
OFFICE

Handed in at.......................................Office....................m. Received....................m.

TO

*Sender's Number	Day of Month	In reply to Number	AAA
RJL 4	19		

sunken road. Mr Clarke reports that there [illegible] held a considerable number of Bosche dead and a few of our dead near CRUCIFIX. Very lights came from his right front as he proceeded up trench estimated at 200 yds distance. He considers that Bosche was not in advance of his rear trench U 21 b. 20.20 to running N.W and S.E.

FROM D. C. C. Coy

PLACE & TIME 2 50 AM. [illegible] Lt

* This line should be erased if not required.

(B 3170) Wt. W. 7196—M957. 250,000 Pads. 10/16. H&S. (E438.) Forms/C 2123/3.

"C" Form
MESSAGES AND SIGNALS.

Army Form C. 2123.
(In books of 100.)

No. of Message..........

Prefix.......... Code.......... Words..........	Received	Sent, or sent out	Office Stamp.
£ s. d.	From D	At ......m.	H. Q. SIGNAL OFFICE 19 MAY 1917
Charges to collect	By DR	To	
Service Instructions. Patrol		By	

Handed in at.......... Office..........m. Received 4.28 a.m.

D

TO COB

*Sender's Number	Day of Month	In reply to Number	AAA
R 7	19th		

Mr NASH reported back from patrol 3.15 am (aaa) He states that (a) certain amount of enemy wire still erect and considerable obstacle (aaa) (b) Enemy heard talking and ~~observed~~ heard passing to & fro along trench about U22C 10.50 (aaa) (c) Considerable number of VERY LIGHTS

FROM
PLACE & TIME

* This line should be erased if not required.

(B 8070) Wt. w. 7496—M357 250,000 Pads. 10/16 H & S (E4994) Forms/C.2123/3.

"C" Form

Army Form C. 2123.
(In books of 100.)

MESSAGES AND SIGNALS. No. of Message........................

Prefix.................Code.................Words..............

£ s. d.

Charges to collect

Service Instructions.

Received
From.................................
By.................................

Sent, or sent out
At.............................m.
To.................................
By.................................

Office Stamp.

Handed in at..Office.......................m. Received..............................m.

TO CQB

*Sender's Number	Day of Month	In reply to Number	AAA

Sent up by enemy and rifle fire opened aaa MR NASH reported back 3.15 am aaa I will send him to BN. HQ

FROM D COY

PLACE & TIME 4.5 am

[signature] Lieut

* This line should be erased if not required.

(B 8070) Wt. w. 7496—M357 350,000 Pads. 10/16 H & S (E4024) Forms/C.2123/3.

CO

1 Composition Sgt Nash & 3 bombers.

2 Task To reconnoitre Boar's trench condition of wire & whether trench held & if not to enter ~~[illegible]~~

3 Time & point of departure 1.15 am
U 21 d 7010

4 On bearing of 28 found little wire in good condition but
Very lights from several places in trench
& fired on by rifles several from front [illegible]
no MG fire Heard [illegible] walking about & a
muttered conversation Lay listening Then came back
&

5 Got in at 3 at U 21 d 7070

"C" Form
Army Form C. 2123.
(In books of 100.)

MESSAGES AND SIGNALS. No. of Message........................

Prefix / Code Words	Received	Sent, or sent out	Office Stamp.
Prefix.............. Code.............. Words..............	From..............	At..............m.	
£ s. d. Charges to collect	By..............	To..............	
Service Instructions. Patrol D		By..............	

Handed in at..............Office..............m. Received..............m.

TO COB

*Sender's Number	Day of Month	In reply to Number	AAA
K 3	9th		

MR SMART and patrol reported back 3.30 am. and He states (a) enemy wire sound and still an efficient obstacle (aaa) (b.) by the number of very lights fired from different points and the number of shots fired at him he infers that the trench

FROM D COY
PLACE & TIME

* This line should be erased if not required.

(B 8070) Wt. w. 7496–M857 250,000 Pads. 10/16 H & S (E4244) Forms/C.2123/3.

"C" Form
Army Form C. 2123.
(In books of 100.)

MESSAGES AND SIGNALS. No. of Message........................

Prefix.............Code.................Words...........

Received From............................ By............................

Sent, or sent out At..........................m. To............................ By............................

Office Stamp.

£ s. d.
Charges to collect

Service Instructions.

Handed in at...Office........................m. Received..........................m.

TO COB

*Sender's Number | Day of Month | In reply to Number | AAA

is held ~~by~~ [by] some force aaa On return journey he worked across further to the W than intended and was bombed ~~[illegible]~~ by the WEST RIDINGS from their lines aaa He reports right of WEST RIDINGS about 150 yds W of CRUCIFIX aaa MR SMART set out at 1.30 am

FROM
PLACE & TIME D. Coy [signature]

* This line should be erased if not required.

(B 8070) Wt. w. 7496—M857 250,000 Pads. 10/16 H & S (E4964) Forms/C.2123/3.

1/ Composition } 6 Rfn } bombers under 2/Lt Smart.
of Party } 2 NCOs }

2/ Reconnoitre wire & strength of [illegible] Bovis trench
[illegible] occupied to block

3/ 1.20 am U 21 d 40 30

4/ on a bearing of 18 Reached
wire & found it in good condition
[illegible] about 50-60x [illegible]

2/Lieut. Smart.

Patrol. B. Left at 1.20 a m on a bearing 18° Magnetic and reached enemy wire & moved down the ^wire^ about 50x to W. Patrol was Very light were sent up from BOVIS trench & rifle fire came from front, & ~~flanks~~ half right & half left and a machine gun opened on patrol from right front. Patrol returned via Crucifix. x [illegible]

x/ Then picked up by flares fired on from front & either side. Trench apparently held in considerable strength judging by volume of fire & number of very lights put up. Machine gun traversed apparently from U22b ^[illegible]^ as ~~light~~ dawn approaching, came back but missed [illegible] West & came against post [illegible] post [illegible]

330 U 27 b 17.80

/

S E C R E T.
Reference Map

174th. Infantry Brigade-Instructions No.1 for Forthcoming Enterprise.

---

1. An attack on BOVIS Trench will take place probably on 20th and be carried out by ~~you~~. Latest air photograph shows trench and wire much damaged. Patrols have reported wire no obstacle.

2. Ammunition and Equipment.
Early preparation must be made today for the collection of ammunition, tools and stores required for the attack on BOVIS trench, and formation of forward dump of bombs and wiring material and everything must be in readiness so that the attacking Companies may be complete with their battle equipment on the man as soon as possible after dark. Staff Captain will arrange for carrying parties required. 300 German egg grenades will be issued to attacking Companies. Two bombs carried on the man will include proportion of P bombs.

3. Reconnaissance.
Every Officer and as many N.C.O's as possible of the attacking companies will study the ground today very carefully, noting any landmarks or any wire still standing, position of dugouts etc., and have a complete picture in their mind of the ground to be gone over, not only for purposes of attack but for the purposes of forming up.

4. Plan of Attack.
(a) Objective. BOVIS Trench from U.22.c.45.47 - U.21.d.50.62 (roads on either flank inclusive).

(b) Two companies to carry out the attack, each in two waves on a two platoon front.

(c) Attack will be delivered at dawn after a hurricane bombardment lasting ~~xxxxxxxxx~~ three minutes. Troops to be formed up and ready not later than 3 a.m. Zero to be notified. Probably 3.20 a.m.

(d) On the right tasks to be noticed are those of clearing the road itself, and mopping up any of the enemy who may be left in BOVIS Trench between U.22.c.6.4. (our most westerly point in BOVIS) and the road. Our posts in BOVIS Trench will put down a heavy barrage of bombs and rifle grenades on this part of the trench from Zero - Zero 4. At Zero plus 4 nearest post will attack it over the open with the bayonet and make it good up to a point just W of the road. A strong patrol will also move up this road on the right of the attacking waves.

(e) In the centre it will be necessary to block the C.T. turning north from U.22.c.07.50 unless it is completely destroyed. Lewis Guns will be pushed well in front of BOVIS Trench all along to cover consolidation and to sweep approaches. Well defined enemy tracks are reported as follows

(1) U.21.d.50.50 - U.22.a.10.00 - U.22.a.10.10 - N.E. to U.22.a.65.90 (Joins C.T. to HENDECOURT.)
(2) U.17.a.70.10 - U.22.b.60.30 - U.22.c.80.90.

(f) On the left a special party of one platoon will be echelonned in depth along the CRUCIFIX - FACTORY Road. They will move along the road at Zero until they reach BOVIS Trench. Here they will turn north west along the trench and form a block at U.21.d.35.77. A bombing post and Lewis Guns will be left at U.21.d.30.30.

(g) ~~62nd Division~~ 186th Inf Bde will be demonstrate on our left against trenches in U.21.

5. Machine Guns.
(a) O.C. 198th Machine Gun Company will site 4 guns in present front line so as to protect it completely in case of necessity with crossed belts of fire.

(b) The gun in the strong point at about U.27.b.25.90 will be carefully laid to sweep enemy front and support line in N.W.corner of square U.21.d. 62nd Division will be asked to cooperate on this flank.

(c) 175th Infantry Brigade will be asked to cooperate by placing a gun at about U.22.d.60.30 to enfilade the whole front attacked.

(d) Four guns behind Railway embankment in U.27.c. open fire at Zero, and maintain until Zero plus overhead barrage fire (frequent long bursts) along the approximate line U.22.a.95.00 - 70.10 - 27.32, two guns being laid to shoot, one along BULLECOURT - FACTORY Road, one along BEEF ALLEY.

(e) ALL RANKS WILL BE WARNED OF THIS OVERHEAD FIRE, AND INFORMED THAT THE OVERHEAD BULLETS THEY WILL HEAR HAVE ABSOLUTELY NO DANGER FOR THEM.

6. Artillery.

(a) Will open hurricane bombardment from Zero - Zero plus 3 on part of BOVIS Trench to be attacked.

(b) Will lift to form protector N. of BOVIS Trench.

(c) Will fire on U.22.a. and b, Sunken Road U.15., and will smother trenches in U.21.

(d) Details to be notified.

~~Xxxxxxxx~~

	Artillery Action.	Infantry Action.
0	Barrage comes down on BOVIS Trench.	Move forward towards objective.
0 + 3.	Barrage lifts beyond " " .	Assault BOVIS TRENCH.
0 + 3 - 0 + ?	Protector.	Consolidate.

Captain.
Brigade Major.
174th. Infantry Brigade.

19/5/1917.

To C.O.B.

My Bombing & Lewis Gun Post on the sunken road has had to withdraw as one of our own guns shelled it every few minutes.

Nothing else to report but a long way off on my left I saw a small party of Germans going along ~~with~~ waving a white flag —

R J Lattitney Lt

H. Q. SIGNALS
21 MAY 1917

"A" Form.

Army Form C. 2121.
(In pads of 100.)

MESSAGES AND SIGNALS.

No. of Message

Prefix............Code..............m | Words. | Charge.

Office of Origin and Service Instructions.

SECRET

DR

Sent
At...............m.
To..................
By..................

This message is on a/c of .... Service.

(Signature of "Franking Officer.")

H.Q. SIGNALS OFFICE
Recd. at 1.45 a m.
Date 21 MAY 1917
By

TO { 6th London Regt — 8th ~~London Regt (for information)~~
7th " " — 198 M G Coy
5th " " (for inf) — 174 LTM Batty

Sender's Number.	Day of Month.	In reply to Number.	AAA
* BMT 182	21/5		

RUTH reports V Corps reports 9.40 p.m. AAA Prisoner of 225 R.I.R. whose other information appears reliable stated that the intention had been to withdraw to DROCOURT LINE on 18th inst AAA The date had been changed to the 19th and then to the 21st. AAA Prisoner did not know the reason for postponement AAA The intention was to go right back to DROCOURT LINE and not to stop on the VIS-EN-ARTOIS Switch AAA Another prisoner gave similar information AAA Both were N.C.O's AAA Ends AAA Every endeavour must be made to keep the closest touch with enemy today by means of patrols and observation posts and frequent situation reports at least one every two hours from battalion in the line will be sent in

From 174th Inf Bde
Place
Time 2.10 a.m.

The above may be forwarded as now corrected. (Z) R. Barrington-Ward Capt

BM 174 IB

Censor. Signature of Addressor or person authorised to telegraph in his name.

* This line should be erased if not required.

(3198.) Wt. W 12952/M1294. 375,000 Pads. 1/17. H. W. & V., Ld. (E. 818.)

"A" Form.

Army Form C. 2121.
(In pads of 100.)

MESSAGES AND SIGNALS.

No. of Message...............

Prefix..........h. Code...............m	Words.	Charge.		
Office of Origin and Service Instructions.	Sent		This message is on a/c of:	Recd. at ....m.
B.R. SECRET	At..............m.		..........................Service.	Date................
	To..................			From ....
	By..................		(Signature of "Franking Officer.")	By..................

TO: CONE
CoB

Sender's Number.	Day of Month.	In reply to Number.	AAA
* BmT 196	21/5		

1. Ref. Bde. Order no. 22. para 5. Owing to inevitable delay in ~~the~~ start of relief tonight compliance with above para. may bring patrolling dangerously near daylight. In such a case it will be at the discretion of C.O.'s concerned to begin bombing before completion of relief if posts are found.

2. The Division are anxious, whatever the success of the enterprise that a post should be established on the highest local piece of ground at or about U.21.d.3050. Every endeavour should be made to do so tonight.

3. Officer leading the 175th Inf Bde – patrol has been killed. It is feared they will be unable to accomplish much to help us.

From
Place
Time

The above may be forwarded as now corrected. (Z)

Censor. Signature of Addressor or person authorised to telegraph in his name.

* This line should be erased if not required.

(3198.) Wt. W 12952/M1294. 375,000 Pads. 1/17. H. W. & V., Ld. (E. 818.)

"A" Form.

Army Form C. 2121.
(In pads of 100.)

MESSAGES AND SIGNALS.

No. of Message..............

Prefix..........Code..............m	Words.	Charge.	*This message is on a/c of:*	Recd. at ....m.
Office of Origin and Service Instructions.	Sent		.... *Service.*	Date..............
	At..............m.			From ....
	To..............			
	By..............		(Signature of "Franking Officer.")	By..............

TO

* Sender's Number.	Day of Month.	In reply to Number.	AAA

4. Information from air reconnaissance [illegible] has been sent you by PRIORITY wire. [illegible] information and for communication to any concerned of your division [illegible] AREAS [illegible] that will LEAVE [illegible]
Addressed [illegible]

From 174 Inf Bde

Place

Time 12. 20 p.m.

The above may be forwarded as now corrected.

(Z) [illegible]

Censor. Signature of Addressor or person authorised to telegraph in his name.

* This line should be erased if not required.

(3198.) Wt. W 12952/M1294. 375,000 Pads. 1/17. H. W. & V., Ld. (E. 818.)

SECRET   Copy No. 2...

174th Inf. Bde. Order No. 22.

1. 7th London Regt. will relieve 6th London Regt. in the BULLECOURT Sector tonight.
2. All arrangements to be made direct between C.O.'s concerned.
3. On relief the 6th LONDON Regt. will be disposed as follows:-
   2 Platoons. Railway U.27.d.
   1½ Coys. ECOUST. Billets now occupied by 7th London Regt.
   HQ and 1 Coy ECOUST. Caves under Church.
   1 Coy. VAULX VRAUCOURT – ST LEGER Road.

4. The attack on BOVIS Trench this morning did not succeed, but posts of our men appear to be established in the above trench at U.22.c.3545 and U.21.d.4065.
   Under arrangements made between O.C. 6th and O.C. 7th LONDON Regt. continuous and active patrolling will be carried on from dusk without interference by the relief.
   The objects of patrols will be:
(a) to gain touch with above-mentioned posts.
(b) to keep watch on the enemy's movements
(c) to re-establish if possible, the situation in BOVIS Trench.
   175th Inf. Bde. have been ordered to patrol ~~west~~ towards

along BOVIS Trench from U.22.c.9530 in order to gain touch with post at U.22.c.3545.

Patrols from 174th Inf. Bde. towards U.22.c.3545 and U.21.d.4065, and patrol of 175th Inf. Bde. towards former point will start out at 9.15 p.m. From this hour machine gun emplacement at U.21.d.2590 will be kept under shrapnel fire.

If posts are found to be established at the two above-mentioned points strong bombing attacks will be made inwards along BOVIS Trench and the trench cleared of the enemy. Commanders of Bombing Patrols must meet and concert a plan of action beforehand.

5. O.C. 6th and O.C. 7th London Regt. will maintain the closest touch throughout with O.C. Left Battalion, 175th Inf. Bde.

The bombing attack mentioned in para. 4 will not take place until after the completion of the relief.

6. The vital importance of sending back information as soon and as ~~[illegible]~~ accurately as possible must be impressed upon all engaged in this enterprise. Battalions will render hourly reports to this office. Completion of relief to be reported by wire in BAB code.

7. ACKNOWLEDGE BY WIRE.

R.M. Barrington-Ward Capt.
Bde. Major 174th Inf. Bde.

Issued to Signals at 6.20 p.m.

Copies to:

1. G.O.C.
2. 6th London Regt.
3. 7th " "
4. 198 M.G. Coy.
5. 174. L.T.M. Batty.
6. Staff Capt.
7. 175 Inf Bde.
8. 187 " "
9. 58th Division.
10. War Diary.
11. File.
12. Field Artillery Group.

H.Q. SIGNALS
21 MAY 1917
OFFICE

7.30 pm

"A" Form.

MESSAGES AND SIGNALS.

Army Form C.2121
(in pads of 100).
No. of Message..........

Prefix .... Code .... m.	Words	Charge	This message is on a/c of:	Recd. at .... m.
Office of Origin and Service Instructions.	Sent		.... Service.	Date ....
	At .... m.			From ....
	To			
	By		(Signature of "Franking Officer.")	By ....

TO { O.C. 8/ Batt.

Sender's Number.	Day of Month.	In reply to Number.	AAA
* RJ 6	21st	O.C.	

The stamp lost in question is at U.21.d.2.2. ([illegible] defences 1-5000 15-5-17) AAA I have sent to the HQ 2 No 3 section to find out where the remainder of their guns are and will send this information to you on receipt AAA May [illegible] the [illegible] the eight remain [illegible] [illegible] [illegible] shelled [illegible] yesterday AAA

From O.C. No 2 Section CLUSTER
Place
Time 10.40 am.

The above may be forwarded as now corrected. (Z) R. [illegible] Lieut.

.... Censor. Signature of Addressor or person authorised to telegraph in his name.

* This line should be erased if not required.

750,000. W 2186—M509. H. W. & V., Ld. 6/16.

O.C. 2/6th Bn.

"A" Form.

MESSAGES AND SIGNALS.

Army Form C.2121 (In pads of 100).

No. of Message ....

Prefix .... Code .... m. | Words | Charge

Office of Origin and Service Instructions.

Sent: At 9:50 m. To 5t 7/6 By ....

This message is on a/c of: .... Service.

(Signature of "Franking Officer.")

Recd. at .... m. Date .... From .... By ....

TO: OC 2/6th L.R.

Sender's Number.	Day of Month.	In reply to Number.	AAA
*	21st		

The Detachment of 2/7th L.R. informs me that he has been informed by the Coy Commander that the enemy ~~is~~ has been ~~been~~ congregating in road running from U22c.5.5. to U22 ~~[illegible]~~ a.5.0.

Can I have some support AAA. 2/7th has not been able to get into touch with 175th Bde Com

? Observation Officer.

From: 2/Lt Wilkinson

Place

Time

The above may be forwarded as now corrected. (Z)

.... Censor. Signature of Addressor or person authorised to telegraph in his name.

* This line should be erased if not required.

750,000. W 2186—M503. H. W. & V., Ld. 6/16.

"A" Form.

Army Form C.2121 (in pads of 100).

MESSAGES AND SIGNALS.

No. of Message

Prefix ... Code ... m. Words Charge

Office of Origin and Service Instructions.

Sent At ... m. To ... By ...

This message is on a/c of: ... Service. (Signature of "Franking Officer.")

H. Q. S. G. ... OFFICE 21 MAY 1917

Recd. at ... m. Date ... From Recd By 5.47AM

TO Cob

Sender's Number.	Day of Month.	In reply to Number.	AAA
* A Coy 2/7	21/5/17	—	

One platoon Lewis Gun & bombers sent forward to reenforce advanced platoon. Only one platoon in support now. Right Flank platoon suffered severely & is of little use

From Cone.

Place Coy H Q.

Time

The above may be forwarded as now corrected. (Z) [illegible] Mitchell O.C. A Coy 2/7

Censor. Signature of Addressor or person authorised to telegraph in his name.

* This line should be erased if not required.

160,000. W 2186—M509. H. W. & V., Ld. 5/16.

(In books of 100.)

SIGNALS. No. of Message.....................

Prefix......Code......Words......	Received	Sent, or sent out	Office Stamp.
£ s. d. Charges to collect	From......... By.........	At.........m. To......... By.........	Recd 6.35 am
Service Instructions.			

H.Q. SIGNALS 21 MAY 1917 OFFICE

Handed in at.................Office.........m. Received.........m.

TO CoB.

*Sender's Number	Day of Month	In reply to Number	AAA
EHS 16	21st	AHO 5	

My OP's have not been able to ascertain this aaa At present there is no movement visible at all in objective aaa

FROM D. Coy

PLACE & TIME 6.25 am

* This line should be erased if not required.

(B 8070) Wt. w. 7496—M357 250,000 Pads. 10/16 H & S (E436,) Forms/C.2123/3.

COB.

"A" Form.

MESSAGES AND SIGNALS.

(in pads of 100)
No. of Message

Prefix ....Code ....m. | Words | Charge | This message is on a/c of: ....Service. (Signature of "Franking Officer.") | Recd. at ....m. Date 3.19pm From 21 MAY 1917 By

Office of Origin and Service Instructions.

Sent
At ....m.
To ....
By ....

TO O.C. D Coy

Sender's Number.	Day of Month.	In reply to Number.	AAA
* AHQ 28	21	EHS 20	

Message	not	wholly	understood	aaa
Have	you	withdrawn	platoon	from
front	aaa	Have	you	been
relieved	aaa	What	is	present
position	of	platoon	with	map
reference	aaa	from	whom	was
report	about	[illegible]	received	

From COTS
Place
Time 3.15 pm

The above may be forwarded as now corrected. (Z)

Censor. Signature of Addressor or person authorised to telegraph in his name.

* This line should be erased if not required.

750,000. W 2186—M509. H. W. & V., Ld. 6/16.

PATROL REPORT. D.

Date 20:5:17

Jamieson

1 Composition of party

1 Corp + 13 (Bombers, L Gun + Rifles)

2 Task: to ascertain state of wire in front of BOVIS trench + location of anything going on there

3. T + point of dep

2. AM. U22C 30.10.

4. W. up road to wire + worked along wire 200 x westwards. Very much broken up, numerous craters.

Heard voices to R nothing to left

No offensive action

5. Made a detour + returned same place at 3.30 AM.

Found LMG very unwieldy in the very broken ground

D Lovis [illegible]

O.C. B Coy

To O.C. 2/5 Lan R.

All platoons report them-selves all right & no casualties. One L.G. team has gone up to D Coy

[illegible signature]
Capt
O.C. B Coy

May 20/17

8.10 am

Bosche barrage dawn 20/5/17

"C" Form

Army Form C. 2123.
(In books of 100.)

MESSAGES AND SIGNALS.

No. of Message..........

Prefix.......... Code.......... Words..........
£ s. d.
Charges to collect
Service Instructions.

Received
From..........
By..........

Sent, or sent out
At.......... m.
To..........
By..........

Office Stamp.
H. Q. SIGNALS
20 MAY 1917
OFFICE

Recd
12.15pm

Handed in at.......... Office.......... m. Received.......... m.

TO

Attack on Bovis

*Sender's Number	Day of Month	In reply to Number	AAA
	20		

2.

Apply to Lient Keller at "A" Company Hd. Qrs. ~~who~~ he is ~~now~~ in command of that Company.
The Platoon should remain with you until actually required to join "A" Coy. Arrange for a guide to come to you to guide ~~platt~~ platoon to ~~Com~~ "A" Coy. lines.

FROM

PLACE & TIME

* This line should be erased if not required.

(B 3070) Wt. w. 7496—M857 250,000 Pads. 10/16 H & S (E436.) Forms/C.2123/8.

...Message......................

Prefix..............Code..............Words..........	...ed	Sent, or sent out	Office Stamp.
£ s. d. Charges to collect	From............ By............	At.............m.	
Service Instructions.		To............ By............	

Handed in at..................Office..........m. Received..........m.

TO O.C. B

*Sender's Number	Day of Month	In reply to Number	AAA
[illegible] 14	20		

[illegible]	an	[illegible]	of	a
platoon	to	reinforce	D Coy	[illegible]
called	upon			

Bosch barrage dawn 20/5/17

FROM C Coy

PLACE & TIME

* This line should be erased if not required.

(B 3070) Wt. w. 7496—M857 250,000 Pads 10/16 H & S (E436.) Forms/C.2123/3.

"C" Fo[rm]

MESSAGES AND SIG[NALS]

Prefix.............Code.............Words.............

£ s. d.

Charges to collect

Service Instructions.

Received From............ By............

Sent, At............m. To............ By............

H.Q. SIGNAL OFFICE 20 MAY 1917

Handed in at............Office............m. Received............m.

TO C.D.B.

*Sender's Number	Day of Month	In reply to Number	AAA
[illegible] 14	20		

Situation is quite normal again [illegible] and the [illegible] standing down. Three men have been slightly hit. [illegible] in touch with D Coy and have sent a runner to D Coy H.Q. A few gas shells came over in the night [illegible] the space of five minutes. The [illegible] most of the shelling was shrapnel. On the [illegible] rifle fire [illegible] have some rifle fire but have seen nothing.

FROM [illegible] Coy

PLACE & TIME [illegible]

* This line should be erased if not required.

(B 3070) Wt. w. 7496—M857 250,000 Pads. 10/16 H & S (E436.) Forms/C.2123/3.

awaiting disposal.

"C" Form

Army Form C. 2123.
(In books of 100.)

MESSAGES AND SIGNALS. No. of Message........................

Prefix........Code........Words........	Received	Sent, or sent out	Office Stamp.
£ s. d. Charges to collect	From........ By........	At........m. To........ By........	
Service Instructions.			

Handed in at........Office........m. Received........m.

TO CO B

*Sender's Number	Day of Month	In reply to Number	AAA
K 18	20th		

All OK at present Mr. JAMISON holding Strong point but no news from him of enemy movements

Bosche barrage 20/5/17

FROM D Coy

PLACE & TIME 6.35 am

* This line should be erased if not required.

(B 8070) Wt. w. 7496—M857 250,000 Pads. 10/16 H & S (E4984) Forms/C.2123/3.

Army Form C. 2123.
(In books of 100.)

[MESSAG]ES AND SIGNALS. No. of Message........................

Prefix.........Code.........Words......... £ s. d. Charges to collect	Received From.............. By..............	Sent, or sent out At..........m. To.......... By..........	Office Stamp.
Service Instructions.			Boesche [?] 20/5/17

Handed in at.......................Office..........m. Received..........m.

TO COB

*Sender's Number	Day of Month	In reply to Number	AAA
K25	20th		

Situation for past twelve hours very violent hostile shelling of whole coy area especially heavy on road 27B70 48 north west to crucifix (aaa) Shells of large and small calibre employed (aaa) I propose to hold the crucifix strong point by night only owing to

FROM
PLACE & TIME

* This line should be erased if not required.

(B 8070) Wt. w. 7496—M857 350,000 Pads. 10/16 H & S (E4964) Forms/C.2123/3.

Co B.

Form

Army Form C. 2123.
(In books of 100.)

MESSAGES AND SIGNALS. No. of Message..................

Prefix................Code................Words..........

£ s. d.

Charges to collect

Service Instructions.

Received

From..................

By..................

Sent, or sent out

At..................m.

To..................

By..................

H.Q. SIGNALS 20 MAY 1917 OFFICE

Office Stamp.

Handed in at..................Office..................m. Received..................m.

TO

*Sender's Number	Day of Month	In reply to Number	AAA

the certainty of being observed by day aaa my original L.G. position will be used by day aaa lull in shelling at time of writing aaa

FROM PLACE & TIME: D Coy. 5.0 am. [signature]

* This line should be erased if not required.

(B 8070) Wt. w. 7496—M857 250,000 Pads. 10/16 H & S (E4904) Forms/C.2123/3.

SECRET.

Copy No............

174th. Infantry Brigade Order No. 21.

Reference Sheet, 57c N.W. 1/20,000; and
Trench Map ECOUST-ST-MEIN 1/10,000.

1. 174th. Inf. Brigade has been ordered to attack and capture the trench known as BOVIS Trench from U.22.c.6040 to U.21.d.5060. The attack will be carried out by the 6th London Regt. on May 20th.

2. Plan of Attack.
(a) The 6th London Regt will attack with two companies. The front
of the assault will be from U.22.c.4345 to U.21.d.4760, the
BULLECOURT – FACTORY and CRUCIFIX – FACTORY Roads being both included
in this front.
These two companies will find no carrying parties and will be at
full strength.
Assaulting troops will form up with leading wave on a line 200 yards
S. of and parallel to the front to be assaulted. They will be in
position by Zero minus one hour.
The attack will be carried out under a hurricane bombardment of
BOVIS Trench lasting four minutes.
At Zero the barrage will be put down on BOVIS Trench. Simultaneously
the attacking troops will begin to move forward at a steady pace
towards their objective. They will move up to a position as close
as possible to the barrage. Immediately the barrage lifts they will
assault and capture the trench.
(b) As soon as the trench is captured Lewis Guns will be pushed
forward to form a chain of posts on a parallel alignment about 100
yards North of the trench. These posts will be joined up to form a
continuous line as soon as the situation permits.
(c) Special care will be paid to the task of mopping up BOVIS Trench
after capture. Every dugout entrance in the trench will be immediately
picketed, men from the line of moppers-up being told off to this
duty beforehand.
(d) Consolidation will be vigorously prosecuted as soon as the trench
is mopped-up. Every man of the rear wave will carry a spade. Wire
will be put out as soon as possible.
(e) Special parties will be told off to certain duties as follows:-
(i) The posts already established in the Eastern end of BOVIS
Trench from U.22.d.0030 to U.22.c.7535 will open an intense
barrage at Zero with bombs and rifle grenades on the German post
EAST ~~west~~ of the road at U.22.c.4742. Every man will ~~xxxxxxx~~ throw
as many bombs as possible. At Zero plus 4 minutes this barrage
will cease and the post will be rushed. Touch will immediately
be gained with our troops in the trench further West.
(ii) A strong patrol with Lewis Gun will move on the right of the
leading wave up the BULLECOURT – FACTORY Road with the object
of protecting the right flank of the attack.
(iii) One of the Lewis Gun posts ordered to be pushed forward will
be told off to establish itself in the old communication trench
joining BOVIS Trench at U.22.c.0752.
(iv) A special party of one strong platoon will be echeloned in
depth along the CRUCIFIX – FACTORY Road on the left of the
attacking waves.
The 186th Inf. Brigade has established a post at U.21.d.3035.
This platoon will take over this post as a bombing post with
Lewis Gun tonight as already ordered.
At Zero this platoon (less personnel manning the above post
which will remain in position) will move forward with the
attacking waves. It will mop up dugouts in CRUCIFIX – FACTORY
Road about U.21.d.6067 and establish a block and bombing post
L HINDENBURG Support in/trench about 100 yards from the above mentioned road.
This platoon will be plentifully supplied with P bombs.

3. A hurricane bombardment by the Field Artillery will open on BOVIS
Trench at Zero, as stated.
At Zero plus four it will lift to form a protective barrage along
the general line U.21.central – BEEF ALLEY in U.21.b. – along
tramway to U.22.b.5730 – thence along road to about U.22.d.2055.
The trenches about U.21.central will be smothered with artillery
fire.
The V Corps Heavy Artillery will bombard enemy assembly areas in
rear of his front line and search roads and approaches.

4. Our present front line will be held by machine guns from Zero onwards. Six machine guns on the railway embankment will provide an overhead barrage during the assault. Machine gun near CRUCIFIX will maintain fire on trenches in U.21.a. on the left of the attack. Two machine guns will be ready to move to N.W. corner of the village after BOVIS Trench has been captured.
Machine Guns of the 175th and 186th Inf. Brigades will cooperate. Detailed instructions have been issued to the O.C. 198th M.G.Coy.

5. O.C. 174th. L.T.M.Batty. will move 2 Stokes Guns tonight to a position of readiness in N.W. corner of BULLECOURT at approximately U.21.d.5040.
These guns will be in position by 2 a.m. tomorrow and will protect left flank of the attack, and engage any hostile counter-attack coming down either side of the two trenches leading into the CRUCIFIX - FACTORY Road in U.21.d.
They will ~~xxxxxx~~ reserve their fire until a counter-attack begins from the flank.

6. 7th Battalion The London Regt. will be prepared to move at any time after Zero.
5th and 8th Battalions The London Regt will be at half an hour's notice from Zero.
No working party will be N. of ECOUST after Zero.

7. O.C. 511th Field Coy.R.E. will arrange to reconnoitre as early as possible a communication trench running back from BOVIS Trench to BULLECOURT ~~in~~ order that work may begin on it tomorrow night.

8. G.O.C. 174th. Inf. Brigade has a direct call on the Tunnelling Company now in ECOUST. The necessary personnel will be ready to proceed to BULLECOURT at short notice and reconnoitre dugouts in BOVIS Trench.

9. A contact aeroplane will be in the air from about 3.45 a.m. Leading troops when summoned by ~~the~~ KLAXON horn or light signals from the aeroplane, will light flares or make other signals at once.

10. Watches will be synchronised with Bde.H.Q. by telephone by the Field Artillery Group, and by O.C. 6th and 7th Battalions The London Regt, 198th M.G.Coy., 174th L.T.M.Batty. before one a.m.

11. Advance Bde.H.Q. will open at the Report Centre ECOUST at Zero minus three hours. All reports will be sent there. Special reports will be rendered as required and hourly situation reports will be rendered by the leading battalion.

12. Zero will be at 3.20 a.m.

13. ACKNOWLEDGE BY WIRE.

R.M.BARRINGTON WARD, Captain,
Brigade Major,
174th. Infantry Brigade.

20th May,1917.
ISSUED to Signals at 12.15 pm.

Copies to:-
1 G.O.C.
2 5th London Regt.
3 6th London Regt.
4 7th London Regt.
5 8th London Regt.
6 198th M.Gun Coy.
7 174th L.T.M.Bty.
8 Staff Captain.
9 Brigade Sig.Officer.
10 511th Field Coy. R.E.
11. 58th. Divn. "G".
12 58th.Divn. "Q".
13 173rd Inf. Bde.
14 183th Inf. Bde.
15 174th Tunnelling Coy.
16 Field Artillery Group.
17 War Diary.
18 File.
19 175th Inf. Bde.
20 C.R.E.

SECRET. Copy No......3...

Amendment No.1 to
174th. Inf. Brigade Order No:21.

1. Add to para. 3 after line 5 "The protective barrage will be maintained until Zero plus one hour."

2. Under same para. add:-
"62nd Division will cooperate by placing barrage of 18 pounders on enemy's front line from U.21.d.3030 to U.20.b.2050 at Zero. At Zero plus 4 this barrage will lift to support line within above limits where it will remain until Zero plus one hour and ten minutes.

3. Under same para. add:-
"Enemy post in wood at U.22.a.5075 will be engaged by a 4.5" howitzer until Zero. At Zero plus 1 section 18 pounders will take over the task and maintain fire as long as the protective barrage lasts."

4. Please acknowledge.

R.M.BARRINGTON WARD, Captain,
Brigade Major,
174th. Infantry Brigade.

20th May, 1917.

Copies to :- All recipients of
174th. Inf. Brigade
Order No:21.

"A" Form.

Army Form C.2121
(In pads of 100).
No. of Message ....

MESSAGES AND SIGNALS.

Prefix .... Code .... m. | Words | Charge | This message is on a/c of: .... Service. | Recd. at .... m.

Office of Origin and Service Instructions.

SDR
SECRET

Sent
At .... m.
To ....
By ....

(Signature of "Franking Officer.")

Date ....
From ....
By ....

TO COB

Sender's Number.	Day of Month.	In reply to Number.	AAA
* BMT 175	20/5		

VII Corps (33rd Div.) on our left has attacked this
morning and captured the HINDENBURG front line
between the CROISILLES-HENDECOURT and CROISILLES-
FONTAINE Roads and has reached the support line AAA
This may possibly induce enemy to withdraw to
SWITCH Line from RIENCOURT to FONTAINE AAA B.G.C.
directs that ~~[illegible]~~ BOVIS Trench be occupied by
you as soon as possible AAA If this is not possible in
your opinion by day you will submit your plans to the
B.G.C. forthwith for the capture of BOVIS Trench by strong
patrols as soon as it is dark, in order that arrangements may be made with the artillery AAA Last night's patrol
reports show wire no obstacle W. of BULLECOURT-FACTORY Rd.
AAA Heavies will fire on BOVIS trench from 5.15 to 8 p.m.
unless you report beforehand that trench has been occupied
AAA If other means of clearing up the situation fail
you will carry out the attack postponed from last night
under similar arrangements AAA Orders attached AAA Acknowledge

From CLAUD
Place
Time 11.40 a.m.

The above may be forwarded as now corrected.

.... Censor.

(Z) R. M. Barrington Ward Capt

Signature of Addressor or person authorised to telegraph in his name.

* This line should be erased if not required.

750,000. W 2186—M509. H. W. & V., Ld. 6/16.

D. D. & L., London, E.C.
(6561). Wt. W8419/M920 50,000 Pads. 11/16 E 500.

Army Form C 2122.

"B" Form.

MESSAGES AND SIGNALS.

No. of Message..................

Prefix XB Code EIP m.	Words	Received	Sent	Office Stamp.
Office of Origin and Service Instructions.	37	At 6.55 m. From WDD By [illegible]	At............m. To............ By............	WDU 20/5/17

TO { C O B

Sender's Number	Day of Month	In reply to Number	AAA
9022	20		

Cancel my BMT 175 AAA
DR2982. 8826 AAA Order
no 21 will be carried out
AAA DR4521 2 Before
that BMT AAA Reference
Conversation with MAJOR
Collins AAA Acknowledge

From
Place CLAUD
Time 5.45 PM

* This line should be erased if not required.

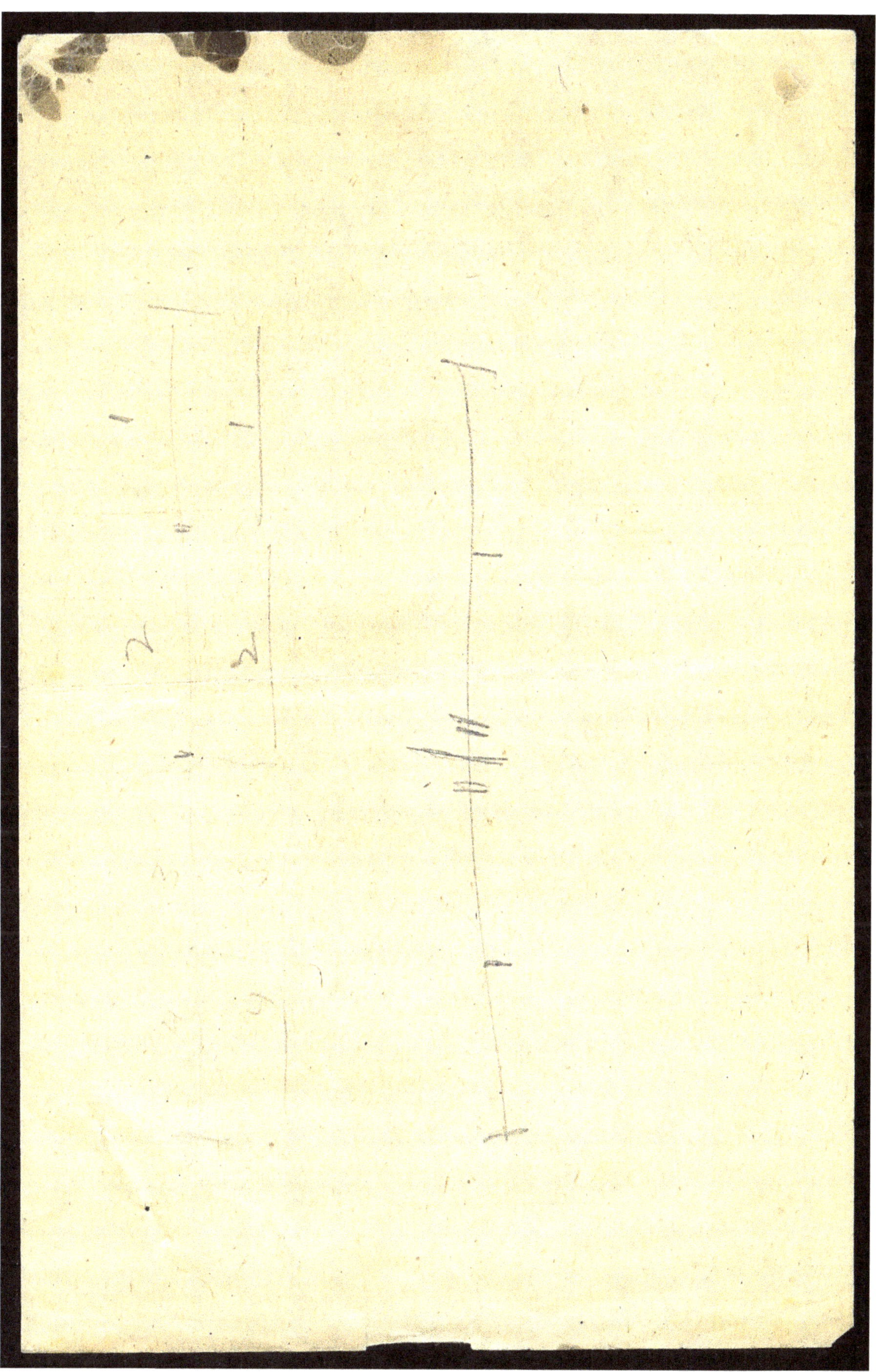

"A" Form.

MESSAGES AND SIGNALS.

Army Form C.2121
(in pads of 100).
No. of Message

Prefix Code m. | Words | Charge

Office of Origin and Service Instructions.

Sent
At m.
To
By

This message is on a/c of: Service.

H. Q. SIGNALS
20 MAY 1917
OFFICE

(Signature of "Franking Officer.")

Recd. at 6.20 P.m.
Date 19.5.17
From
By

TO COB.

Sender's Number.	Day of Month.	In reply to Number.	AAA
* 1.0.13.	20/5		

Cancel my B.M.T. 175 aaa
Patrols will not go out aaa
Order NO 21 will be carried out. aaa
no action ~~before~~ (before) that time aaa
Reference conversation with Major Collins
Acknowledge

From CLAUD.
Place
Time 5.30 pm.

The above may be forwarded as now corrected.

(Z) C A Montgomery 2nd Lt
for Bde Major

Censor.

Signature of Addressor or person authorised to telegraph in his name.

* This line should be erased if not required.

750,000. W 2186—M509. H. W. & V., Ld. 6/16.

H. Q. SIGNALS
21 MAY 1917
OFFICE

To O. C. 2/6 L. R.

From M. O.

Will you please apply for a M. O. to reinforce me as soon as possible. I have kept up thus far on my own but am almost exhausted.

9 gas cases in all sent back.

Thank you,
O Dinnitt
Capt RAMC.

20/5/17.
1 50 AM

In the other map there is new work shown on the Factory Road at U.22.c.55.70 probably a M.G. emplacement. I have arranged for 2 guns to keep on this point.

Let me know by bearer any points you want information on.

I am sure it will be a success. The great thing is correct forming up & previous reconnaissance.

C J Higgins

19.5.17
5pm

Dear Ford

Provl. Orders stand good

(1) with no important modification of any kind.

(2) Zero 3.20 at which time guns will open intense fire & keep it up for 4 minutes during this time the infy to push up as close as possible to barrage.

(3) About the Wire the heavies will be firing on Boris Tr. from 11.30 pm – 2. a.m tonight so your patrolling should be finished

by that hour (11·30 pm).

If you want longer for them, you must let me know.

Please let me know results of wire patrols at once as I must let Divⁿ know & impress on people who are doing it the importance to their own regiment of accurate information.

(4) I enclose 2 good aeroplane maps you will notice the large dug outs in Sunken on your left flank in one map these will need special attention with P. bombs

To C.O.B. 21/5/17

One or two wounded have come back from Lt Clarke's party, & apparently he and most of the party entered the trench but met with opposition from bombs. Cannot obtain any further particulars

R/ Matthew, Lt

5.15 A.M.

My men are alright

"C" Form

MESSAGES AND SIGNALS.

Army Form C. 2123.
(In books of 100.)

No. of Message.....................

...Code.............Words..........	Received	Sent, or sent out	Office Stamp.
£ s. d.	From.....................	At..................m.	Recd
...Collect	By.......................	To.......................	3.2 pm
...e Instructions.		By.......................	

H. Q. SIGNALS
21 MAY 1917
OFFICE

Handed in at.......................................Office..................m. Received........................m.

TO C O B

*Sender's Number	Day of Month	In reply to Number	AAA
	21		

Have [illegible] altered arrangements and 186th Bde post is being relieved by 2Lt Clarke at the same time as he takes up his position for the attack. He left the ~~Cru~~ CRUCIFIX with his party by 2 AM.

Attack on BOVIS
21/5/17

FROM C Coy [illegible]

PLACE & TIME

* This line should be erased if not required.

(B 3970) Wt. w. 7196—M857 250,000 Pads 10/16 H & S (E436.) Forms/C.2123/3.

"C" Form.
Army Form C. 2123.
(In books of 100.)

MESSAGES AND SIGNALS.

No. of Message..........

Prefix........Code........Words........	Received	Sent, or sent out	Office Stamp.
£ s. d. Charges to collect	From........ By........	At........m. To........ By........	
Service Instructions.			

Handed in at .... Office........m. Received........m.

TO O.C. 2/6th LR

*Sender's Number	Day of Month	In reply to Number	AAA
	21st		

In reply to (a) No 1 Platoon occupied strong point last night and [illegible] from it this morning (b) Four sections attached (c) Sgt Wal Cpl Dice Cpl Auston L/C Turner (d) None (e) No (f) It would involve great risk to reoccupy it by day AAA

Is there any truth in a persistent rumour that we are being relieved by 2/7th LR tonight AAA

FROM 2/Lt. Wilkinson

PLACE & TIME 4.15 pm

*This line should be erased if not required.

(B.O 10651 Wt. 498 M 5?? 195,000 ... & Co. Ltd 10/1? ... Forms C. 2123/2

Army Form C.2121
(in pads of 100).
No. of Message

[MES]SAGES AND SIGNALS.

Prefix ....Code ....m. | Words | Charge | This message is on a/c of: ....Service. | Recd. at ....m.

Office of Origin and Service Instructions.

Sent
At............m.
To ....
By ....

(Signature of "Franking Officer.")

Date ....
From ....
By ....

TO 2/Lt Wilkinson Brook Bovis

Sender's Number.	Day of Month.	In reply to Number.	AAA
* AHD27	21		

Information	is	needed	at once	on
the	following	points		
(a)	What	Platoon	occupied	strong
point	(previously	held	by No 1)	last
night	and	attacked	from	it
this	morning			
(b)	How	many	sections	attacked
(c)	What	NCOs	went	with
	the	attackers		
(d)	How	many	sections	remained
	behind			
(e)	Are	the	sections	mentioned
	in (d)	still	occupying	S/Point
(f)	If	not	it	must
	be	reoccupied	Can	it
	be	done	by	day?

From COB
Place
Time 3pm

The above may be forwarded as now corrected.

Censor.

(Z) Mr Sgts 2/Lt Adj Adj

Signature of Addressor or person authorised to telegraph in his name.

* This line should be erased if not required.

750,000. W 2186—M509. H. W. & V., Ld. 6/16.

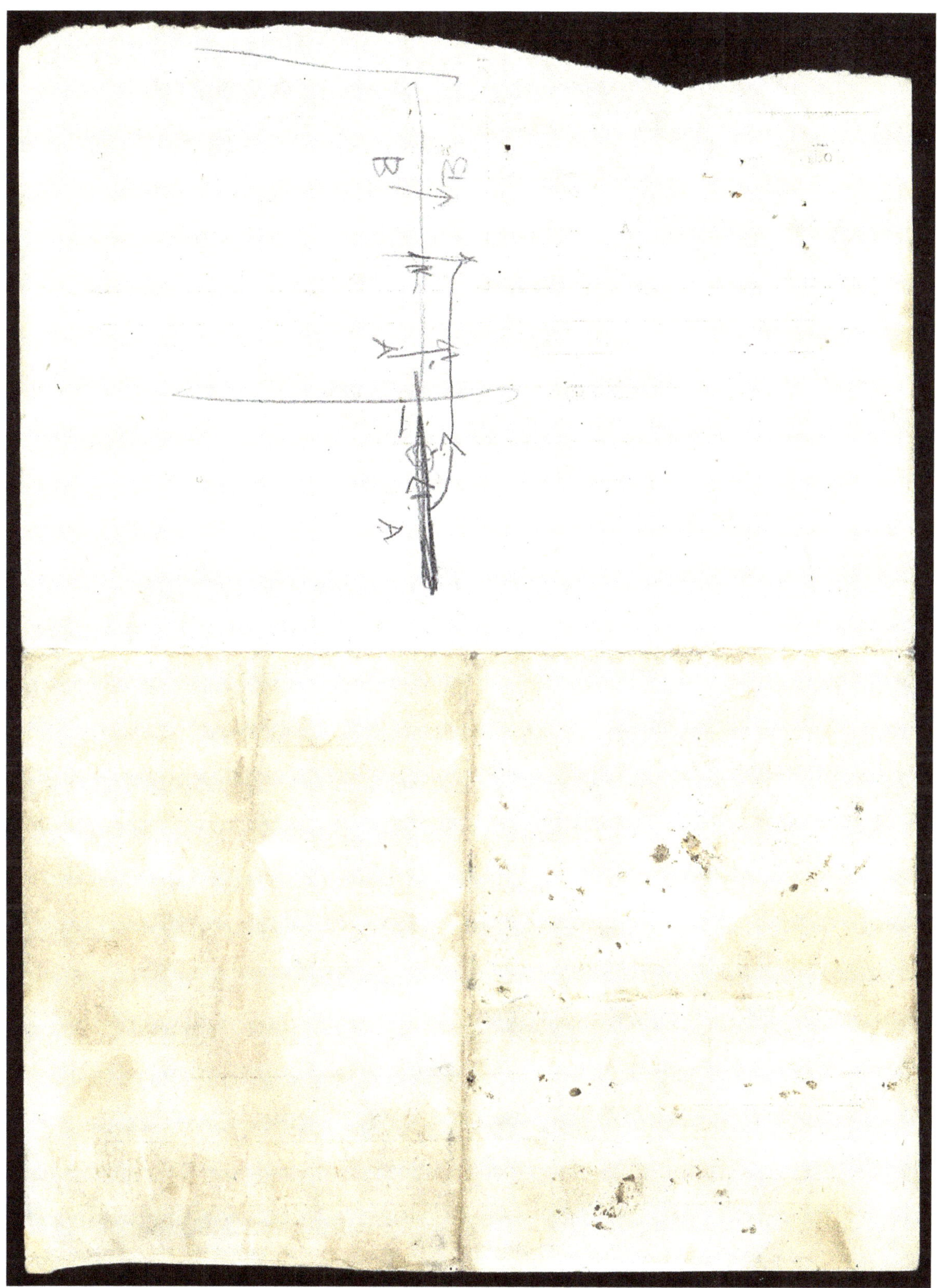

2/6th

174th. Infantry Brigade.

The following pieces of information were obtained from wounded Officers and men of the 2/6th Battalion The London Regt. who took part in the attack on BOVIS Trench on 21/5/17.

2/Lieut. Pickup (Severely wounded).
Right Company in attack. Was wounded before entering BOVIS Trench but went on. Wounded again in trench. Was taken prisoner by Germans. Had his compass, revolver etc., taken by them. Released owing to two of his guard being shot by some of our men. Claims to have killed 5 Germans himself. Crawled back later. Saw a thin wire running from BOVIS Trench towards BULLECOURT. Did not follow it up as far as our trenches. States no hitch in forming up or advance - German wire no obstacle. Saw no dug-outs in BOVIS Trench. BOVIS Trench strongly held. Germans lying just behind it. Heard them call out to our men who got in "Dig in". Machine guns are on Sunken road and just East and West of it in BOVIS Trench U.22.c.3. as shown on map of 20/5/17. Germans were wearing white patches on helmets. Believes from various things that the Germans were preparedand waiting for our attack. Believes we killed a number of Germans. Right flank platoon of right flank Company.

2/Lieut. Wilmot.
Right Company in attack. Wounded by a bullet soon after advancing. No hitch in forming up. Men followed the barrage well.

Sergt. Garlick (?).
Left of attack. Advanced up Sunken road in U.21.d. Jumped into trench almost same time as barrage lifted off it. Was bombed almost immediately from rear of trench and wounded. Says they have machine guns as shown on map of 20/5/17 i.e. on Sunken road and West of it in (U.21.d.2.6.) States BOVIS Trench very strongly held. Lay in a shell hole about 20 yards from BOVIS Trench until 11 p.m. that night. Was going to try and get away just when the Bosche barrage and our own started about 9 p.m. On his way back nearly crawled into a Bosche listening post in a shell hole between BOVIS Trench and our lines. Was challenged but they did not fire. Enemy kept the Sunken road in U.21.d. under intermittent ~~fx~~ bursts of machine gun fire directly our barrage lifted. Mr Clarke's Platoon

Corpl. ________________ ?.
Left attack - advanced up Sunken road in U.21.d. Got into BOVIS Trench and was wounded there - Crawled back and got in somewhere by CRUCIFIX. Confirms positions of Machine guns given and says trench was strongly held.

Mr Clarke's Platoon

REPORT ON THE ATTACK MADE ON BOVIS TRENCH BY THE 2/6th BATTN. LONDON REGT. on the 21st MAY 1917.

LINE HELD.

Ran approximately as shown on sketch attached from East end of sunken road U 22 c 7520 to CRUCIFIX at U 27 b 22. A post was held in German trench at U 22 c 7535. Touch maintained with 176th Brigade on right at crossroads U 22 d 0025, and with 180th Brigade on left at U 21 d 3035.

TASK

(a) To capture BOVIS trench from U 22 c 4545 to U 21 d 4760, roads on either flank inclusive.
Troops to be formed up one hour before zero.
Attack to be carried out under a hurricane bombardment of BOVIS trench lasting 4 minutes, troops moving forward as barrage commences and assaulting trench as it lifts.

(b) The posts in eastern end of BOVIS trench between U 22 d 0030 to U 22 c 7535 to open an intense barrage at zero with bombs and rifle grenades on the German post East of the road at U 22 c 4742. At zero plus 4 minutes barrage to cease and post to be rushed and touch at once gained with troops in the trench further West.

(c) A strong patrol with Lewis Gun to move on the right of the leading wave up the BULLECOURT-FACTORY road with the object of protecting the right flank of the attack.

(d) A Lewis Gun to be pushed forward and established in the old communication trench joining BOVIS trench at U 22 c 0752.

(e) A special party of one strong platoon to be echelonned in depth along the CRUCIFIX-FACTORY road on the left of the attacking waves to take over the post at U 21 d 3036 as a bombing and lewis gun post. Remainder of platoon to move forward at zero with attacking waves, to mop up dugouts in CRUCIFIX-FACTORY road about U 21 d 0037 and establish a block and bombing post in HINDENBERG support trench about 100^x from above mentioned road.

DISPOSITIONS.

Task (a) allotted to A Coy less 1 platoon with 1 platoon of C Coy on the right, and B Coy on the left. Dividing line between Companies TOAST ALLEY inclusive to A Coy.
(b) One platoon of A Coy
(c) One platoon of D Coy
(d) To be arranged by A Coy
(e) One platoon of C Coy

Tape was laid out 300^x from the main objective and troops ordered into position 1 hour before zero.

ACTION. Troops were extended on tape as ordered except that flanking patrols to push up roads (tasks (c) & (e)) moved up just before.
At zero the artillery opened a hurricane bombardment lasting 4 minutes on BOVIS trench and M.G. emplacements located in neighbourhood. A Coy (with 1 platoon of C Coy) and B Coy followed the barrage closely. The platoon of D Coy in post at U 22 c 7535 put down a barrage of bombs and rifle grenades on enemy posts E of road (U 22 c 4742) and attacked over the open.
Enemy Machine Guns were active in spite of barrage and enemy counter barrage came down quickly. From evidence gathered from N.C.Os and men it appears that heavy casualties were suffered in the centre and touch was lost between right and left.

RIGHT. The right Coy advanced over the objective which they were unable to recognize and continued forward about another 200^x losing direction and swinging half right.

The right flank platoon (moving up road) suffered severely and were carried away to the North East by the right of the main attack swinging.

The right platoon working from U 22 c 7535 moved South West and then attacked northwards, passing over their objective and mixing with right of main attack.

LEFT. The left of main attack met with severe machine gun fire and apparently could not reach objective. It also lost direction and moved northwest leaving a large gap between it and the right Coy.

The left patrol (e) unable to make ground along the sunken road owing to machine gun fire moved up out of it Eastwards and delivered a frontal attack on the enemy posts at U 21 d 6065 in conjunction with the left of B Coy, but suffered heavily from machine guns working from a bank at about U 21 d 4075, from shell fire and from bombs.

CENTRE. Owing to casualties and especially Officer casualties and loss of touch between left and right and loss of direction the centre of BOVIS trench at U 22 c 0752 was not reached.

The enemy apparently held the left strongly but retired from the right to a line of consolidated shell-holes in rear and advancing again threatened to work round to the left flank of our right Coy who were digging in. Machine guns and well posted snipers caused heavy losses and the right, unable to hold their ground gradually withdrew to the original position on the road from U 22 c 7580 to U 22 c 5010 which had been taken over by a platoon of the 7th LONDON when the attack began. Some portion remained out until night and apparently all but one became casualties in an attempt to rejoin Battalion. Isolated men of the left Coy and of the left flanking platoon including wounded crawled back to our front line during the morning, the remainder stood their ground until the evening when the enemy attacked in strong force from both flanks and drove them back.

The arrangements made for communication failed as the telephone instrument was smashed by shell fire and the pigeon men were apparently put out of action.

The causes of failure appear to be

(1) failure to recognise objective owing to the effect of our shell fire and advancing too far

(2) Heavy casualties from machine guns which had not been put out of action by our artillery (especially in the centre and on left flank)

(3) Heavy losses in Officers.

(4) Gap in the centre owing to casualties, and

(5) Loss of direction in consequence of (3) & (4).

The men lined up on the tape at the point of assembly correctly, and made a good start.

Of the 111 men reported missing, 4 have since reported and evidence points to the fact that the remainder were either killed or so severely wounded as to be unable to get back to our lines. Of 11 Officers who went over only 3 have returned, all of them wounded.

From the statements of all N.C.Os and men who have returned it seems probable that the enemy suffered heavily.

A. G. Foord

Major.

27/5/17.

Comdg. 2/6th Bn. The London Regt.

A

Copy No:.....9

SECRET

2/6th LONDON REGT. ORDER NO. 1.
(Ref. Map 57c N.W. 1/20000 and Trench Map).
(ECOUST ST. MAIN 1/10000)

29/5/17.

1. The Battalion will relieve the 2/7th London Regt:-
   (a) In the Left Sub-Sector tonight 29/30 May.
   (b) In Right Sub-Sector Line on the night 31 May/1 June.
2. The starting point will be the Quartermasters Stores.
3. The Battalion will leave Camp in the following order:-
   "C" Coy to billets in ECOUST, to pass starting point at 9.0 p.m.
   "D" Coy to Caves in ECOUST, to pass starting point at 9.5 p.m.
   "B" Coy to Shelters on W. of MORY-ECOUST road, to pass starting point at 9.10 p.m.
   "A" Coy to Trenches on VRAUCOURT-St. LEGER Road, to pass starting point at 9.15 p.m.
   Bn. H.Q. to Caves in ECOUST, to pass starting point at 9.20 p.m.
   200 yards distance to be maintained between Companies on the march, and 50 yards distance between Platoons.
4. O.C. Coys and 1 N.C.O. A & B Coys, 4 N.C.Os from "C" and 5 N.C.Os from "D" will be at ECOUST at 6.30 p.m. today 29th May, to reconnoitre the Left Sub-Sector Support. These Officers and N.C.Os will afterwards proceed to their respective positions, and later the N.C.Os will be sent to meetthe leading platoons of their respective Companies as under:-
   "B" Coy.....9.40 p.m.) At cross-roads
   "A" " .....9.45 ") B.17.b.2.3.
   "C" " .....10.30 ") Crater Dump
   "D" " .....10.35 ") ECOUST.
   Bn. H.Q.....10.40 ")
   The extra N.C.O. of D Coy will act as guide to Bn. H.Q.
5. Completion of reliefs will be reported to Bn. H.Q. by runner, duplicate messages being sent at 10 minutes interval.
6. At the earliest possible moment after relief O.C. Coys will send in to Bn. H.Q. a sketch map showing accurate disposition of platoons and location of Coy H.Q.
7. All ranks are to be warned against:-
   (a) Collecting at the entrances of dugouts. The location of these are known to the enemy and they are consequently liable to be accurately shelled.
   (b) Unnecessary movement during hours of daylight.
   This order must be strictly enforced at all times.
8. All men will be in possession of:-
   Trench rations for two days
   Full water bottles
   50 extra rounds S.A.A.
   tonight and when going into the Left Sub-Sector Line on night 31 May/1 June.
9. Water for troops in Left Sub-Sector Line will be brought up by the 1st line Transport to the Crater Dump, ECOUST, in petrol tins at the rate of:-
   "A" Coy ...... 8 tins
   "B" " ...... 8 tins
   "C" " ......12 "
   "D" " ......8 "
   H.Q. .... 7 "
   " (reserve).. 4 "
   Medical Off... 3 "
   Carrying parties will be provided by "A" & "B" Coys. No. petrol tins will be handed over full by carrying parties until an empty one is received in exchange. The 1st line Transport will wait for the returned empties at theCrater Dump.

Order No. 1 (Contd.) 29/5/17.

Company Q.M. Sgts will accompany all carrying parties whether for water or stores.
Petrol tins in accordance with above distribution will be sent up tonight 29th May under arrangements to be made by the Quartermaster & Transport Officer.
O.C. Coys will arrange for the collection of their own water supply and "D" Coy that of Bn. H.Q. and Medical Officer in addition.

10. All S.A.A., Grenades, tools and trench stores will be taken over from Companies ~~Xc~~ being relieved. A duplicate list will be forwarded to Bn. H.Q. within 12 hours of relief. O.C. Coys should keep a copy of this list.
Company dumps will be formed at once and protected from shell fire.
There are many tools, arms, ammunition, bombs and equipment yet to be salvaged in BULLECOURT,- this must be undertaken without delay after taking over the front line. O.C. Coys will be responsible for this in their Company areas.

11. Latrine accomodation will be arranged at once and carefully supervised by O.C. Coy. Any refuse found lying about must be buried immediately and O.C. Coys will select the site for this purpose.
When selecting sites for Latrines and Refuse pits, the health of the troops must be the first consideration. The removal system should be adopted for Latrines.

12. In addition to improving sanitary conditions, efforts will be concentrated on improving our defences, especial attention being paid to improvement of our front line trenches and communications both lateral and from front to rear and wiring.
Every opportunity must be seized for work of this nature and strict attention will be paid to continuity of work. O.C. Coys will obtain particulars of work commenced when taking over from the Battalion relieved.

13. The burying of dead in BULLECOURT will be carried out in accordance with instructions already issued.

14. Paras 7 to 13 will apply both in Support and in the front line.

15. The necessity for taking the strictest precautions in the use of the telephone or buzzer in forward areas cannot be too firmly impressed upon all ranks. The use of all telephones and buzzers will be carefully supervised by the senior officer on the spot. He will endorse all written messages before allowing them to be sent by telephone or buzzer and a note of any message to be sent verbally by telephone ~~or buzzer~~ will be made and sanctioned by his signature beforehand. In the case of telephones forward of Bn. H.Q. as a general rule the senior officer on the spot only should use the telephone and its use must be restricted to messages of an urgent nature.. All other messages will be sent by runner.

16. Acknowledge.

(Sgd.) S.W.F.Crofts.
2/Lt. & A/Adjutant.

Issued by runner at 5.10 p.m.

1. O.C. Bn.
2. Adjutant.
3. "A" Coy
4. "B" Coy
5. "C" Coy
6. "D" Coy
7. 174th Inf. Bde.
8. File.

9. War Diary } Typed later.
10. " " }

RIGHT FRONT COMPANY

WORK COMPLETED.

(a) The communication trench linking up my position with BULLECOURT AVENUE has been deepened and widened for a distance of some 40 yards; a sandbag traverse has been constructed in main trench to give further protection from enemy's enfilade artillery and M.G. fire. The main trench has been lowered and the parapet and parados improved by sandbagging. Sandbag steps up ba k of Sunken Road have been made for more easy access to posts. One additional temporary shelter has been hollowed out in bank and sandbagged. 12 sections of baby elephants have been carried up to my position ready to be built in.

(b) WORK COMMENCED BUT NOT FINISHED Nil.

(c) WORK PROPOSED.

(1) Linking up by C.T. Coy H.Q. and main trench leading to posts also connecting this to C.T. running to BULLECOURT AVENUE. Assisting R.E. to put in elephants on sunken road.

(2) The wiring of the entire front of my position with knife rests as the condition of the ground prevents other methods being effectively put up. Continuing of filling shell-holes in front with wire obstacles of any description.

(3) The construction of a latrine for use of Officers, suitable position is not yet decided upon.

W I R I N G.

A reconnaisance of my front and examination of the wire showed that owing to the crumbly nature of the ground it was inadvisable to fix apron wire. Two 10 ft. lengths of this already fixed could be easily lifted out, about 40 feet front has loose wire obstacles placed in the shellholes, and I continued this same method last evening.

In my opinion the best method would be to put out knife rests and if the frames could be made 6 feet long and sent forward to the front line they could be wired, taken out and picketed down.

S A N I T A T I O N.

Two F head latrines have been constructed:- one leading out of C.T. just south of where it crosses sunken road to my position, one leading out of main trench on left of my position (see rough sketch). The tins supplied are being used and in the absence of lids the tins are covered with a sandbag. Under cover of darkness and during the day if necessary, these tins are emptied by the sanitary men and buried in shell-holes in rear of sunken road. All tins and rubbish are collected and put into sandbags hung up in trenches for the purpose, and are also buried in rear under cover of dark.

LEFT FRONT COMPANY.

I was handicapped in my work by the fact that throughout each night there was frequent shelling and M.G. fire and that the moon was very bright, and behind us. The casualties suffered in No. 9 platoon did not help matters. Wiring could not be carried out though attempts were made.

(a) WORK COMPLETED. Trench held by No. 11 platoon U.27.b.0.8. has been completed, no work is required upon it except rivetting possibly in parts.

(b) WORK COMMENCED BUT NOT COMPLETED.
Trench held by No. 9 Platoon U.27.b.90.85. Trench deepened sufficiently but has only a fire step in parts. More work required on this. This trench has been knocked about by shell fire, and part of parapet knocked in on two occasions. This has been partly repaired.
Strog point held at night by No. 10 Platoon U.21.d.9.1. Good work has been put into this but there is still much to be done. Two of th arms of the strong point are roughly completed and three sides of the centre square. Trench held by this platoon by day has been deepened but not enough U.22.b.55.30
Trench held by No. 12 Platoon U.27.b.15.80 consisted of a row of funk holes dug in ground. These have been deepened and are being linked up. This has not been finished.

(c) WORK PROPOSED.
(1) Coy. H.Q. required rebuilding. Strut should be put in and elephants used. A sapper's job. A shallo C.T. to be dug between Coy H.Q. and No. 11 Platoon U.27.b.0.8. As communication by day is very exposed. A C.T. to be dug from Coy H.Q. to left support line.
(2) Wire to be put up in gap between U.27.b.4.8. and U.27.b. 90.85.
(3) A small trench T shaped to be dug at each post for a latrine.

W I R I N G. Nil.

S A N I T A T I O N.
Latrines are situated in the trench in each case and are dug in the side of the parados like a funk hole, and the bucket placed there. They are emptied into holes dug in the botton of shell craters and covered up. Tins and rubbish are collected in sandbags and are put in shell holes and covered well up.

RIGHT SUPPORT COMPANY.

(a) WORK COMPLETED.

(i) L.G. Posts at U.28.a.9.5. and U.28.a.8.7. have been provided with fire steps and completed sufficiently to provide fire positions and protection for gun teams. Several lengths of communication trench were completed sufficiently to allow safety for traffic, but have since been filled in by shell bursts, notably between C.H.Q. at U.28.a.4.2. and proposed strong point at U.28.a.6.5. A sandbag fire step for Riflemen completed opposite dugout entrance at U.28.a.8.5. to the right of L.G. post.

(b) WORK COMMENCED BUT NOT COMPLETED.

Deepening and widening trench between U.28.a.4.2. and about 100 yards right towards L.G. post at U.28.a.8.7. Work was only possible on one night and was then twice interrupted by heavy shelling.

(c) WORK PROPOSED.

It seems of first importance to deepen and widen the whole length of trench between U.28.a.3.1. and U.28.a.8.7. Next build fire steps at intervals in parapet between those points so that garrison can man parapet in the event of an attack. This includes digging corpses from parapet, parados and bottom of trench, of which there are still many between U.28.a.6.5. and U.28.a.8.7. Permanent latrines need to be built at a safe sanitary distance from dugout and the removal system for both urine and excreta installed. Not advisable at present on account of enemy observation and accurate shelling along the whole of this sector. The strong points require traverses putting in and ammunition dumps provided, and bomb stores and bombing posts dug.

W I R I N G.

The whole sector should be wired, the strong point coming first in order of importance, and then wire in between them.

S A N I T A T I O N.

Everything that comes under the above heading is required in this sector, the most important being the digging out and reburying of corpses and the provision of fly-proof latrines.

3 latrines have been dug from leading off trench at a safe distance from C.H.Q. and 5 & 6 platoons dugouts. Earth pits for excreta with earth for covering after use. Urine buckets are removed nightly and emptied in shell holes a good distance from trench and filled in with earth. All tins and rubbish are collected during the day and buried by night. Have also buried 8 sandbags full of latter left in dugout by previous occupants.

G A S   A P P A R A T U S.

This is entirely lacking and at present there is no protection for dugout entrances. This requires immediate attention. I understood from the 7th London Bn. that the necessary apparatus had been indented for.

S A L V A G E.

An enormous amount requires to be done in this direction

LEFT SUPPORT COMPANY.

(a) WORK COMPLETED. Nil.

(b) WORK COMMENCED BUT NOT COMPLETED.

(1) Work has been done at various parts of the trench to make it deeper (from U.27.b.10.65. to U.27.b.55.30.) There is not much more work to be done between U.27.b. 10.65. and U.27.b. 3.4. There is a good deal to be done between U.27.b.3.4. and U.27.b.55.30; some of the worst parts in this piece have been done, but there is a strip of about 30 yards which requires digging to at least a depth of 3 feet, and there is another strip of about 20 yards close to the road U.27.b.[illegible] which requires digging to some depth.

(2) Trench across road at U.27.b.[illegible].15. This is about [illegible] feet deep by 2 feet wide. This requires deepening and broadening.

(3) Communication trench U.27.b.40.37 running to front line has been started but will require another working party for 2 or 3 nights. There is another communication trench started at U.27.b.35.15 which only runs about 20 yards and is about 2 feet deep.

W I R I N G. Nil.

S A N I T A T I O N.

Latrine arrangements are one small pit with two seats in a small trench running off main trench. This is unsatisfactory and I have started another length of trench. The present latrine is like this and is exposed besides being too small.
I have started making another arm to the small communication trench like this and intended putting a couple of pails at the end of the head.
This requires to be done immediately and old latrine filled in - it will take about [illegible] men one night.
There are four urine buckets, two per platoon, down the trench. These are emptied at night in shell holes well to the rear of trench. Tins and rubbish have been collected in sandbags by each platoon, and will be buried at night in selected places. Situation of latrine U.27.b.30.45.

Remarks. Another latrine needs to be built (for a strong company) somewhere about U.27.b.r.o. The most important work is to get a good trench all along so that movement cannot be observed. A trench requires to be made at U.27.b.15.35. to connect with strong point. There is still a lot of work to be done to put support trench in a satisfactory state of defence and I consider this is the most important piece of work.

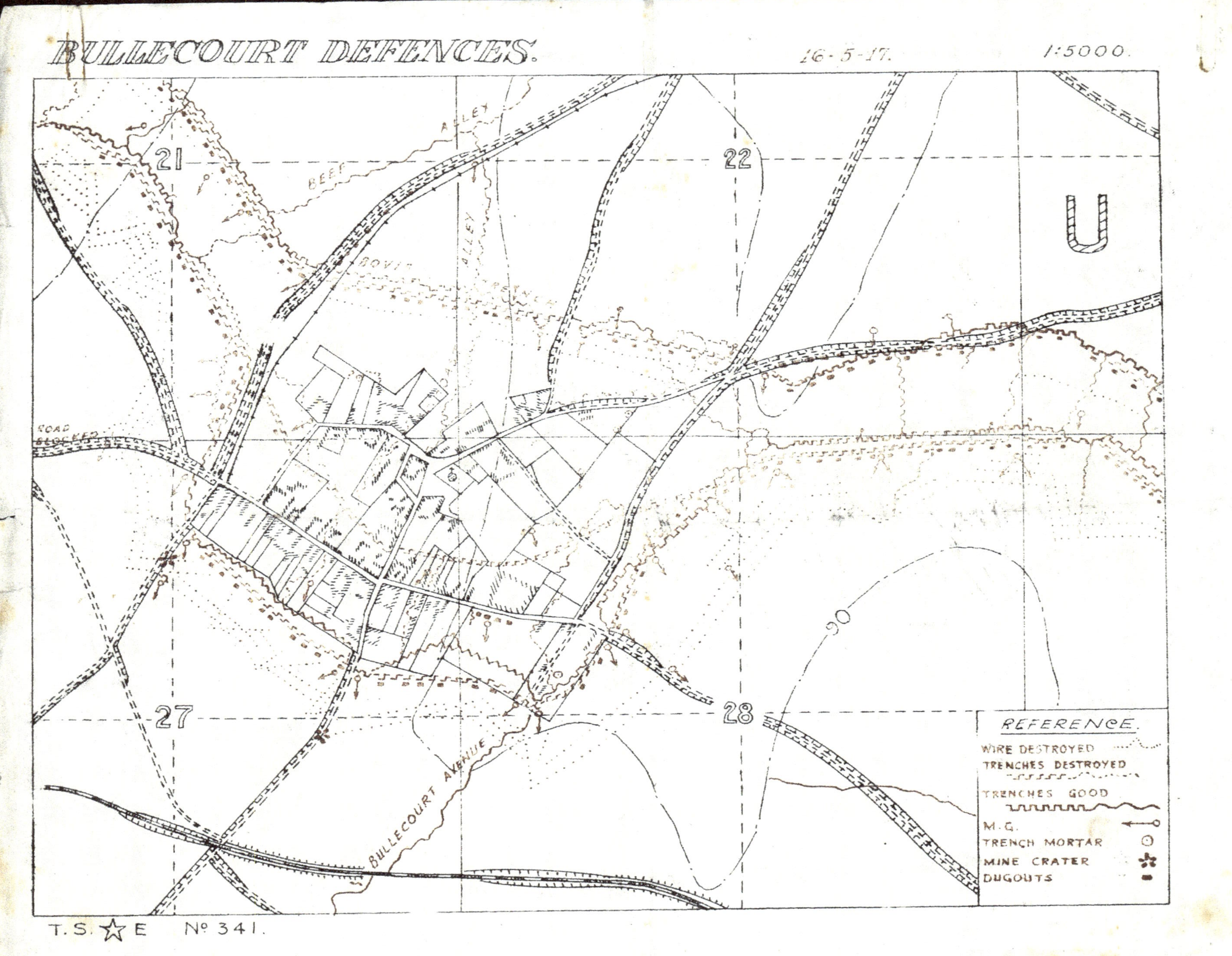
BULLECOURT DEFENCES.
16-5-17.
1:5000.
21
22
27
28
U
BEEF ALLEY
ALLEY
BOVIS TRENCH
ROAD BLOCKED
BULLECOURT AVENUE
90
REFERENCE.
WIRE DESTROYED
TRENCHES DESTROYED
TRENCHES GOOD
M.G.
TRENCH MORTAR
MINE CRATER
DUGOUTS
T.S.☆E Nº 341.

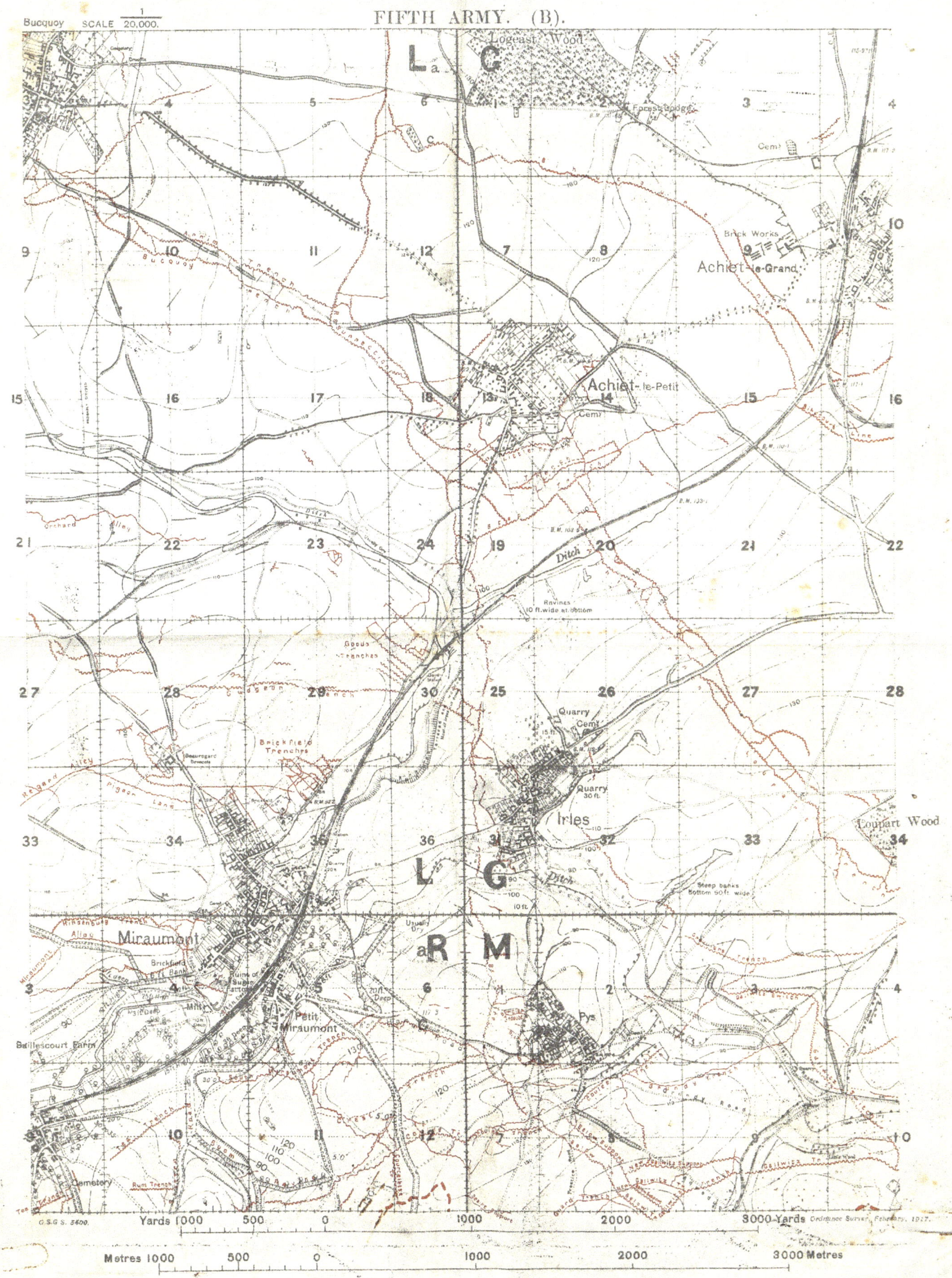

FIFTH ARMY. (B).
Bucquoy SCALE 1/20,000.
Logeast Wood
Forest Lodge
Brick Works
Achiet-le-Grand
Achiet-le-Petit
Bucquoy Trench
Orchard Alley
Ditch
Ravines 10 ft. wide at bottom
Goods Trenches
Brickfield Trenches
Quarry
Cem.
Irles
Loupart Wood
Steep banks bottom 50 ft. wide
Miraumont
Brickfield
Petit Miraumont
Pys
Baillescourt Farm
Cemetery
Usually Dry
G.S.G.S. 3500.
Yards 1000 500 0 1000 2000 3000 Yards
Ordnance Survey, February, 1917.
Metres 1000 500 0 1000 2000 3000 Metres

O.C. D Coy

Please mark in on this sketch map your dispositions by Platoons with Lewis Guns shown. Also posts strongpoints both belonging to ~~[illegible]~~ your sector & adjoining it

To be at Battn H.Q by 2.45 pm

Show also position of Coy H.Q please

[illegible] 2/Lt
Actg Adjt
2 pm

1 – Strong Point – (13 Plat)

2 – Day Post for Strong Point Garrison

3. Company H Q

4. 15 Platoon

5 – 14 Platoon (trenches near to church)

6 – Reserve dugouts (unoccupied)

·X L. M. G.

21

27

28

Scale 1:10000

BULLECOURT

To COB

MAP

BULLECOURT
21
22
27
28
10 ft
not steep
6 ft
12 feet
Crucifix
10 ft steep
low
CLAUD III
SCALE 1:5000

O.C. 'C' Coy 21/5/17

Please mark in on ~~this~~ sketch map your dispositions by Platoons with Lewis Guns shown. Also ~~[illegible]~~ posts & strong points both belonging to your sector & adjoining it.

To be at Battn H.Q by 2.45 pm

Show also position Co H.Q please

[signature] Lt. Actg Adj
2 pm

L.G.

B.P.

12

12

½ section

STRONG POINT

9

10.

Coy H.Q

11. PLATOON

11.

1 section

O.C. D Coy 2/7th Batt. Please mark in on this sketch map your dispositions by Platoons with Lewis Guns shown. Also posts & strongpoint [illegible] belonging to your sector & adjoining it.

BULLECOURT

Scale 1 : 10,000

Yards 500

Please also position Coy H.Q. please.

21/5/17
2.10 pm

[illegible]
Lt
Adjt
2/6

21

22

27

28

Cutting posts in ruins

Coy HQ

X strong point
— [illegible]

S.C.G.
[illegible]
Lt

116
85
31 5

O.C. 'A' Coy 2/7th Battn Please mark in on this sketch map your dispositions by Platoons with Lewis Guns shown also posts & strongpoints both belonging to your sector and adjoining

21/5/17 [illegible] Actg Adjt

2.10 pm

Shew also posn Coy H.Q. please.

BULLECOURT

Scale 1:10,000

Yards 100 50 0 500

LG
x Bombing Posts

BULLECOURT (in ruins).

To HENDECOURT

Reproduced by 2/6th London Regt. Int.

2/6th London Rgt

June 1917

Index

SUBJECT.

No.	Contents.	Date.
	70/2976—3000.	

(49,674). Wt.42,605—128. 2000. 4/20. Gp.164. A.&E.W.
(51,507). „ 6005—137. 500. 5/20. „ „

Confidential

Vol 6

War Diary

of

2/6th London Regt.

from 29.5.17

to 30.6.17

Army Form C. 2118.

Instructions regarding War Diaries and Intelligence Summaries are contained in F. S. Regs., Part II. and the Staff Manual respectively. Title pages will be prepared in manuscript.

WAR DIARY
or
~~INTELLIGENCE~~ SUMMARY.

(*Erase heading not required.*)

Place	Date	Hour	Summary of Events and Information	Remarks and references to Appendices
	May 29th	9pm	Left camp S. of MORY & relieved 2/7th Bn Londons in ECOUST. Hd Qtrs & 1 Coy in caves under church, 1 Coy in billets in village, 1 Coy on ~~[illegible]~~ Road S.E. of village. 1 Coy at L'HOMME MORT	See Order No 1 App^x A
	June 1		2nd Lieut COLTMAN died of wounds.	
	1/2	night	Relieved 2/7th Bn in BULLECOURT. D Coy right front. B Coy right support. C Coy left front. A Coy left support. Left support in new position further East. Bn Hdqtrs in new position near Embankment. 1 O/R killed 5 wounded	Appendix A.
	3		2nd Lieut A.S. HILL died of wounds. 6 O/Ranks killed & 9 wounded.	
	3/4	night	Relieved by 2/9th Bn LONDONS. Relief complete by 1.15 am 4th June. 1 O/R wounded	Order No 2 Appen^x B.
	4	3am	Reached camp South of MORY (H36 b 5 8. Ref. 57c N.W)	
	13		B Coy attached to 2/8th Bn LONDONS passed under orders 173 Bde & occupied posts in line East of CROISILLES.	
	14	10pm	Moved from camp to ST. LEGER & occupied sunken road South of village.	Order No 3 Appen^x C.
			173rd Bde attacked HINDENBURG front line from HUMP to KNUCKLE inclusive. Successful.	
	15		C Coy attached to 2/2nd Bn LONDONS (173rd Bde) took over posts North of B Coy. 4 O/R killed 2 wounded	
	15/16	night	Bn (less B & C Coys) moved to Railway Embankment in T24d (Ref 51B S.W) & came under 173 Bde	
	16		173rd Bde attacked HINDENBURG support line. Partially successful.	
	16/17	night	174th Bde relieved 173rd Bde. B & C Coys still holding posts in front. A & D Coys & Bn Hd Qtrs in Embankment.	Map appendix C
	17		1 O/R killed. 11 wounded.	

T2134. Wt. W708-776. 500000. 4/15. Sir J. C. & S.

Instructions regarding War Diaries and Intelligence Summaries are contained in F. S. Regs., Part II. and the Staff Manual respectively. Title pages will be prepared in manuscript.

WAR DIARY
or
INTELLIGENCE SUMMARY.
(Erase heading not required.)

Army Form C. 2118.

Place	Date	Hour	Summary of Events and Information	Remarks and references to Appendices
	June 22		1 O/R killed 1 wounded	
	23/24	night	Bn. relieved by 21st MANCHESTERS & moved to MORY COPSE camp. Relief complete by 12.20 am 24th	Order No 44 Appendix "D"
	24	10 am	Bn. moved into quarters at COURCELLES vacated by 21st MANCHESTERS.	
	28		Bn. inspected by G.O.C. 174th Brigade.	

[illegible signature]
A/Adjt.

T2134. Wt. W708—776. 500000. 4/15. Sir J. C. & S.

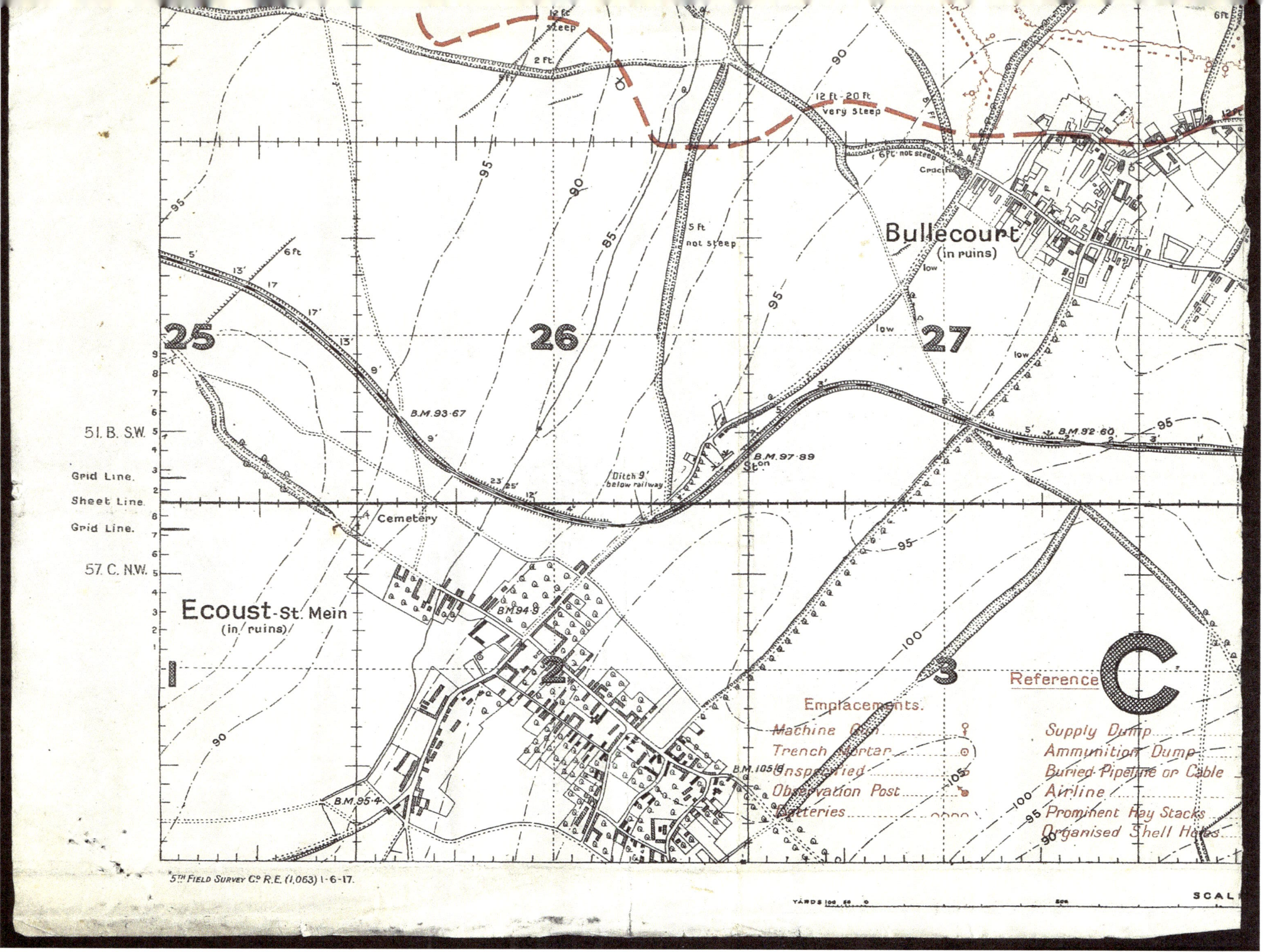
Bullecourt
(in ruins)
Ecoust-St. Mein
(in ruins)
Cemetery
25
26
27
C
2
3
51. B. S.W.
Grid Line.
Sheet Line.
Grid Line.
57. C. N.W.
12 ft 20 ft
very steep
12 ft
steep
5 ft
not steep
6 ft not steep
Crucifix
Ditch 9'
below railway
B.M. 93·67
B.M. 97·89
B.M. 92·60
B.M. 94·9
B.M. 95·4
B.M. 105·8
Reference
Emplacements.
Machine Gun
Trench Mortar
Unspecified
Observation Post
Batteries
Supply Dump
Ammunition Dump
Buried Pipeline or Cable
Airline
Prominent Hay Stacks
Organised Shell Holes
5TH FIELD SURVEY Co R.E. (1,063) 1-6-17.
SCALE

No 4 Ptn.
No 2 Ptn.
A Coy HQ
No 3 Ptn
No 1 Ptn
A Coy HQ
Trench Traced Only.
No 5 Ptn
No 6 Ptn
No 7
No 8
B Coy HQ
Bn. HQ
R.A.P.
M.G. Coys.
12 Ptn
11 Ptn
10 Ptn
9 Ptn
C Coy HQ
C
13 Ptn
D Coy HQ
14 Ptn
15 Ptn
16 Ptn
D
40,000
2/7/17.
Office Copy.

B.

Copy No 4

3/6/17.

2/8th Bn. London Regt. Order No. 2
(Ref. map 57C NW 1/20000 and Trench Map)
(ECOUST ST. MEIN 1/10000)

---

1. The Battalion will be relieved by the 2/9th Bn. London Regt. tonight. The disposition of the 2/9th Bn. in the line will be:-

Right) B Coy line at present held by D Coy - 3 platoons
Front)
near TANK CRATER & old B Coy H.Q. - 1 platoon.

Left Front.
C Coy line held by C Coy except
CRUCIFIX POINT & reserve position - 1 platoon

2. Guides will be supplied as follows:-

C Coy will detail (a) 2 guides for 1 platoon of C Coy 2/9th for N.W. post.
(b) 3 guides for 3 platoons of C Coy
(c) 2 guides for 1 platoon of D Coy 2/9th Bn. for Crucifix Post &reserve.

A Coy will detail (d) 3 guides for 3 platoons of D Coy.
C & A guides to be at CENTRAL CRATER U 27.d.50.95 at 10.15 p.m.
D Coy will detail (e) 3 guides for 3 platoons of B Coy 2/9th Bn.
B " " " (f) 1 guide for 1 platoon of B Coy for old B Coy H.Q. position.
B " " " (g) 4 guides for 4 platoons of A Coy 2/9th
D & B Coy guides to be at TANK CRATER at 10.15 p.m.
The guides for serial letters (a) (e) & (f) will be given special instructions to prevent their guiding the wrong platoons.

3. All companies will report relief complete to Bn. H.Q. and will proceed on relief to ECOUST, A & C Coys along the track west of FIRS ROAD (BULLECOURT ECOUST Road) and B & D Coys by the track on East side of BULLECOURT AVENUE. Platoons will march at 200x distance

4. At ECOUST, Lewis Guns, empty water tins & salvage will be loaded on limbers at CRATER DUMP & Coys will march to camp vacated by 2/10th Bn. London Regt. at H.3.b.5.8. with not less than 200x distance between Companies & 50x between platoons.

5. Baths will be available for the Battalion for the whole day on 5th June.

(sgd) S.W.F. Crofts.
2/Lt. & A/Adjutant.

Issued by runner at

1. O.C. Bn.
2. A Coy
3. B "
4. C "
5. D "
6. File.
7. } Wardiary
8. }

Headquarters.
174th Infantry Brigade.

The attached copies of reports from Company Commanders on the work done in BULLECOURT during the Battalion's tour of duty in the front line, and the present position of the defences, are forwarded for information.

Major.
Comdg. 2/6th Bn. London Regt.

4/6/17.

SECRET.

CURL OPERATION ORDER No. 11.

13th June, 1917.

Copy....

1. The Battalion and 1 Coy. 2/6th Battn. will relieve the 2/7th London Regt and 1 Coy. 2/1st London Regt in the left sector, Right subsector trenches tonight. Relief to be completed by 2.30 a.m. 14th June. Completion to be wired to Bn.H.Q. using code word CLOSE.

2. O.s.C. Coys will arrange for guides with their opposite numbers and will choose their own route to the trenches keeping 100 yds between platoons.

3. Companies will leave camp at the times stated below :-

H.Q.	under 2/Lieut Mumford	........8. 0. pm.
Coy. 2/6 London Regt.		........8.15. pm.
D. Coy.		........8.30. pm.
C. "		........8.45. pm.
B. "		........9. 0. pm.
A. "		........9.15. pm.

The R.S.M., Rfn Gibney, Cpl Gander and Cpl Grey will proceed to Bn.H.Q. in advance and take over.
Sigs Officer will arrange to take over by 9.0. p.m.

4. The T.O. will detail 1 Limber for H.Q., and 1 for each Coy. which must be loaded by 8.0. pm. with L.G.'s, Officers' Kits and Mess Baskets.
Sigs Equipment and M.O. Stores will be loaded on H.Q. Limber.
The T.O. will arrange for a N.C.O. to be at the Transport Lines to superintend loading from 7 - 8 p.m. All carrying parties should report to him. O.S C.Coys will each tell off 2 O.R.'s to proceed with their Coy. Limber.

5. 2 Limbers of the 2/6th Battn., with two loaders per limber will report to the T.O. at 2/8th Lines at 8.30 pm. This limber will proceed to point U 25.a.6.5. and unload. H.Q., A and C Coy. limbers will dump at point ~~XXXXXXXXX~~ U 25.d.1.9., and B and D Coys. at point C 2 a.3.5.
The T.O. will arrange for limbers to be at their respective dumps at 10.0. pm.

6. Packs will be dumped by Coys at Q.M. Stores by 6.30 p.m..
Water bottles must be filled between 6 - 7 p.m.
Water for any other purposes must not be drawn during this hour.

7. Coys. will each send 4 runners to Bn.H.Q. as soon as their relief is complete.

8. Two days rations will be carried on the man and 3 sandbags per man will be carried.
The Q.M. will arrange for H.Q. and D Coy. to each take 10 tins of water.

9. All trench stores will be taken over and the receipt sent to Bn.H.Q. as soon as possible.

10. The same daily repots and returns will be sent to Bn.H.Q. at the same times as during the last tour.

11. The present camp must be completely cleared by 7.0. pm. tonight and the Battn. formed up in mass on the Battn. Parade Ground facing the Transpott Lines.
The camp must be left absolutely clean.

BY ORDER.

Copies to 1. War diary.
2. O.C. "A" Coy.
3. " "B" "
4. " "C" "
5. " "D" "
6. L.G.O.
7. T.O.
8. Q.M.
9. M.O.
10. Sigs. Officer.
11 2/6th Bn

2/7th Bn

Bde No 7.

Operation Order 24

SECRET

Ref maps. ECOUST ST MEIN 1/10000
173rd BDE Disposition map No 2.
57 C NW 1/20000

1 Relief — The Battalion (less A Coy) will be relieved in the line tonight by 2/8th LONDONS.
A Coy will be relieved by a company of 2/6th LONDONS

2 Guides — B & A Coy will provide guides as arranged with O.C. the relieving Coy. O.C. B Coy will be notified later of the guides required from his Coy. O.C. C Coy will provide a guide for each of his posts & one for his HQ, to be at the SW end of PELICAN AVENUE at 10 pm.

O.C. D Coy will provide a guide for each post at his HQ at 10-0 pm

3 Route — After relief Coys will return to Camp at MORY (B27 d) by the following routes:-
A Coy - Along valley running from T24 d 82 SSW through T30 a & c B6 a B5-b & c to the ST LEGER-MORY road; thence by the shortest route.
B & C Coys via Sunken Road U25 a 24 - 15 NW of ECOUST; thence via C2 a C2 c C1 d to ECOUST-MORY road.

D Coy & HQ by track from U25 d 19 through U25 c B6 a b to L'HOMME MORT. O's C Coys will have their routes reconnoitred by daylight if necessary.

4 Transport. Officers Mess Cart & Maltese Cart will be at U25 d 10 at 10-0 pm. Limbers for Lewis guns & drums will be at the following points:

A Coy T30 b 48
B " } U25 d 24
D " }
C " C2 a 44.

When loaded all transport will return to Camp under orders of the Transport Officer.

5 Water. O's C A, C & D Coys will ensure that sufficient water for 24 hours is handed over to relieving Coys. The necessary petrol tins will be included as Trench Stores. Coys will carry back to Camp as many tins as they brought up.

6 Trench Stores. O's C Coys will have in readiness for departure by relieving units (a) List of Stores in each post (b) Complete list of Stores in Company Sector. A signed duplicate of the Coy list will be handed in to the Orderly Room on

arrive in Camp

7 Report: Completion of relief will be notified to Battalion HQ. In the line by the code word CARLTON transmitted by quickest means possible. No personal report is required.

[signature] Captain

Capt & Adjt.

Copies as under:-

1 A Coy
2 B "
3 C "
4 D "
5 Signals Officer
6 C.C. Details
7 2/6 LONDONS } For information
8 2/8 " }
9 173rd BDE }
10 174th BDE }
11 War Diary
12 File.

13-6-17

"A" Form.

Army Form C. 2121.
(In pads of 100.)

MESSAGES AND SIGNALS.

No. of Message..............

Prefix............Code..............m | Words. | Charge.

Office of Origin and Service Instructions.

SECRET

S.D.R.

Sent
At..............m.
To..............
By..............

This message is on a/c of:
.... Service.
(Signature of "Franking Officer.")

Recd. at.........m.
Date..............
From..............
By..............

TO 6th LONDON Regt.

Sender's Number.	Day of Month.	In reply to Number.	AAA
* BMT 256	13/6		

Reference para 4. this office BM 7/11 of yesterday (174th Inf. Bde. Warning Order) your Battalion less one Coy now in Right Subsector will now move to ST LEGER to arrive at 11-30 p.m. June 14 and will come under orders of B.G.C. 173rd Inf. Bde. from that hour AAA For your information AAA Orders follow

From 174th I.B.
Place
Time 11. 36 p.m.

The above may be forwarded as now corrected.

(Z) R.M. Barrington Ward Capt. BM 174 I.B.

Censor. | Signature of Addressor or person authorised to telegraph in his name.

* This line should be erased if not required.

(3198.) Wt. W 12952/M1294. 375,000 Pads. 1/17. H. W. & V., Ld. (E. 818.)

"A" Form.

Army Form C. 2121.
(In pads of 100.)

MESSAGES AND SIGNALS.

No. of Message...............

Prefix............Code..............m | Words. | Charge. | This message is on a/c of: | Recd. at ....m.

Office of Origin and Service Instructions.

Sent At................m. To................ By................

........................Service.

(Signature of "Franking Officer.")

Date................ From .... By..................

SECRET.

S.D.R.

TO All recipients of this office B.M./7/11.

Sender's Number.	Day of Month.	In reply to Number.	AAA
* A.B.M.58	13th		

Reference	this	office	B.M./7/11
para 1.	aaa	Instructions	for
one	Company	of	6th
London	Regt.	to	move
today	are	confirmed	aaa
Addressed	all	recipients	of
this	office	No. as	above.

From 174th. Inf. Brigade.

Place

Time 12 noon

The above may be forwarded as now corrected. (Z)

.... Censor.

Captain,
Brigade Major,
174th Infantry Brigade.

Signature of Addressor or person authorised to telegraph in his name.

* This line should be erased if not required.

(3198.) Wt. W 12952/M1294. 375,000 Pads. 1/17. H.W. & V., Ltd. (E. 818.)

Copy.

2/6th London Regt. - Order No. 3
(Ref. Map 57 c N.W.)

14/6/17.

1. The Battalion less B Company will move to St. LEGER to arrive there at 11.30 p.m. on night June 14/15.

2. The starting point will be the Quartermasters stores.

3. The Battalion will leave Camp in the following order:-

Bn. Hd. Qtrs.)	to shelters in (	to pass starting point at 10.0 p.m.
"D" Coy)	sunken road in (	do 10.3 "
"C" ")	B.4.b & d. south (	do 10.6 "
"A" ")	of St. LEGER. (	do 10.9 "

200 yards distance to be maintained between companies on the march & 50 yards between platoons.

4. Guides from advance party will meet Companies on sunken road at B.4.d.3.9.

5. All movement is to be reduced to a minimum during hours of daylight and men are forbidden to leave their quarters without permission from the Company Commanders.

6. All ranks are to be warned against the possibility of gas shells and box respirators will be worn in the alert position at all times.

7. All men will be in possession of:-
Trench rations for two days (in addition to ordinary iron rations)
Full water bottles.
50 extra rounds S.A.A. & 3 sandbags.

8. 10 tins of water per Company will be taken up tonight to St. LEGER and can be drawn from limbers at Bn. Hd. Qtrs. in sunken road. Corpl. & 2 men of the R.A.M.C. (water duties) will accompany the Battalion and will be responsible for chlorinating all drinking water drawn from the source of supply.

9. Salvage work will be continued as usual and dump will be at Bn. Hd. Qtrs.

10. Latrine accomodation will be arranged at once and carefully supervised by Os.C. Coys. When selecting sites the health of the troops must be the first consideration. Refuse found lying about must be collected and burned in the incinerator.

11. Regimental aid post will be in the sunken road.

12. Bn. Signalling Officer will arrange to send 8 runners to report at advanced Bde. Hd. Qtrs. at T.30.a.15.10 (4 to remain and 4 to return to Bn. Headquarters) as soon as the Battalion is established in quarters.

13. Acknowledge.

(Sgd.) S.W.F. Crofts.
2/Lt. & A/Adj.

Issued by runner at
1. O.C. Bn.
2. Adjutant.
3. O.C. A Coy.
4. O.C. B Coy.
5. O.C. C Coy.
6. O.C. D Coy.
7. 174th Inf. Bde.
8. 173rd Inf. Bde.
9. Files)
10. War Diary) Typed afterwards.
11. War Diary.)

No. of Message 410

Prefix .... Code .... m	Words.	Charge.	This message is on a/c of:	Recd. at .... m.
Office of Origin and Service Instructions.	Sent		.... Service.	Date
	At .... m.			From
	To			
	By		(Signature of "Franking Officer.")	By

H. Q. SIGNALS 15 JUN 1917 OFFICE

TO COB

Sender's Number.	Day of Month.	In reply to Number.	AAA
* BM192	15		

Your Head Quarters and two Companies will leave ST LEGER at 11 pm tonight and move to Sunken Rd T 23 d & 30 a taking over HQ and shelters of Coys of BRAN which are now in residence.

From BERNARD
Place
Time 8 pm

The above may be forwarded as now corrected. (Z)

Censor.

Signature of Addressor or person authorised to telegraph in his name.

* This line should be erased if not required.

(3198.) Wt. W 12952/M1294. 375,000 Pads. 1/17. H. W. & V., Ld. (E. 818.)

"A" Form.

Army Form C. 2121.

MESSAGES AND SIGNALS.

No. of Message............

Prefix........... Code............m. | Words | Charge | This message is on a/c of .... Service. | Recd. at ....m. Date 15 JUN 1917 From .... By ....

Office of Origin and Service Instructions.

Sent At ....m. To .... By ....

(Signature of "Franking Officer.")

[Stamp: SIGNALS OFFICE 15 JUN 1917]

TO { To O.C. C O.B

Sender's Number	Day of Month	In reply to Number	AAA
* WD 75	15		

Ref B 189 from 173rd Inf Bde your Coy will be used for garrisoning L12 strong points + 4 posts of 1 section each namely L10 L9 L7 + L6 and there is a Lewis gun in L7 + one in L6 . and L12 is a big post + could accommodate a Coy. and your Coy could move under cover all the way along the ST LEDGER. CROISILLES road to the Factory area just beyond the Factory there is a communication trench leading to L12 post at T 24 b 35 . 25 and

From
Place — Supplied by return of C. Coy.
Time

The above may be forwarded as now corrected. (Z)

Censor. Signature of Addresser or person authorised to telegraph in his name.

* This line should be erased if not required.

(A1) O. Ltd., London— W.14042/M.44. 150,000 Pads. 12/15. Form C.2

Army Form C. 2121.
(In pads of 100.)

MESSAGES AND SIGNALS. No. of Message..............

Prefix..........Code..........m Words. Charge.
Office of Origin and Service Instructions.
Sent At..........m. To.......... By..........
This message is on a/c of: .... Service.
(Signature of "Franking Officer.")
Recd. at ....m. Date.......... From.......... By..........

H.Q. SIGNALS OFFICE 15 JUN 1917

TO { COB BRUSH

Sender's Number.	Day of Month.	In reply to Number.	AAA
* B189	15		

Please detail 1 Coy to report in platoons at ½ hour intervals to OC 2/4th Bn at RY EMBANKMENT T 24 d 7.3. AAA This Coy will only be used to garrison our original posts AAA authority has been obtained from RUTH AAA Added COB repeated BRUSH.

From BERNARD
Place
Time 11.45 am

The above may be forwarded as now corrected. (Z) [signature]

Censor. Signature of Addressor or person authorised to telegraph in his name.

* This line should be erased if not required.

(3198.) Wt. W 12952/M1294. 375,000 Pads. 1/17. H. W. & V., Ld. (E. 818.) [handwritten] 173.

"A" Form.

Army Form C. 2121.
(In pads of 100.)

MESSAGES AND SIGNALS.

No. of Message..............

Prefix.......... Code......... m	Words.	Charge.	This message is on a/c of:	Recd. at .... m.
Office of Origin and Service Instructions.	Sent		.... Service.	Date..............
SECRET	At..............m.			From ....
S.D.R.	To................			
	By................		(Signature of "Franking Officer.")	By ....

TO { 5th London Regt. 58th Division
6th " "
173rd Inf. Bde.

* Sender's Number.	Day of Month.	In reply to Number.	AAA
BmT 262	16/6		

Enemy by a counter-attack has succeeded in reoccupying right part of the line captured by 173rd Inf. Bde yesterday morning AAA 6th London Regt. (less 2 Coys.) now in ST LEGER has been ordered to move forward AAA 6th London Regt. will be replaced in ST LEGER by 5th LONDON Regt AAA 5th LONDON Regt. will leave its present camp at SIX a.m. today and will march to ST LEGER by platoons at 100 yards distance AAA ROUTE road through B.10. central and B.4.d AAA 5th London Regt. passes under command of B.G.C. 173rd Inf. Bde. at six a.m. AAA Arrival at ST LEGER will be reported to 173rd Inf. Bde. and repeated to this office AAA Two bombs and one extra bandolier per man

From
Place
Time

The above may be forwarded as now corrected. (Z)

Censor. Signature of Addressor or person authorised to telegraph in his name.

* This line should be erased if not required.

(3198.) Wt. W 12952/M1294. 375,000 Pads. 1/17. H. W. & V., Ld. (E. 818.)

"A" Form.

Army Form C. 2121.
(In pads of 100.)

MESSAGES AND SIGNALS.

No. of Message..............

Prefix.......... Code.............. m | Words. | Charge.

Office of Origin and Service Instructions.

Sent
At..............m.
To..............
By..............

This message is on a/c of:

.... *Service.*

(Signature of "Franking Officer.")

Recd. at ....m.
Date..............
From..............
By..............

TO (2)

Sender's Number.	Day of Month.	In reply to Number.	AAA
*BMT 262 Cont'd			

will be taken AAA Advance party will be sent to ST LEGER to take over accommodation there and care will be taken that troops on arrival move straight to their shelters etc. AAA Advanced HQ 173rd Inf. Bde. are at T.30.c.3090 in SUNKEN ROAD AAA Added 5th LONDON Regt. to acknowledge by bearer repts. ~~to~~ 58th Division 173rd Inf Bde and 6th London Regt.

From 174th Inf Bde

Place

Time 1.15 a.m.

The above may be forwarded as now corrected. (Z) [signature] Capt

Censor. | Signature of Addressor or person authorised to telegraph in his name.

* This line should be erased if not required.

(3198.) Wt. W 12952/M1294. 375,000 Pads. 1/17. H.W.&V. Ld. (E. 818.)

BM 174 IB

"A" Form.

Army Form C. 2121.
(In pads of 100.)

MESSAGES AND SIGNALS.

No. of Message..............

Prefix.......... Code.......... m | Words. | Charge.

Office of Origin and Service Instructions.

SECRET.
S.D.R.

Sent
At..............m.
To..............
By..............

This message is on a/c of:
.... Service.
....
(Signature of "Franking Officer.")

Recd. at.......m.
Date..............
From..............
By..............

TO O.C. 5th London Regt.
OC 6th " "

Sender's Number.	Day of Month.	In reply to Number.	AAA
* BMT 265	16/6		

1. You will not now relieve any posts of 6th London Regt. in the Left ~~Sect~~ Sub-section tonight

2. Your ~~reserve~~ support coy. will move up as soon as possible and as far as is possible by daylight towards position of readiness ~~about~~ in U.14.c.

3. It will form four patrols each consisting of a platoon under an officer complete with Lewis Gun, four bombs per man and 2 days rations and water.

4. Two of these patrols will enter HINDENBURG Support Line as soon as darkness permits from junction of trench with FAG ALLEY and work Southwards. Two will enter ~~[illegible]~~ from junction of trench with CRUMP ALLEY and work northwards. They will reinforce

From
Place
Time

The above may be forwarded as now corrected. (Z)

Censor. | Signature of Addressor or person authorised to telegraph in his name.

* This line should be erased if not required.

(3198.) Wt. W 12952/M1294. 375,000 Pads. 1/17. H. W. & V., Ld. (E. 818.)

"A" Form.

MESSAGES AND SIGNALS.

Army Form C. 2121.
(In pads of 100.)

No. of Message...............

Prefix.........Code.........m	Words.	Charge.	This message is on a/c of:	Recd. at ....m.
Office of Origin and Service Instructions.	Sent At.........m. To......... By.........		.................Service. (Signature of "Franking Officer.")	Date......... From .... By.........

TO (2)

Sender's Number.	Day of Month.	In reply to Number.	AAA
* Point 265 contd			

existing posts in HINDENBURG Support Line between these points and establish them also in the gap which apparently exists in our line between U.14.d.2.0. and U.14.d.1.5 approximately and clear it of any enemy that may be encountered

5. Patrols will report as soon as they are established along the above line. O.C. 5th London Regt. will arrange to reinforce them at once with a Coy. from the HINDENBURG Front ~~Support~~ Line. and The [illegible] forward extra bombs and water [illegible].

6. The HINDENBURG Support line will be held as our front line. A defensive flank will be formed along the Road from U.14.a.8.0 to U.14.c.0.9. from Bty Embankment

7. O.C. 6th London Regt. will detail two platoons with 25% picks and 75% Shovels to report at

From
Place
Time

The above may be forwarded as now corrected. (Z)

Censor. Signature of Addressor or person authorised to telegraph in his name.

* This line should be erased if not required.

(3198.) Wt. W 12952/M1294. 375,000 Pads. 1/17. H. W. & V., Ld. (E. 818.)

"A" Form.

Army Form C. 2121.
(In pads of 100.)

MESSAGES AND SIGNALS.

No. of Message..............

Prefix............ Code.............. m | Words. | Charge.

Office of Origin and Service Instructions.

Sent At..............m. To.............. By..............

This message is on a/c of: .... *Service.*

(Signature of "Franking Officer.")

Recd. at ....m. Date.............. From .... By..............

TO (3)

Sender's Number. | Day of Month. | In reply to Number. | AAA

* BMT 265 cont'd

HQ 2nd London Regt. in GUARDIAN Trench at 10 p.m. O.C. 2nd London Regt. is to arrange for an officer to lead them to and point out their task. It is all-important that the communication should be dug through along this line tonight. Posts will be established along this line by O.C. 5th London Regt.

8. Acknowledge.

Addressed 5th repeated 6th London Regt.

From 174th I.B.

Place

Time 7.55 p.m.

The above may be forwarded as now corrected. (Z)

Censor.

Signature of Addressor or person authorised to telegraph in his name. [illegible] Capt. [illegible] 174 I.B.

* This line should be erased if not required.

(3198.) Wt. W 12952/M1294. 375,000 Pads. 1/17. H. W. & V., Ld. (E. 818.)

"A" Form.

Army Form C.2121
(in pads of 100).

MESSAGES AND SIGNALS.

No. of Message ....

Prefix .... Code .... m.	Words	Charge	This message is on a/c of:	Recd. at .... m.
Office of Origin and Service Instructions.	Sent		.... Service.	Date ....
Runner	At .... m.		SECRET	From ....
	To			
	By		(Signature of "Franking Officer.")	By ....

TO CLAUD

Sender's Number.	Day of Month.	In reply to Number.	AAA
* W.B. 27	17	Para Y BMT 265	

The Officer i/c party states that he reported at rendezvous as instructed. The garrison there could give him no instructions & the Officer who was to meet & point out the task could not be found. He waited 1 hour & 10 minutes and then returned owing to the relief by CASE being in progress.

An Officer was detailed to reconnoitre this morning from LONE TRENCH to THE BLOCK and onwards. He reports that ~~from~~ a party of R.E. ~~[illegible]~~ way through THE BLOCK & onwards to about U.14.c.10.97. last night & that the work was being continued towards THE HUMP. (Vide attached Map.)

From COB.

Place

Time 2.20 P.M.

The above may be forwarded as now corrected. (Z) .... Censor.

A. G. Foord Lt Col
Signature of Addressor or person authorised to telegraph in his name.
Commdg

* This line should be erased if not required.

750,000. W 2185—M502. H. W. & V., Ld. 6/16.

SECRET D Copy No. 8.

2/6th Bn. London Rgt. Order No. 4.
Ref. maps sheets 57.C. S.W. and 57C. N.W. 1/40,000
Trench Map. ECOUST - ST MEIN.

22.6.17.

1. The battalion will be relieved by the 21st MANCHESTER REGIMENT in the LEFT SECTOR SUPPORT on the night 23/24th June and will withdraw to the COURCELLES area on relief.
2. Movements in connection with this relief will take place in accordance with the attached March Table.
3. All Trench Stores, maps, Aeroplane Photographs, Standing Orders and Defence Schemes will be handed over. Receipts in duplicate will be forwarded to Battalion Headquarters within 12 hours of relief. Details of work in progress will be carefully handed over.
4. Companies will march at 200 yards distance with 50 yards between platoons on the march to MORY COPSE, and at 200 yards distance between companies on the march from MORY COPSE to COURCELLES. 1st line transport will march at 200 yards distance between pairs of vehicles.
5. Acknowledge.

[illegible signature] 2Lieut.
A/Adjt. 2/6th Bn. London Rgt.

Issued to Signals at

Copies to:-

1. Adjutant
2. A Company
3. B "
4. C Company
5. D "
6. 21st Manchester Rgt.
7. 174th Inf Bde.
8. War Diary
9. File

SECRET March Table to accompany 2/6th London Regt. Order No. 4

Serial No	Date	Unit	From	To	Guides	Route	Remarks
1.	June 22.	A Coy less party in Sunken Road (the Tooth) in T.30.a	Railway Embankment	MORY COPSE	—	along valley B.5 T.30 - B 4.d. .50 - thence by road through B.10 central	
2.	23	B. Coy	Posts L1, L3, L4, L5 and L8, dugout position about U.19 C.40.23 and Railway Embankment	MORY COPSE	One for each post & one for dugout position to be at T.30.a .1.2 7.30 pm	-do-	On relief by 21st Manchester Regt. To take over camp at MORY COPSE vacated by 21st Manchester Regt.
3.	23	C Coy	Posts L6 and L7 position in Sunken Road about U19.C.22.12 and Railway Embankment	do.	One for each post and one for position in Sunken Road about U19.C.22.12	-do-	
4.	23	D Coy less party in Sunken Road (the Tooth) in T.30.a	Railway Embankment	do	—	do.	
5.	23	Parties of A & D Coys. X	Sunken Road (the Tooth) in T.30.a	do.	—	do.	X On completion of water carrying vide 174th Inf. Bde. instruction Q 58/718 dated 22/6/1917.
6.	23.	Battalion Headquarters	Railway Embankment	do.	—	do.	
7.	23	Battalion medical officer and personnel	R.A.P. T. 24. b.35.30	do.	—	CROISILLES - ST. LEGER	

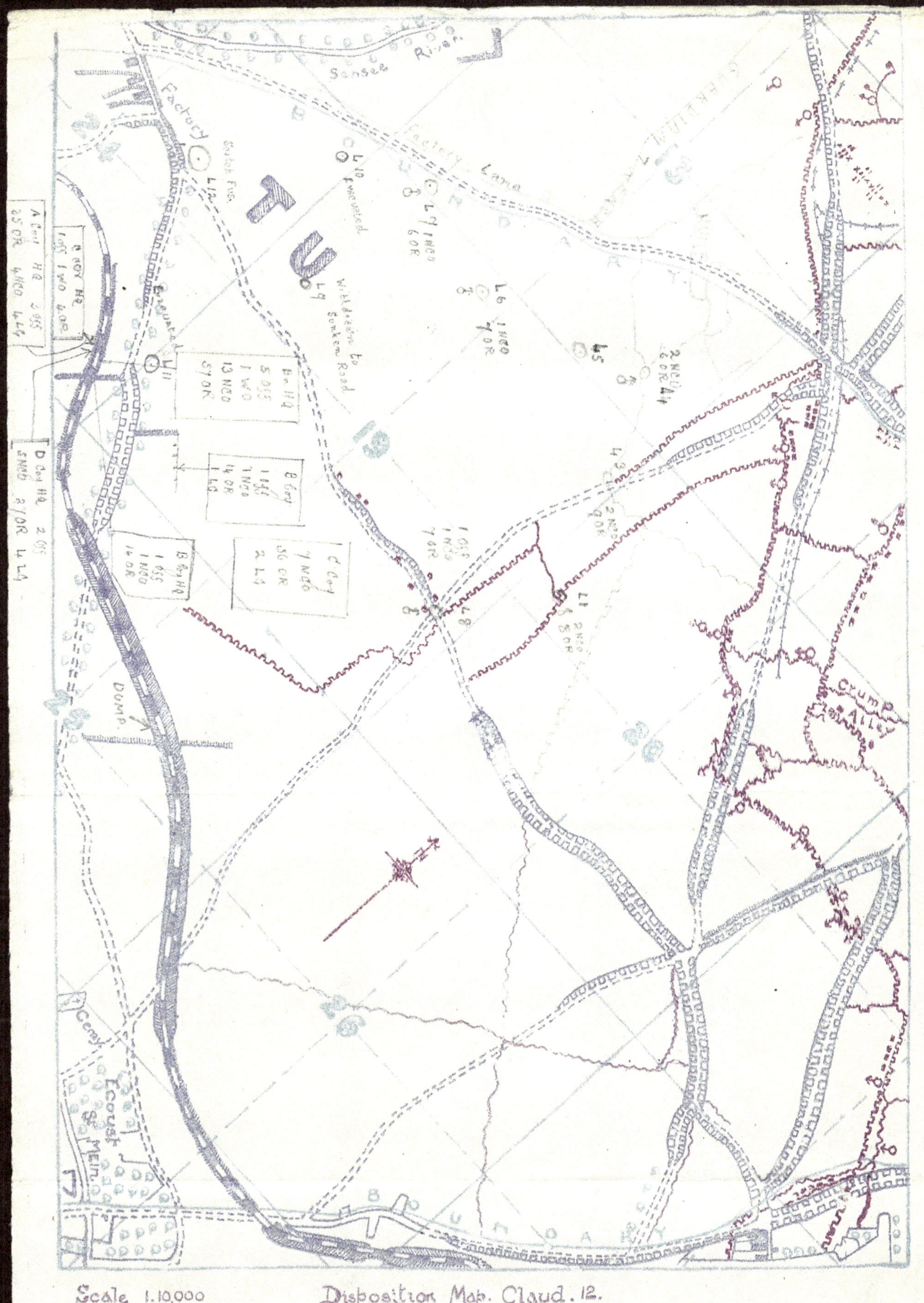

Scale 1.10,000

Disposition Map. Claud. 12.
New Works in Purple.

Remainder of A Coy	1 NCO 44 OR	} Road T 30 d.
D "	1 Off 8 NCO 37 OR	

No 1
Appendix C1.

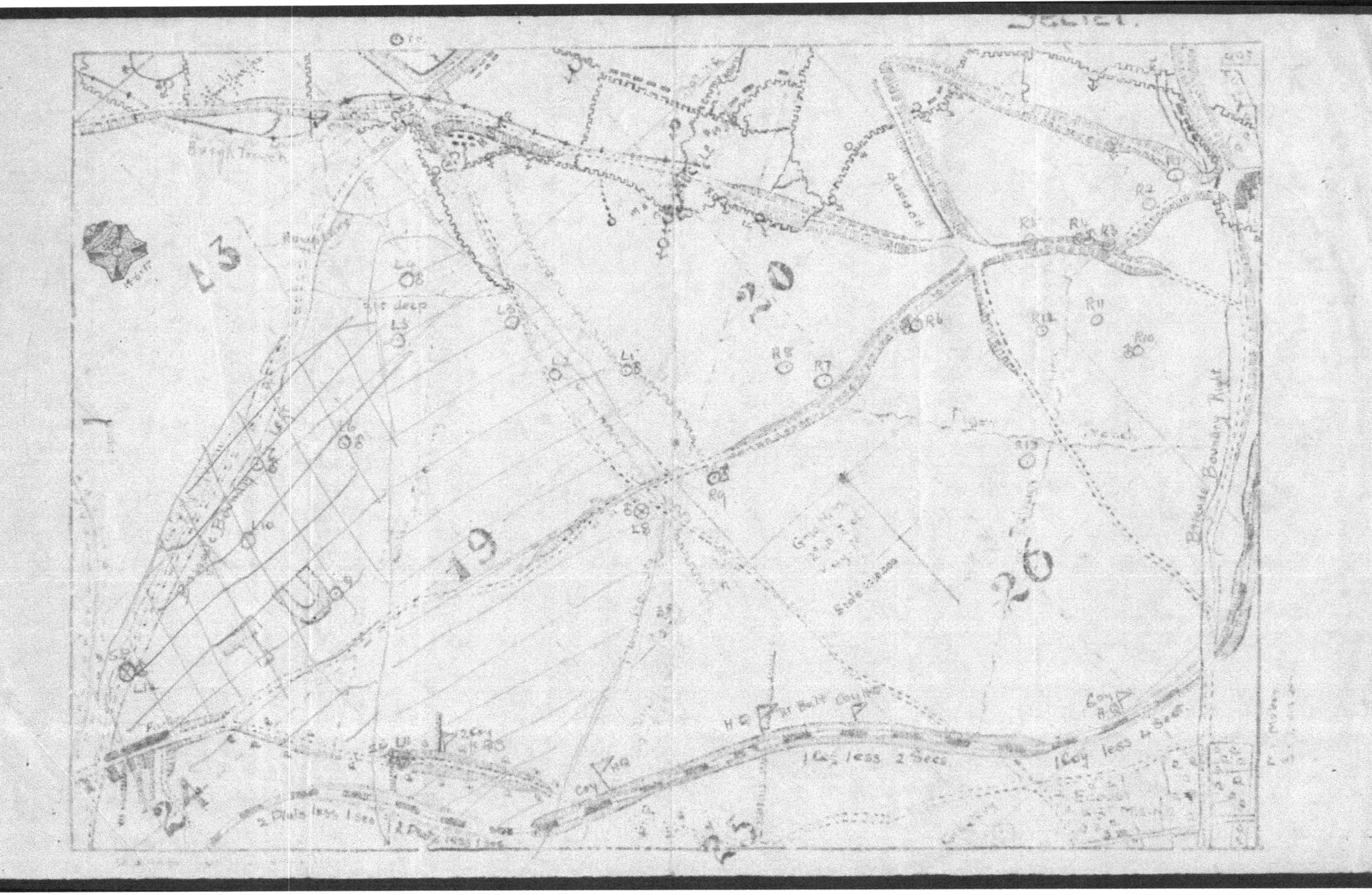

T – U

1

Secret

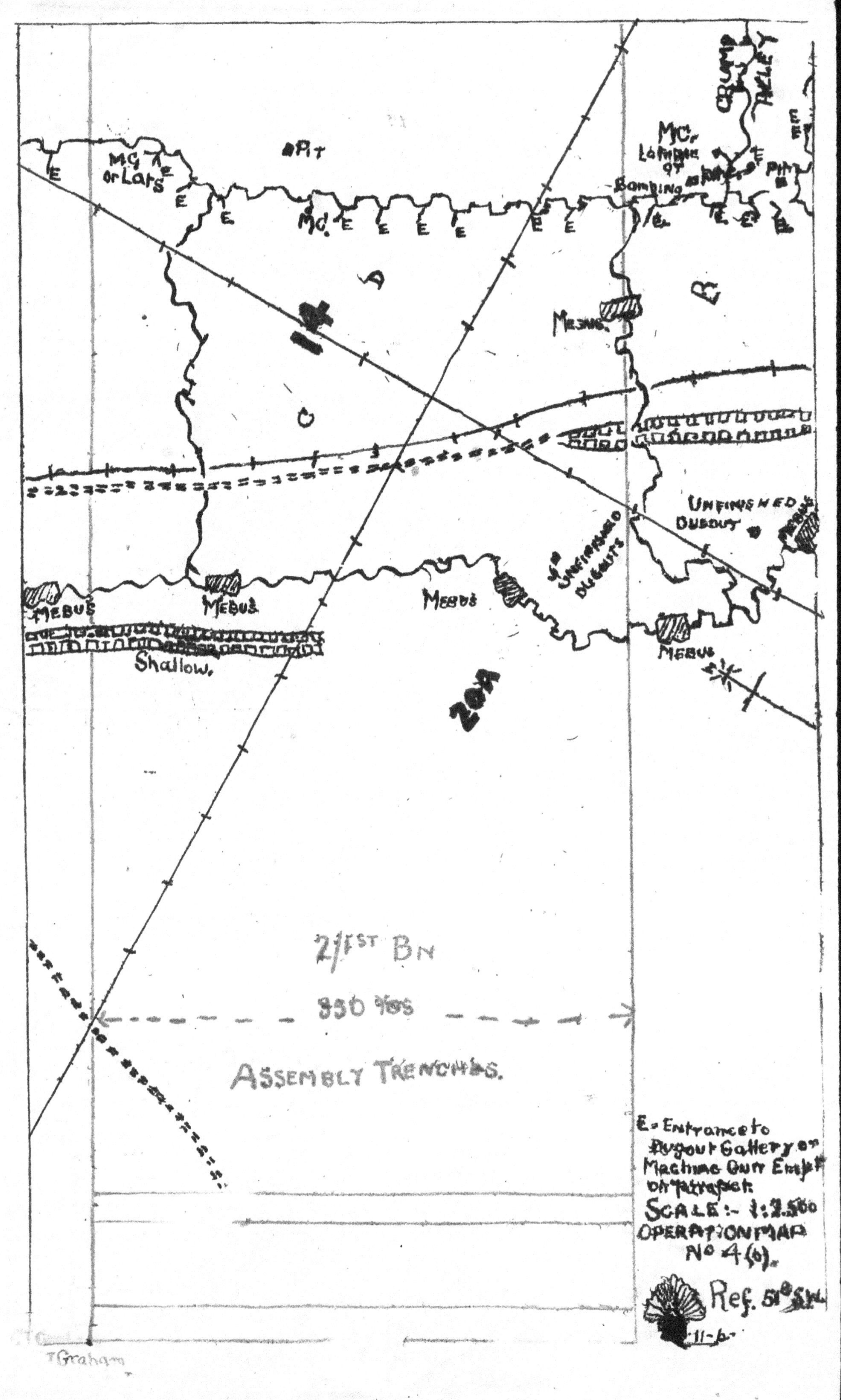

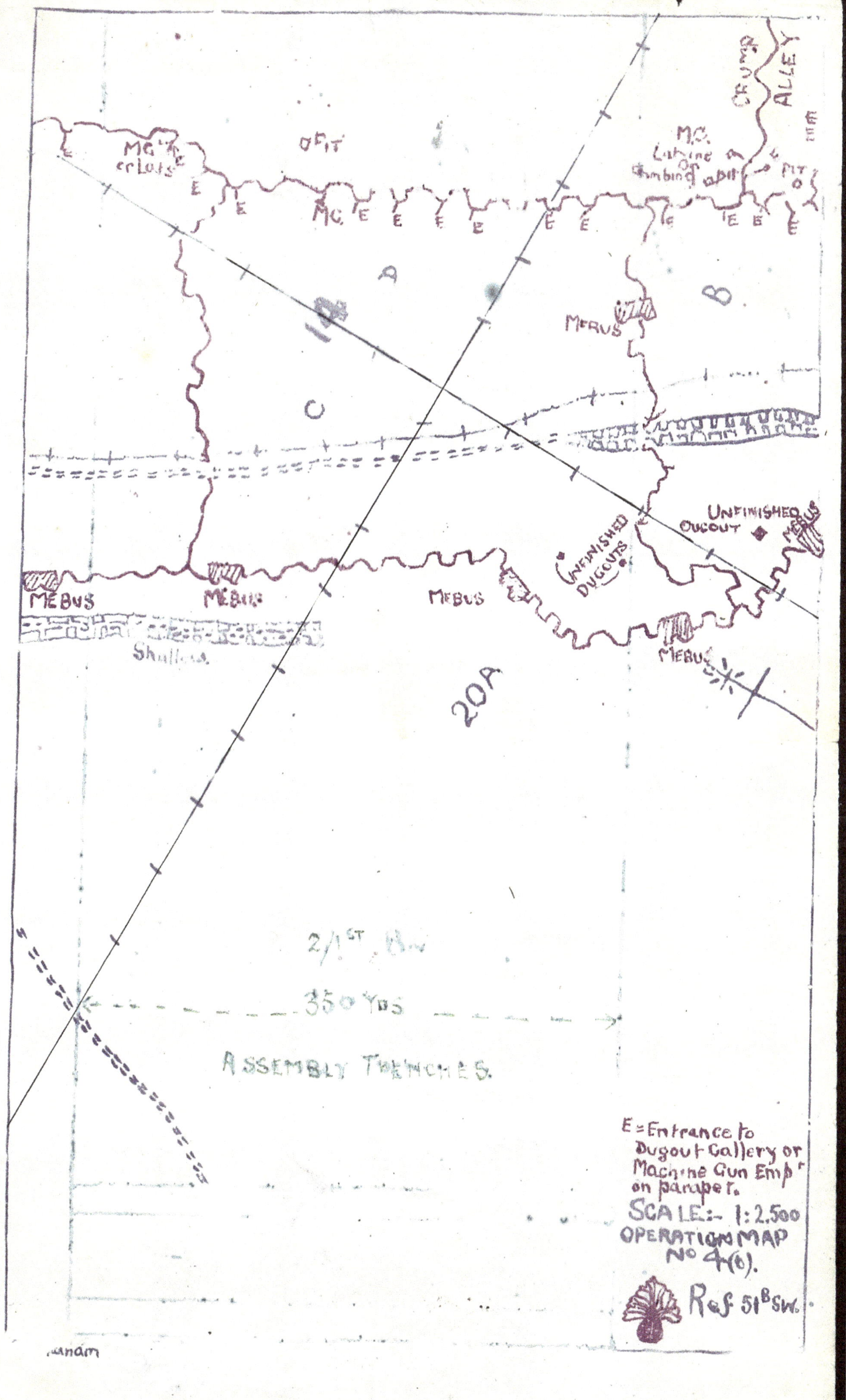

CRUMP ALLEY
A
B
C
MEBUS
UNFINISHED DUGOUT
UNFINISHED DUGOUTS
20A
350 YDS
ASSEMBLY TRENCHES
E = Entrance to Dugout Gallery or Machine Gun Empt on parapet.
SCALE:- 1:2,500
OPERATION MAP No 4(b).
Ref 51B SW.

S E C R E T /

ADMINISTRATIVE INSTRUCTIONS
issued in conjunction with
21st Battalion Manchester Regiment
OPERATION ORDERS Nos. 62 & 63.

Copy No. 14...

THURSDAY, June 21st, 1917.

1. PERSONNEL. The following personnel will not go into action and will be accomodated in Camp at B. 27. a. 5. 7. remaining under orders of ~~xxxx~~ Lieut: W.B.PURVIS:-

Transport	40.	
Water Squad	5.	
Q.M.Stores.	4.	
Postmen.	2.	
Workshop.	8.	
Pioneers,	6.	
Sock Washers.	4.	
Canteen.	2.	
Instructional Staffs.	6.	
Trained L.Gunners.	16.	(1 per L.G.Team).
Drums.	16.	
Servants.	4.	(H.Qr's & Chaplains).
Orderly Room	3.	
Awaiting Commission	1.	(Sgt. Bristow).
For Courses.	8.	(As per list forwarded to O.C.Coys).
M.O.Staff.	1.	
C.Q.M.S's & Storemen	8.	
Cooks,-Coy & H.Q.	12	

2. DETAIL. The following will be the detail for June 22nd 1917:-
(a) Blankets rolled in bundles of 10 and dumped at Q.M.Stores by 2.0 p.m.
(b) Company boxes, officers mess boxes, officers valises dumped at Battalion Headquarters by 2.30 p.m.

The Transport Officer will arrange to convey (a) & (b) to Camp at MORY COPSE.
O.C.D.Company will detail a party of 1 N.C.O. and 10 men to report to R.Q.M.S. at Q.M.Stores at 2.0 p.m.. to act as loading party.
O.C.D.Company will detail 1 N.C.O. and 10 men to act as unloading party at Camp at MORY COPSE. This party to arrive there not later than 2.30 p.m.

(c) The R.Q.M.S. will arrange for rations for consumption on 23rd to be issued on 22nd after arrival at camp at MORY COPSE.
(d) Billeting Representatives i.e.C.Q.M.S's and 1 N.C.O. from Headquarters will report to Sec: Lieut: G.H.POWER at Camp at MORY COPSE at 2.0 p.m. and will arrange to guide their Companies into their Company Lines.

3. Officers Commanding Companies will detail one man per Company to remain in present billets to hand over to incoming Unit. These men to rejoin wagon line at B.27. a.5.7 . on completion of duty.

4. DETAIL. The following will be the detail for June 23rd 1917 at MORY COPSE Camp:-
Blankets, Officers Mess Boxes, Company Boxes, Officers Valises will be dumped at Guard Tent by 3.0 p.m.
The transport officer will arrange with R.Q.M.S. ~~tox~~ store ~~xxx~~ all this kit either at Q.M.Stores or at Brigade Stores which are situated at Billets Nos. 40 and 42 ERVILLERS.

~~Rations for consumption on 24th instant~~

The following transport will accompany the Battalion to Railway Embankment:-
1 Pack Animal per Company) tox carry officers trench
1 Pack Animal for Bn.Hd.Qtrs.) and Mess Kits.
14 Pack Animals carrying petrol tins for water.
Grenade Waggon will follow Battalion as soon as it is dark.
Rations for consumption on 24th instant will be carried on the man and will be issued before leaving MORY COPSE on 23rd instant.

5. SUPPLY OF S.A.A., BOMBS, R.E. MATERIAL etc.
D.A.C. is at B. 25. d.
Brigade Stores are at U. 25. b. 2. 5. and T.30. a. 1. 2.
Battalion Dump at Battalion Headquarters at T.24. d. 7. 2.
R.E.Yard is at B. 16. d. 7. 2.
Forward R.E.Dump is at C. 1. d. 2. 4.

6. MEDICAL.
Regimental Aid Post is at T. 24. b. 30. 45.
Advanced Dressing Station is on ST LEGER Road at B. 4.b.3.4.

7. WATER.
There will be a dump of petrol tins at Battalion Headquarters at T. 24. d. 7. 2. and there is a well in ST LEGER at T. 23. c. 2. 2.

8. BILLETS.
Special care must be taken that all billets and camp areas occupied by the Battalion are handed over in a clean condition.

Time of issue..10.15am....

(Signed) E.F.ORGILL,
Lieutenant & Adjutant.

.....

Copy No. 1. Commanding Officer. 14. O.C. 2/6th London Regt.
2. O.C.A.Coy.
3. B. "
4. C. "
5. D. "
6. Transport Officer.
7. R.Q.M.S.
8. Medical Officer.
9. H.Q.21st Infy, Bde.
10. File.
11. do.
12. War Diary.
13. do.

OPERATION ORDERS No.63
by
Lieut: Colonel C.E.N.LOMAX,M.C.
....

No. 11

Reference Map. 51. b. S.W. Ed. 4. a.
" " 57. c. N.W. Ed. 6. a.

21st JUNE. 1917.

....

1. The 7th Division is relieving the 58th Division on the 5th Corps Front.
On the nights 22/23 - 23/24th June 1917 the 91st Infantry Brigade will relieve the 174th Infantry Brigade on the left Sector with the following boundaries:-
Right Boundary of Brigade:-
ECOUST - CRUCIFIX- FACTORY Road.
Left Boundary of Brigade:-
From U. 14. a. O. 1. S.W. along N.W. side of track to Factory at T. 24. b. 1. 4.
Boundary between Battalion Sub-Sectors:-
From U. 25. a. 5. 6. on a line to U. 30. b. 8. 3. (inclusive to Left Sub-Sector.)

2. 21st Battalion Manchester Regiment at MORY COPSE will relieve the 6th LONDON Regiment in support on night of 23rd June, 1917 and after relief will be disposed as follows :-
Bn. Hd. Qtrs. will be at T. 24. d. 7. 2.
A. Company will take over line of posts at the following points:- U. 19. d. 9. 7. - U. 20. a. 2. 2. - U. 19. b. 80. 75. - U. 13. d. 75. 30. - U. 13. d. 5. 1. - U. 13. c. 3. 1. U. 19. a. 9. 9. - U. 19. a. 3. 3. with Coy. Hd. Qtrs at T. 24. d. 7. 4.
B. Company will be accomodated as follows:-
1 Platoon in dugouts at U. 19. c. 35. 35.
1. Platoon in Sunken Road from U. 19. c. 0. 4. to U. 25. a. 4. 6.
C. Company will be situated along the Railway Embankment in U. 24. d. (approximately).
D. Company will be situated in Sunken Road at about T. 30. c. 4. 8.

3. Guides from 6th LONDON Regt., at the rate of 1 per post, one per platoon and one per Company Headquarters will be at T. 30. c. 4. 8. at 7.30 p.m.

4. For the purpose of holding the posts referred to in para 2. O.C. D. Company will detail one Lewis Gun Section complete to work under the orders of O.C. "A" Company.

5. Companies will move off from camp at MORY COPSE at the following times and will proceed to new positions by the following route:-
Road from MORY COPSE to B. 10. b. 45. 95. and thence along N. slope of the valley running N.E. from about B. 10. b. through b. 5. Central and T. 30. central:-

Bn. Hd. Qtrs.		6.45 p.m.
A.	Company.	7.0 p.m.
B.	"	7.20 p.m.
C.	"	7.40 p.m.
D.	"	8.0 p.m.

6. Completion of relief will be reported in code to Bn.Hd. Qtrs.

(Signed) E.F.ORGILL,
Lieutenant & Adjutant.

Issued at 3.45 p.m.
....

No. 1. Commanding Officer.
2. O.C. A. Coy.
3. B. "
4. C. "
5. D. "
6. Transport Officer.
7. Q.M.Sgt.
8. M.O.
9. 91st Infantry Bde.
10. File.
11. O.C. 2/6th LONDON Regt

OPERATION ORDERS No.62
by
Lieut. Col. C.E.N. DOMAX M.C.
....

No. 14.......

Ref. Map 57.c.N.W. - Edition 6.a.

21st JUNE, 1917.

1. The 21st Battalion Manchester Regiment will proceed to camp at MORY Copse on afternoon of 22nd JUNE, 1917.

2. Quartermaster's Stores, Staff, Transport and personnel detailed in administrative Orders No.62 will proceed to camp at B.27. a. 5. 7.

3. Companies will pass the starting point at U. 15. d. 5. 7. at the following times:-

Headquarters	5.30 p.m.
A. Company.	5.35 p.m.
B. "	5.45 p.m.
C. "	5.55 p.m.
D. "	6. 5 p.m.

Route via U. 16. d. 0. 4 - FAIRWEATHER TRACK through ERVILLERS.

4. The following transport will accompany the Battalion:-
Lewis Gun Limbers (with Companies).
Cookers.
Maltese Cart.
Officers Mess Cart.
Remainder of Transport will precede the Battalion independently.

(Signed) E.F. ORGILL,
Lieutenant & Adjutant.
....

Copy No. 1. Commanding Officer.
2. O.C.A.Company.
3. O.C.B. "
4. O.C.C. "
5. O.C.D. "
6. Transport Officer.
7. Quartermaster Sgt.
8. Medical Officer.
9. 91st Infy: Bde.
10. File.
11. File.
12. War Diary.
13. do.
14. O.C. 2/6th London Regt —
issued at [illegible]

21st Bn MANCHESTERS W/115

O.C.
2/6th London Regt.

Your Order NO. 4 dated 22/6/17 received.

I enclose my O.O.'s 62 & 63 and administrative instructions issued in conjunction with these orders.

I have noted that Post 29 has been evacuated and I am awaiting orders from my Brigadier on this point.

Ch[illegible] Lt Col.
Cmd'g 21st Manchester Regt.
(Code Name LAKE)

22/6/17.

2/16 London Rgt

July 1917

Index..

SUBJECT.

No.	Contents.	Date.
	70/2951—2975.	

(49,674). Wt.42,605—128. 2000. 4/20. Gp.164. A.&E.W.
(51,507). „ 6005—137. 500. 5/20. „ „

WAR DIARY Vol 7

of

2/16th London Regt

1/7/17 to 31/7/17

Instructions regarding War Diaries and Intelligence Summaries are contained in F. S. Regs., Part II. and the Staff Manual respectively. Title pages will be prepared in manuscript.

WAR DIARY

or

~~INTELLIGENCE SUMMARY.~~

(Erase heading not required.)

Army Form C. 2118.

Place	Date	Hour	Summary of Events and Information	Remarks and references to Appendices
COURCELLES	1st to 5th July	/	Bn training at COURCELLES	
	6th		Bn moved to BANCOURT by road taking over camp from ~~5th Staffords~~ 2/10th LONDONS	Appendix A
	7		Bn moved to EQUANCOURT by road & took over camp from 2/5th STAFFORDS	Appendix B
	8		Bn moved to DESSARTS WOOD. Bn. less ½ A & B Coy moved to BEAUCAMP Sector and	App^x C
			relieved elements of 2/5th & 2/8th ~~[illegible]~~ SHERWOODS in BROKEN TRENCH & INTERMEDIATE LINE with Bn Hd Qrs in Sunken Road South of BEAUCAMPS	App^x D
	9		Bn Hd Qrs moved to CHARING CROSS & ½ A & B Coy relieved elements of 2/5th LINCOLNS in BROKEN TRENCH	App^x E
			2nd LIEUT LAWRENCE wounded (since died of wounds)	
	10/13		In trenches as above	
	14		Dispositions of Companies changed. Hd Qrs platoon put into line	Appx F
	16		Bn relieved by 2/1st LONDONS (less 3 Coys) & 1 Coy 4th LONDONS & moved to NEUVILLE BOURJONVAL	" G
	18		Bn relieved 2/7th LONDONS in right of CENTRE or TRESCAULT SECTOR	" J
	19		1 O/R Killed 2 wounded	
	20		3 O/R Killed 3 wounded (one died of wounds 21/7/17). A Coy less 1 Plat^n to new positions in Posts 1 & 3	Appx K
	21		~~#~~ Remaining Platoon of A Coy moved to No 2 post. B Coy occupied DERBY Support	
			RESERVE. 1 Platoon of C Coy to right of front line	Appx L

T2134. Wt. W708–776. 500000. 4/15. Sir J. C. & S.

Instructions regarding War Diaries and Intelligence Summaries are contained in F. S. Regs., Part II. and the Staff Manual respectively. Title pages will be prepared in manuscript.

WAR DIARY
or
~~INTELLIGENCE SUMMARY.~~
(Erase heading not required.)

Army Form C. 2118.

Place	Date	Hour	Summary of Events and Information	Remarks and references to Appendices
	23rd July		Bn relieved by 2/5th LONDONS in daylight moved to Divisional Reserve at YTRES.	Appx. M
	24/27		Training at YTRES.	
	28.		Bn. relieved by 4th S. African Infantry Regt. moved to camp vacated by that unit at BERTINCOURT	App. N
	29.		Bn. moved to BERNEVILLE by Bus to BAPAUME, train to BEAUMETZ & march route to BERNEVILLE	App. O.
	30/1		Training – BERNEVILLE	

[signature]
A/Adj.

SECRET. Appendix A.

2/6th LONDON REGT. ORDER NO.5. Copy No.9.
(Ref. Map 57c 1/40,000.)

1. The Bn. will move to BANCOURT tomorrow the 6th inst. and take over the camp at H36.d.9.9. vacated by the 10th London Regt.
2. The starting point will be Road Junction at A16.d.56.
3. The Bn. will pass the XXXXXXXXX starting point in the following order.-

A. Coy. Zero
B. Coy. Zero plus 1½mins
C. Coy. Zero plus 3mins
D. Coy. Zero plus 4½mins.
Transport Echelon A. Zero plus 6mins

Zero hour will be notified later.

All.Headquarters personnel will parade and march with their Coys. with the exception of the Intelligence Officer, who will march with A. Coy.
100yds. distance will be maintained between Companies throughout the whole march and between D. Coy. and Echelon A of Transport. ✕

✕ Leading Company will pass Balloon shed in A23c.5.9. at zero plus 27mins

4. ROUTE. GOMIECOURT - SAPIGNIES - BAPAUME - BANCOURT.
5. HALTS. Halts will take place 10mins. before each clock hour. Every unit in the column will halt without further orders. At the clock hour all units will simultaneously advance.
6. ADVANCE PARTY. An advance party as follows will parade at Bn. H.Q. at 8a.m. under 2/Lieut. Brasher and will arrive at BANCOURT CAMP before 12 noon to take over from the 10th Bn. London Regt.

Headquarters.- 2. N.CO's. and 1 Rfn. as detailed
1 N.C.O. per Company
1 Rifleman per Platoon.

7. ADVANCE BILLETING PARTY. 2/Lieut. Etheridge and 1 Rfn. per Coy. will parade at Q.M. Stores at 9a.m. and will proceed direct by lorry to the new area (EQUANCOURT)(V.16.b.7.2.) The party will act as unloading party and will await arrival of the Bn. on the 7th inst. and 2/Lieut. Etheridge will send one guide to cross roads at V.4.c.3.0. to meet and guide Bn. to Camp. All stores sentforward on lorries will be dumped outside Q.M. Stores of the 5th South Staffs. until the camp is vacated on the 7th inst. This party will carry rations for the 7th July.
8. FIRST LINE TRANSPORT. Echelon A will march with the Bn. as ordered in para. 3 and B. Echelon in rear of the Brigade Transport Officer. Two S.A.A. vehicles per Battalion and four from the M.Gun Coy. will form the Brigade reserve of S.A.A. which will be included in XXXXXXXXXXXX.B. Echelon

A. Echelon.
Pack Animals
Lewis Gun limbers
S.A.A. Vehicles (less Brigade reserve.)

B. Echelon.
Tool carts.
Cookers.
Officers mess carts.
Water carts.
Maltese carts.
Brigade reserve of S.A.A.
Baggage Wagons.

9. DRESS. Marching order. Equipment will be worn in manner demonstrated to units by R.S.M. Payne on July 1st. Steel Helmets will be worn.
10. OFFICERS ~~KITS~~ kits will be stacked outside Headquarters by 12noon.
11. OFFICERS MESS BAGGAGE. The Transport Officer will arrange to collect Officers Mess baggage which will not exceed one box and one basket per Company at zero minus 1 hour.

ORDER NO. 5. cont. 2.

13. BAND. The Band will take up position by the star ing point at zero minus 5 mins., and will march at the head of the 4th Coy., moving forward one Coy. at each halt.

10. BILLETS. All Billets will be left clean and tidy and all rubbish burnt. Company Commanders will render certificates to this effect to Bn. Orderly Room on arrival at new camp.

The Bn. Orderly Officer will inspect all vacated accomodation after the departure of the Bn. and will obtain from the Town Major a certificate in duplicate that Billets etc. have been left clean. He will hand in the certificate to Bn. Orderly Room at BANCOURT by 5p.m.

14. WATCHES. Watches will be synchronised from Bn. Signals at 10a.m.

15. Acknowledge.

Sgd. S.W.F. Crofts.,
2/Lieut.
Acting Adjutant, 2/8th London Regt.

8/7/1917.

Issued by runner at........to.-
1. C.O.
2. O.C. A. Coy.
3. O.C. B. Coy.
3. O.C. C. Coy.
5. O.C. D. Coy.
6. Q.M. & Transport Officer.
7. 174th Inf. Bde.
8. File
9. & 10. War diary.

Appendix B

SECRET. ORDER NO. 6. Copy No. 9.

2/6th BN. THE LONDON REGT.

6/7/1917.

(Ref. Map Sheet 57c. 1/40,000)

1. The Bn. will move to EQUANCOURT tomorrow, the 7th inst. and take over the camp at V.16.b.7.[?] vacated by the 5th South Staffs.

2. The starting point will be road junction at O.2.b.0.8.

3. The Bn. will march in the following order.-

B. Coy.
C. Coy.
D. Coy.
A. Coy.
Transport Echelon A.

B. Coy. will pass the starting point at Zero plus 22mins and 100 yds. distance will be maintained between Companies and between A.Coy. and Echelon A. of Transport.

4. ROUTE. HAPLINCOURT - BERTINCOURT - YTRES - EQUANCOURT.

5. HALTS. Halts will take place 10 mins. before each clock hour. Every unit in the column will halt without further orders. At the clock hour all Units will simultaneously advance.

6. FIRST LINE TRANSPORT. As laid down in Order No. 5. para 3.

7. DRESS. As laid down in Order 5, para 9.

8. BAND. The Band will take up position by the road at the North Easterly corner of camp at zero plus 10 mins. and will play during the march out and will march at the head of A. Coy. moving forward 1 Coy. at each halt.

9. OFFICERS' BAGGAGE. Officers kits will be stacked on the north side of the officers lines at 11 a.m.

10. OFFICERS MESS BAGGAGE. The Transport officer will arrange to collect Officers Mess Baggage at zero minus 1 hour.

11. GUIDE. A guide from the advance ~~party~~ Billeting party detailed on order No. 5, para 7, will meet the Bn. at cross roads V.4.c.4.0. and guide it to camp.

12. CAMP. The camp will be left clean and tidy and rubbish buried or burnt before departure. Coy. Commanders will render certificates to this effect to Bn. Orderly Room on arrival at new camp.

The Bn. Orderly Officer will inspect all vacated accomodation after the departure of the Bn. and will obtain from the incoming Bn. a certificate in duplicate that camp has been left clean. He will hand in the certificate to Bn. Orderly Room at EQUANCOURT.

13. WATCHES. Watches will be synchronised from Bn. signals at 10 a.m.

14. Q.M. STORES & TRANSPORT LINES are at V.3.a.0.3.

15. ADVANCE PARTY. An advance party consisting of the following.-

O.C. A. Coy.
O.C. D. Coy.
An Officer to be detailed by C.Coy.
1 N.C.O. per platoon and 1 Lewis Gun N.C.O. or Rifleman per platoon of C. & D. Coys and for No's. 1 & 2 Platoons of A. Coy. will parade at 1.30 p.m. and proceed direct to the positions in BROKEN TRENCH and the intermediate line which the Bn. will occupy on the night 8/9th inst.

Capt. Martin will be in command of this party.

Guides will be sent back by this party to the extent of 1 per platoon to the camp in DESSARTS WOODS (W.2.c.) to report to Bn. H.Q. by 9 p.m. on the 8th inst. to guide their platoons to their respective positions.

16. Acknowledge.

Sgd. S.W.F. Crofts,
Acting Adjutant, 2/Lieut. 2/6th Bn. London Regt.

Copies issued by runner at.......to.-

1. C.O.
2. O.C. A. Coy.
3. O.C. B. Coy.
4. O.C. C. Coy.
5. O.C. D. Coy.
6. Q.M. & T.O.
7. 174th Inf. Bde.
8. File
9. & 10. War diary.

Appendix C

SECRET.

ORDER NO. 7.
2/8th BN. THE LONDON REGT.

Copy No...9....
7/7/1917.

1. The Bn. will move to camp at W.2.a. in DESSARTS WOODS tomorrow 8th inst.

2. The starting point will be road junction in EQUANCOURT at V.10.d.30.

3. The Bn. will march in the following order
A. Coy.
C. Coy.
D. Coy.
B. Coy.
Headquarters.
A. Coy. will pass the starting point at 4.15 p.m. and 100 yds. distance will be maintained between Platoons and 300 yds. between Coys.

4. ROUTE. EQUANCOURT - FINS - DESSARTS WOOD.

5. BAND. The Band and other details not proceeding to the trenches will move to the Transport lines under orders of the Transport Officer.

6. OFFICERS BAGGAGE. Officers valises and mess baggage not intended for the trenches will stacked in the neighbourhood of the cookers by 5 p.m.

7. OFFICERS MESS BAGGAGE. The Transport Officer will arrange to collect Officers Mess baggage at 3 p.m. and convey it to Transport Lines where it will be loaded on Coy. Lewis Gun Limbers.

8. CAMP. Order No. 6, para 12 applies.

9. ADVANCE PARTY. An advance party consisting of one officer of A. Coy. ~~and one~~ one N.C.O. of A. Coy. of B. Coy. will proceed to the camp of the 6th Sherwoods W.2.a. to arrive by 10 a.m. and will arrange tent accomodation for half of A. Coy. and B. Coy.

10. SIGNALLERS. The Signalling Sergeant and two Signallers to be detailed by him will proceed to Bn. H.Q. at present occupied by the 6th Sherwoods in Q.12.d.52. to reach there by 6.p.m.

11. Acknowledge.

Sgd. S.W.P. Crofts,
2/Lieut.
Acting Adjutant, 2/8th London Regt.

Copies issued by runner at.......to.-
1. C.O.
2. O.C. A.Coy.
3. O.C. B.Coy.
4. O.C. C.Coy.
5. O.C. D.Coy.
6. Q.M. & T.O.
7. 174th Inf. Bde.
8. File
9 & 10. War diary.

SECRET. Scale 1:20,000
28
29
30
Quarry
BOUNDARY
5
6
Derby Support
Derby Res
King's Lane
Reserve
12
Hun Crater
Broken Trench
Sherwood Av
17/7/17. E.G. Godfrey Reproduced from △ CORPS 18.S. 49+51

SECRET Appendix D Copy No. 8

OPERATION ORDER No. 8
2/6th Bn. LONDON REGIMENT
(Ref. Map sheet 57c 1/40000 & Trench Map.)

8/7/17.

1. The Bn. (less 1½ Coys) will move from camp in DESSART WOOD to-night & relieve elements of the 5th & 8th Sherwood Foresters in BROKEN TRENCH and Intermediate line.
2. The starting point will be the track at NW corner of DESSART WOOD W.1.b.0.9.
3. The Bn. will leave camp in he following order:-
   ½ "A" Coy to portion of BROKEN TRENCH in 12 c to pass starting point at 10.30 p.m.
   Hd. Qtrs. to Hd. Qtrs occupied by 8th Sherwoods Q.12.d.
   C Coy to intermediate line in Q.18.c., exclusive /Q.18.a., Q.17.b. from LINCOLN AVENUE to road Q.17.b.8.5. inclusive.
   D Coy to intermediate line in R.13.c. & Q.18.d. to LINCOLN AVENUE inclusive.
   100 yards distance will be maintained between Platoons & 200 yards between Companies. For purposes of this order Hd. Qtrs. will be considered as two platoons, the first under the Intelligence Officer, the second under the R.S.M.
4. Guides. 1 for each platoon will report at DESSART WOOD camp at 9 p.m.
5. RELIEFS. Reliefs will be reported to Bn. Hd.Qtrs by runner as quickly as possible, using the code word DUPLEX.
6. At the earliest possible moment after relief O.C. Coys will send in to Bn. Hd. Qtrs a sketch map showing accurate dispositions of Platoons, (including Platoon H.Q. & Lewis Gun positions) and location of Coy Hd. Qtrs. Platoon Commanders will in every case find accomodation and live in their Platoon sectors.
7. All ranks are to be warned against unnecessary movement and smoke from fires during hours of daylight.
8. All men will be in possession of:-
   Rations for one day
   Full water bottles (not to be touched on the march)
9. Rations will come to:-
   Q.13.d.0.5. for C & D Coys.
   Q.12.c.15.00 for A Coy.
   Q.17.b.2.6. for H.Q.
   on the night of the 9th & following nights.
10. WATER. Water Carts will come up with rations on and after the night of the 9th. There is a good supply of washing water at VILLERS PLOUICH.
11. Trench Stores and defence schemes and aeroplane photographs will be taken over on relief and a copy of list sent at once to Bn. Hd. Qtrs.
12. Q.M. Store & Transport lines will be West of FINS-NEUVILLE Rd. in V.6.c.
13. DRESS. Troops willgo into the line in full marching order and not as on previous occasions in fighting order.
14. The R.A.P. will be at Q.17.b.8.5. at present occupied by 8th Sherwoods.
15. Latrine accomodation will be arranged at once and carefully supervised by O.C. Coys. Any refuse found lying about must be buried immediately & O.C. Coys will select the site for this purpose. The removal system should be adopted for latrines.
16. Work is to be concentrated on the improvement of trenches where these are held by posts, especially in the construction of fire steps & bays.

(Sgd) S.W.F. Crofts. 2nd. Lt.
Acting Adjutant.

Issued by runner to:-
1. O.C. Bn.
2. O.C. A Coy.
3. O.C. B Coy.
4. O.C. C Coy.
5. O.C. D Coy.
6. Q.M. & T.O.
7. 174th Inf. Bde.
8. War Diary.
9. do.
10. File.

P.T.O.

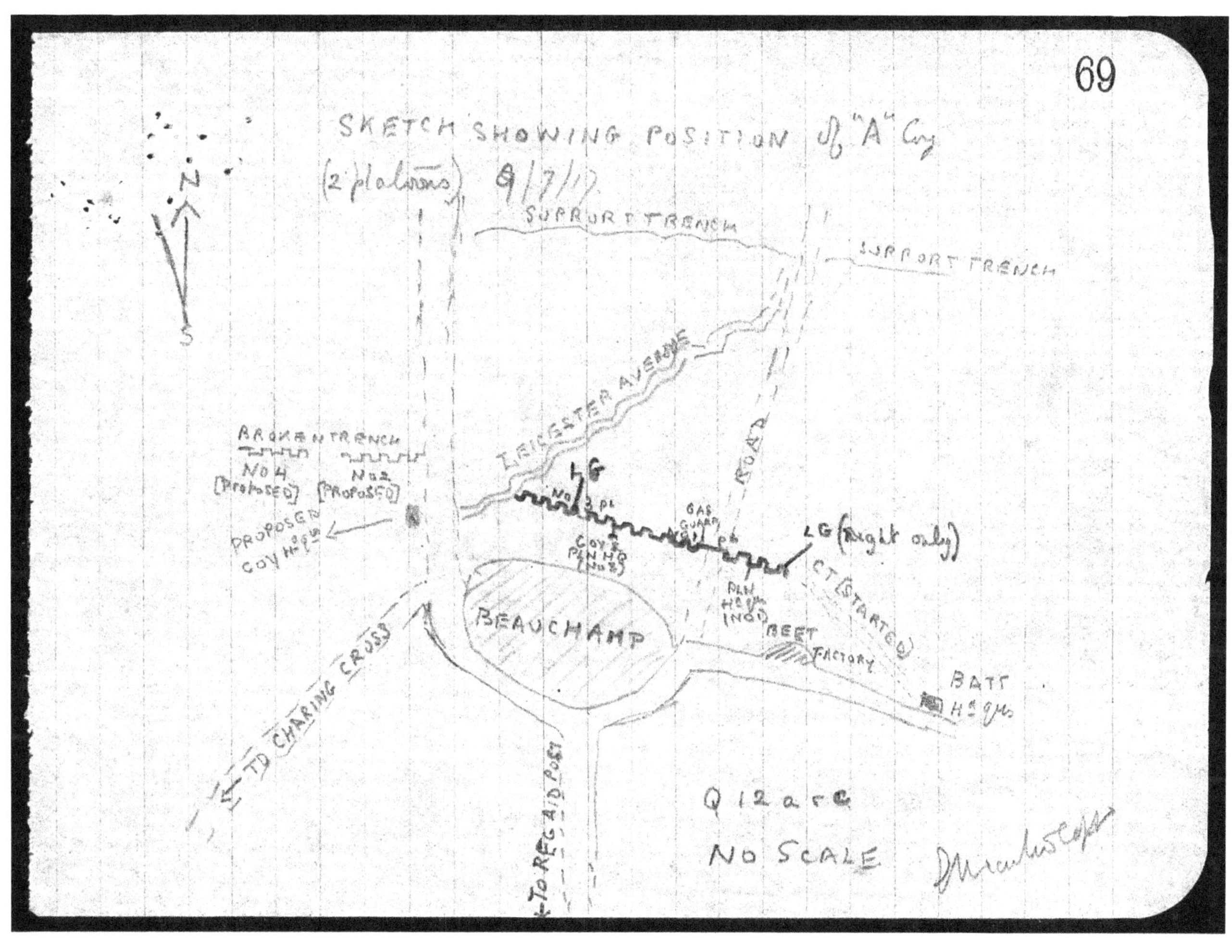
69
SKETCH SHOWING POSITION of "A" Coy
(2 platoons) 9/7/17
N
S
SUPPORT TRENCH
SUPPORT TRENCH
LEICESTER AVENUE
ROAD
BROKEN TRENCH
NO 4 [PROPOSED]
NO 2 [PROPOSED]
PROPOSED COY HQrs
LG
No 3 PL
GAS GUARD
LG (Night only)
COYS PLN HQ (No 3)
PLN HQrs (No 1)
CT (STARTED)
BEAUCHAMP
BEET FACTORY
BATT HQrs
TO CHARING CROSS
TO REG AID POST
Q 12 a c
NO SCALE

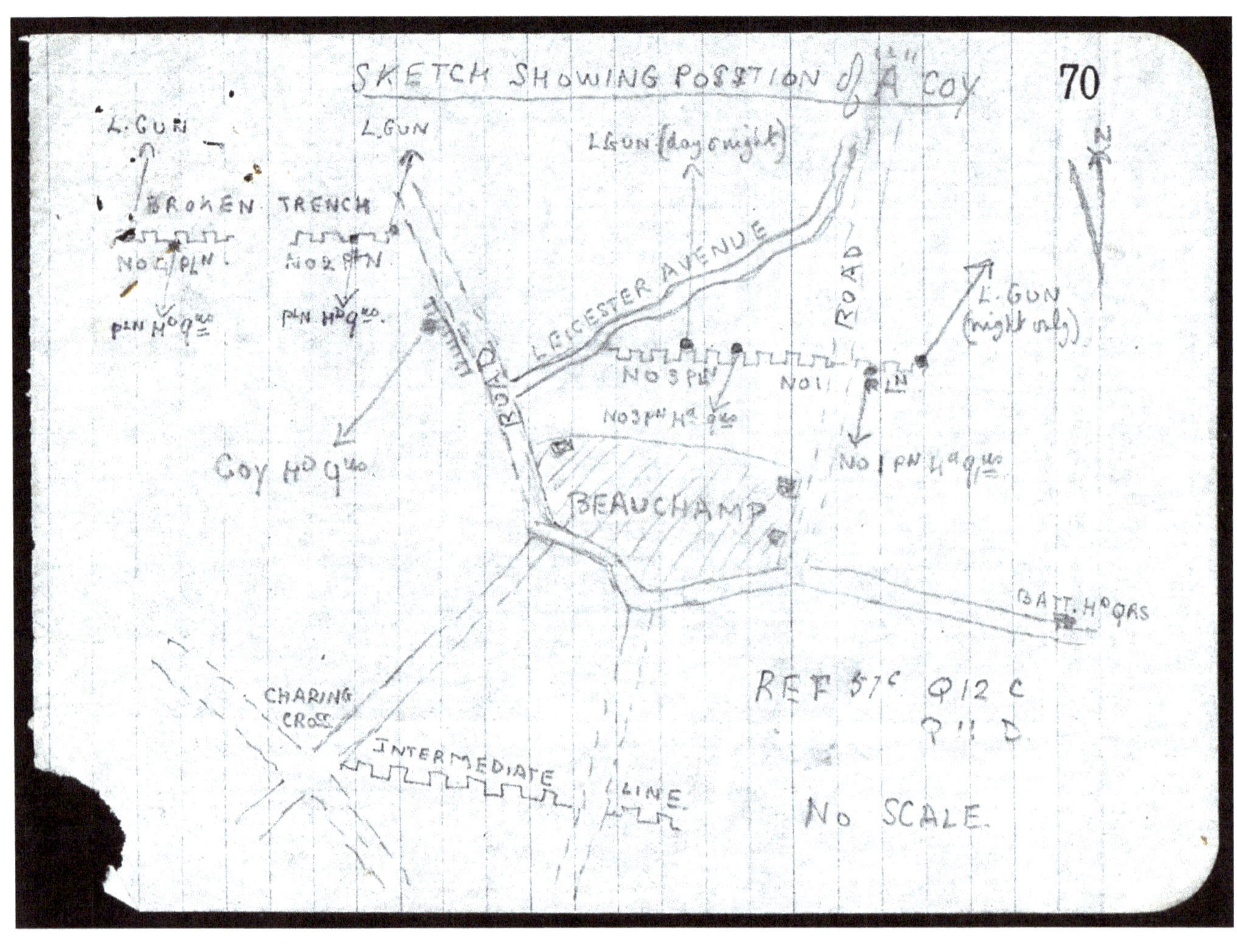
SKETCH SHOWING POSITION of "A" COY
70
N
L. GUN
L. GUN
L GUN (day & night)
BROKEN TRENCH
No 2 PLN
PLN HDQRS
PLN HDQRS
LEICESTER AVENUE
ROAD
ROAD
L. GUN (night only)
No 3 PLN
No 1 PLN
No 3 PLN HdQRS
No 1 PLN HdQRS
COY HdQRS
BEAUCHAMP
BATT. HdQRS
CHARING CROSS
INTERMEDIATE LINE
REF 57c Q 12 C
Q 11 D
No SCALE.

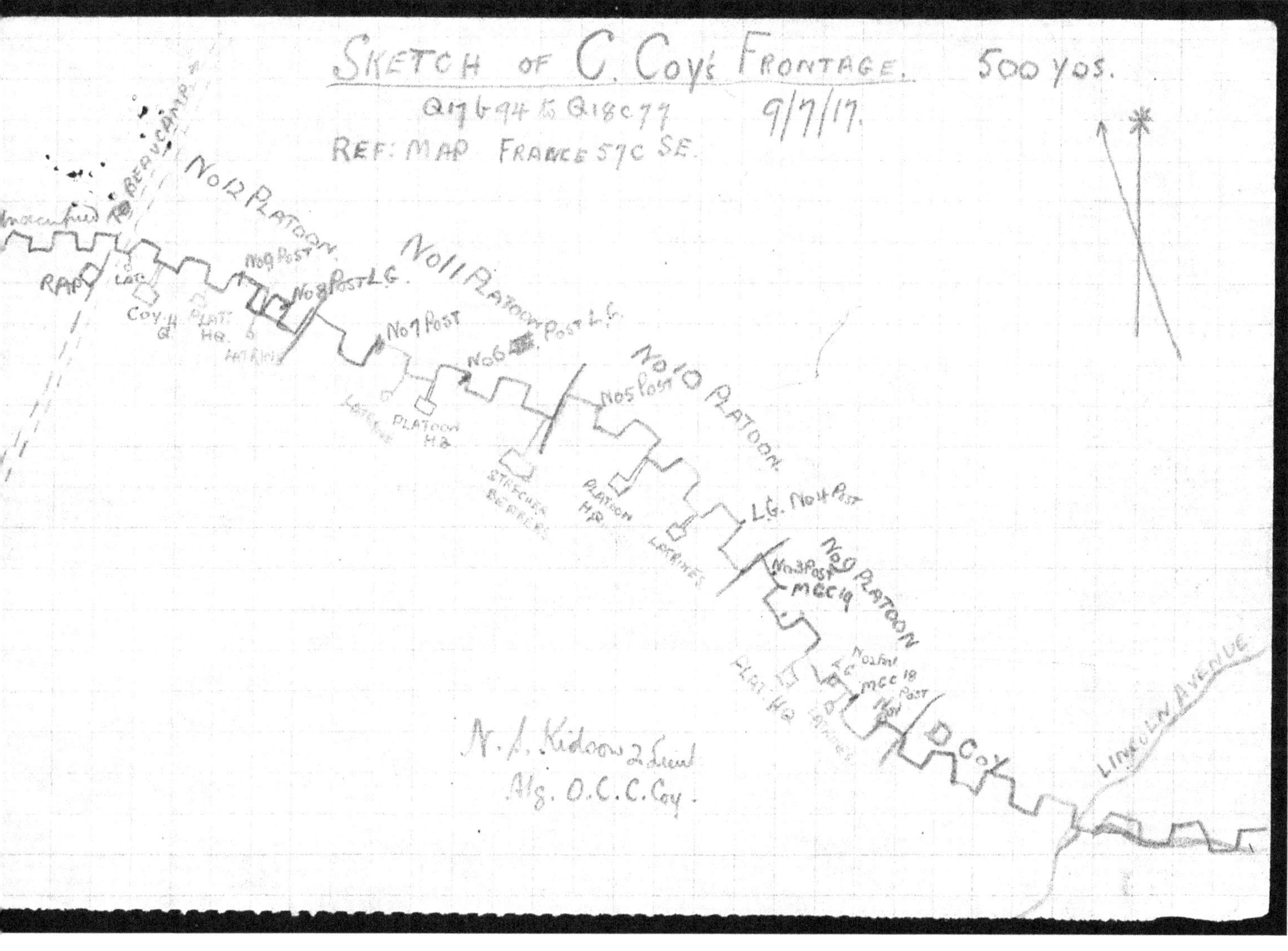
SKETCH OF C. COY'S FRONTAGE.
500 YDS.
Q17b94 to Q18c77
9/7/17.
REF: MAP FRANCE 57C SE.
No 12 PLATOON.
No 11 PLATOON
No 10 PLATOON.
No 9 PLATOON
No 9 Post
No 8 Post L.G.
No 7 Post
No 6
Post L.G.
No 5 Post
L.G. No 4 Post
No 3 Post
MGC 19
MGC 18
RAP
Coy. H.Q.
PLAT. HQ.
LATRINES
PLATOON HQ.
STRETCHER BEARERS
PLATOON HQ.
LATRINES
PLAT. HQ
D COY
LINCOLN AVENUE
N. L. Kidson 2 Lieut
A/g. O.C.C. Coy.

Secret Appendix E Copy No. 9

Order No. 9 9/7/17

(Ref. Map Sheet 57c & Trench Map)

1. Half of A. Coy. & B. Coy. will move from Camp in DESSART WOOD & relieve elements of the 5th LINCOLNS in BROKEN TRENCH & intermediate line.

2. The starting point will be the track at N.W. corner of DESSART WOOD. W.1.b.09.

3. Coys. will march in the following order:-

A. Coy. to BROKEN TRENCH, West of BEAUCAMP.

B. Coy. to intermediate line from Q.17.b.85. to CHARING CROSS.

Leading Coy. will pass starting point at 9.30pm. 100 yds. distance will be maintained between Platoons & 200 yds. between Coys.

4. ROUTE. South-East corner of GOUZEAUCOURT WOOD - QUEENS CROSS. Road junction Q.23.c.72.- Road junction Q.17.d.54. Troops will not appear within 200 yds. of DESSART FARM.

5. Coy. Commanders will arrange for the necessary guides to report to their platoons in DESSART WOOD at 8.30pm.

6. Bn. H.Q. will close at Q.12.d.60 at 9.30pm. & reopen at Q.17.b.36. at the same hour.

7. Relief will be reported to Bn. H.Q. by runner as quickly as possible using code word 'DUPLEX'

8. At the earliest possible moment after

over

Order No. 9 cont. 2.

relief. O.C. Coys will send in to Bn. H.Q. a sketch map showing accurate dispositions of Platoons (incl. platoon H.Q. & Lewis Gun positions) & location of Coy. H.Q. Platoon commanders will in every case find accomodation & live in their platoon section.

9. All men will be in possession of:-
   Rations for 1 day.
   Full water bottles (not to be touched on the march)

10. Trench stores will be taken over on relief & duplicate list sent to Bn. H.Q. at once.

11. Coy. Commanders will arrange for Coy. dumps of S.A.A. Grenades, tools & R.E. material & will report locations to Bn. H.Q.

12. Transport Officer will arrange for transport of Lewis Guns of A & B.

13. Acknowledge.

Sgd. S.H.F. Crofts.
2/Lieut.
Acting Adjutant, 2/6 London Regt.

Copies issued by runner at ..... to:-

1. C.O.
2. O.C. A. Coy (2/Lt. Wilkinson)
3. O.C. B. Coy.
4. O.C. C. Coy.
5. O.C. D. Coy.
6. Q.M. & T.O.
7. 174 Inf. Bde.
8. File
9 & 10. War Diary
11. O.C. A. Coy.

LINCOLNS AVENUE

Coy HQ

LG

13 Platoon

LG

14 Platoon

LG

15 Platoon

LG

16 Platoon

Scale 1/20,000

To The Adjutant.

Herewith rough pencil map showing disposition of platoons and ~~[struck through]~~ lewis guns etc.

N. O. Nash 2/Lt
O.C. D Coy

9/7/~~16~~ 17

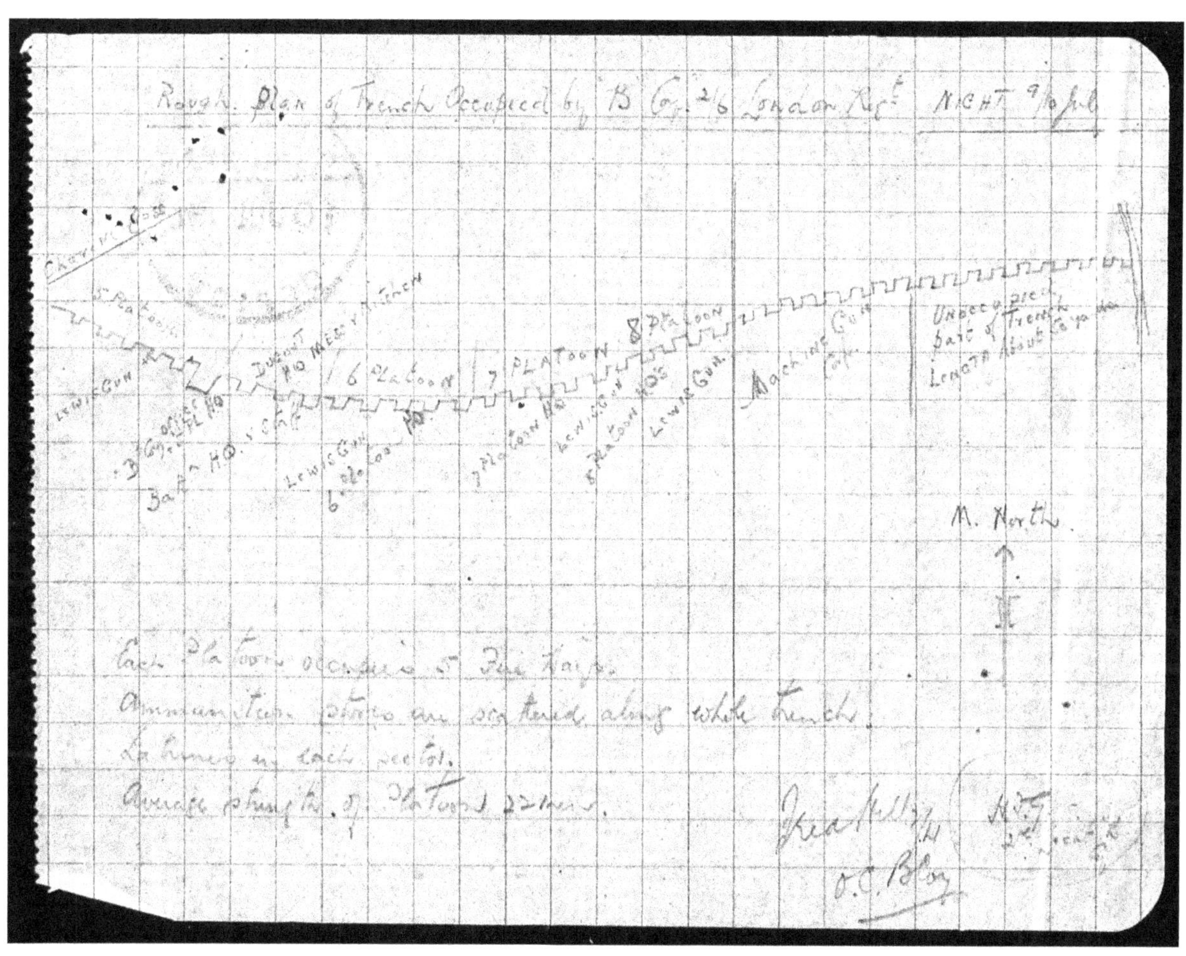
Rough Plan of Trench Occupied by B Coy. 2/6 London Regt NIGHT 9/10 Jul
5th Platoon
Lewis Gun
6 Platoon
7 PLATOON
8 Platoon
Lewis Gun
Machine Gun
Unoccupied part of Trench
M. North
Each Platoon occupies 5 Fire Bays.
Ammunition stores are scattered along whole trench.
Latrines in each sector.
Average strength of Platoons 22 men.
O.C. B Coy

[illegible]

10 JUL 1917
OFFICE

Army Form C.2121
(in pads of 100).
No. of Message

SIGNALS.

Prefix ...... Code L.B.A. m. | Words 32 | Charge

Office of Origin and Service Instructions.

Fuller

Sent
At ...... m.
To ......
By ......

This message is on a/c of: ...... Service.

H. Q. SIGNALS 13 JUL 1917 OFFICE

(Signature of "Franking Officer.")

Recd. at ...... m.
Date ......
From ......
By ......

TO C.G

Sender's Number.	Day of Month.	In reply to Number.	AAA
* 073	13/7		

Daily Sick Return AAA

1. No. of men reporting sick	9 AAA
2. Excused duty slight duty	4 AAA
3. Hospital	2. AAA
4. Medicine & duty	3

From M. G.
Place
Time 10.55 am

The above may be forwarded as now corrected.

(Z) [illegible signature] Adj

Censor.

Signature of Addressor or person authorised to telegraph in his name.

* This line should be erased if not required.

750,000. W 2186—M500. H. W. & V., Ld. 6/16.

Appendix F

Secret.

Order No. 10

Copy No 9

(Ref Map Sheet 57c SE & Trench Map) 14/7/17.

1/ Disposition of Bn. as laid down in Order No. 8, para 3 & Order No. 9, para 3 is cancelled.

2/ "D" Coy will be responsible for the intermediate line from the right of the Divisional Boundary inclusive, to the junction of grid line between Q18a & Q18c & the intermediate line (Q18.a.50) exclusive.

"C" Coy. from last named point inclusive to BEAUCAMP Valley at Q17b.5.6. inclusive.

Headquarters Platoon plus one Lewis Gun section to be detailed by O.C. B Coy. under the command of Bn. L.G. Officer with Sgt Lush as Platoon Sgt., from the last named point exclusive to CHARING CROSS inclusive.

"B" Coy. less one Lewis Gun section will remain as a reserve in the hands of the Bn. Commander.

3/ On receipt of the order "ATTACK — MOVE" fr[illegible] Bn. H.Q., "B" Coy. less 1 section Lewis Gun[illegible] will at once proceed to reinforce A Coy [illegible] in BROKEN TRENCH & H.Q. Platoon plus [illegible] Lewis Gun section from B. Coy and

A. C. & D. Coys. will occupy [illegible] battle positions

4. O.C. A. C. & D Coys will submit [illegible] showing proposed

(a) day

(b) night

(c) battle

8

Order No. 80 cont. 2.

dispositions to Bn. H.Q. by 9 pm. today, 14th inst., with the amount of SAA & bombs proposed for

(a) Posts

(b) Platoon Reserves

(c) Company Reserve, & Ullent for defence

5/ O.C. B. Coy. will reconnoitre lines of advance to BROKEN TRENCH & after consultation with O.C. A. Coy. submit sketch shewing his proposed battle dispositions & SAA & bomb arrangements.

6/ O.C. Coys are responsible that all their Officers are well acquainted with ground over the whole extent of the Brigade front with the positions of all posts & trenches & with the routes leading to the front line system.

7/ Coy. & Platoon Commanders will consider & formulate definite written plans for the defence of their sectors & for counter attack. They will concert measures for mutual support with Commanders of corresponding units on their flanks. These plans will be handed over by units on relief.

8/ Acknowledge.

Copies issued by runner at .... to:-

1. C.O.
2. OC A Coy
3. B.
4. C.
5. D.
6. 2.C.O.
7. 174 I.B.
8. File
9. & 10 War diary.

Sgd. S.W.F. Crofts 2/Lieut.
Acting Adjutant
7th London Regt

Appendix G

Order No 11 — Copy No 9

7th London Regt. [illegible]

(Ref. Map 57c SE & Trench Maps)

1/ The Bn. (less A & B Coys.) will be relieved by 1st London Regt (two Coys) & by one Coy. of 2nd London Regt by day July 1[illegible]

All movement & reliefs of the Intermediate Line will take place via [illegible] AVENUE which will be [illegible]

The Coys in [illegible] TRENCH & Intermediate Line which are to be relieved will withdraw via SHAFTESBURY AVENUE when relief of the other two Coys is complete.

6th London Regt on completion of relief will march by Coys [illegible] at [illegible] [illegible] [illegible] to S. edge of [illegible] WOOD will be [illegible] Brigade reserve.

2/ C & D Coys will leave behind for 24 hrs after relief [illegible] per Coy & 1 man for Lewis Guns

HQ signals will leave behind 1 man

3/ An interval of at least [illegible] will be kept between Coy reliefs. Guides from C & D Coys will be at Bn HQ at [illegible] & these Coys will [illegible] Bn HQ as soon as relief is complete & instructions will be given to all Coys as to moving [illegible] E & NE of the North & South line through [illegible] central will be by [illegible] at 50 yds distance.

The greatest care is to be taken that movement is observed by the enemy. The [illegible]

P.T.O.

Order No. 11 cont. 2

of the S.A.L. strongly impressed upon all ranks. Where the trenches are particularly shallow all ranks will keep below the parapet & in the lower portions of trench. O.C. Companies will see to this [illegible]. Rifles will be carried at the trail.

4. All maps, aeroplane photographs, defence schemes & Standing Orders will be handed over and a receipt obtained.

All trench stores, Very lights & S.O.S. lights, grenades will be handed over by C & D Coys & a receipt in duplicate sent to Bn. H.Q. at once. As A & B Coys are not being relieved the receipt for these stores will be obtained by Bn. H.Q. direct.

5. Particular care will be taken in handing over details of work in progress.

6. B.C. & D. Coys will dump Lewis Guns & Ammunition & trench stores [illegible] packs [illegible] at Bn. HQ (at a spot to be indicated by [illegible]). A Coy will dump theirs by A Coy HQ. 1 N.C.O. & 1 man per Coy will be left in charge of dump which will be collected by limber at night.

7. Transport lines & Q.M. stores remain as at present.

8. Acknowledge.

(Sgd.) S.H.F. [illegible] 2/Lieut

Acting Adjutant 7th [illegible]

Copies issued by runner at ....

To:—

1 C.O.
2 OC A Coy
3 OC B Coy
4 OC C Coy
5 OC D Coy
6 17th Inf Bde
7 QM & TO
8 File
9 & 10 War diary.

Appendix J

SECRET. ORDER NO. 12 Copy No. 9

2/8th BN. THE LONDON REGT.

Ref. Map. 57 c SE and Trench Map. 18/7/17.

---

1. The Bn. will relieve the 2/7th Bn. London Regt, in the right subsector on the 18th inst.
2. The starting point will be cross roads at Q.23.a.13.
3. The Bn. will leave camp in the following order:-

   Headquarters to Q.10.d.38. to pass starting point at 2 p.m.

   A Coy. to STAFFORD RESERVE from SHAFTESBURY AVENUE (inclusive) to SHERWOOD AVENUE (exclusive) to pass starting point at 2.30 p.m.

   to TRESCAULT Rd inclusive

   B Coy. to DERBY RESERVE from SHERWOOD AVENUE inclusive to pass starting point at 3 p.m.

   C Coy. to right front and support line from QUEEN LANE inclusive to BASS LANE exclusive to pass starting point at 3.30 p.m.

   D Coy. to left front and support line from BASS LANE inclusive to TRESCAULT ROAD inclusive to pass starting point at 4.p.m.
4. ROUTE. All Coys. to Bde. H.Q. HAVRINCOURT WOOD Q.15.c.82. by road via METZ thence H.Q., B & D Coys through wood to foot of SHERWOOD AVENUE and via SHERWOOD AVENUE A & B Coys round southern face of woods to commencement of SHAFTESBURY AVENUE, and via SHAFTESBURY AVENUE. 200 yards distance will be maintained between platoons up to Bde. H.Q. which will be passed by H.Q. at 4 p.m. and thence forward Coys. will move by sections at 50 yds distance taking all precautions to avoid enemy observation. Guides from 7th Bn. will be at Bde H.Q.
5. Coy. Commanders and C.S.M. will proceed independently to arrive at their respective sectors by 5.30 p.m.
6. All maps, aeroplane photographs, plans, standing orders and defence schemes will be taken over.

   Trench stores, Very lights, S.O.S. Grenades and hot Food containers will be taken over and receipts forwarded in duplicate to Bn. H.Q. immediately after completion of relief.
7. Completion of reliefs will be reported to Bn. H.Q. by wiring the word LEMBERG (to be confirmed by runner).
8. A sketch map showing dispositions will be forwarded to Bn. H.Q. by 10 a.m. 19th July.
9. All men will be in possession of

   Full water bottles

   Unexpended portion of days rations.
10. DRESS. Full marching order.
11. Bn. H.Q. will be at Q.10.d.38.
12. R.A.P. will be at Q.10.d.69.
13. Rations and water will be brought up nightly by Transport to Q.10.d.38. A & B Coys will supply carrying parties to C & D Coys in the front line. There is a supply of water at TRESCAULT.
14. LEWIS GUNS. Lewis Gun limbers will accompany their Coys. as far as Q.15.c.82 where they will be unloaded. The guns will be carried up from there.

    9 men per Coy. for training as Lewis Gunners will remain in the Transport lines and go through a course of instruction under Sgt. Watkins. The class will be supervised by 2/Lt. Brasher.
15. Acknowledge.

Sgd. R.W.F. Crofts.
2/Lieut.
Acting Adjutant, 2/8th Bn. London Regt.

Copies issued by runner at........to:-

1. C.O.
2. O.C. A Coy.
3. O.C. B Coy.
4. O.C. C Coy.
5. O.C. D Coy.
6. 174th Inf. Bde.
7. Q.M. & T.O.
8. File.
9. & 10. War Diary.

Appendix K.

COPY.

Secret. **ORDER NO. 13** Copy No: 8
(ref. 57c SE and Trench Map) 20/7/17.

A. Coy. less 1 Platoon will move tonight to new positions as follows:-

Company less 2 Platoons to No. 3 Post (Q.10.a.82 to Q. 10.a.91.). 1 Platoon to No. 1 Post (Q.10.b.74 to Q.10.b.9025).

The remaining platoon (No.1 Ptn. 2/Lieut. Anderson) will remain in STAFFORD RESERVE and pass under the orders of O.C. B. Coy. at 1 a.m. 21st July.

O.C. B. Coy. will arrange the disposition of B. Coy. and 1 Ptn. of A. Coy. in DERBY RESERVE and CLAY STREET, and will submit sketch of positions by 12 noon, 21st July.

C. Coy. Hdqtrs. will move temporarily to those at present occupied by A. Coy.

Sgd. S.W.F. Crofts,
2/Lieut.
Acting Adjutant, 2/6th London Regt.

Copies issued by runner at.........to.-
1. C.O.
2. O.C. A. Co.y
3. O.C. B. Coy.
4. O.C. C. Coy.
5. O.C. D. Coy.
6. 174th Inf. Bde.
7. File
8/9 War diary.

... back. I am sure that it is no good trusting to a laddered line being laid before the show as the shell fire will nearly always wipe out the men. Bury cable as far as possible and then trust to a large no of runners and Lucas lamps. Pigeons can then be kept as an emergency means. If every Coy had had a lamp I think that quicker ms. work would have resulted although I do not think communications failed during the entire proceedings.

Asst Sig Sgt
RSO

the lamp sent up by the Bn was in touch with OW within ½ hour of A Coy reaching its objective and remained through during the operations. Personally, I saw no message rockets launched so cannot speak of their efficiency. All the time I was at SPRINGFIELD the Power Buzzer was dis but I believe it got through after I left. The only means of communication left us other than runners were pigeons & dogs. The pigeons were as far as I know a success but the dogs took a long time to

Report on Communications during Operations of 20 [illegible] July 1917

The chief noticeable feature regarding communications was the lack of accomadation for establishing an office. Forward of St Julien it was impossible for a wire to hold for [illegible] even if it ever got laid. The brigade station at SPRINGFIELD had heavy casualties but succeeded in getting a line to MARINE VIEW but there was nothing there which could be manned by an office. The smoke of the barrage prevented a disc being seen but

Appendix L

COPY.

SECRET. ORDER NO. 14 Copy No. 8
(Ref. 57c SE and Trench Map) 21/7/17.

1. No. 1 Platoon will revert from the command of O.C. B. Coy. to O.C. A. Coy. at 3a.m. 22nd July. The Platoon will occupy No. 2 Post in Q.10.b.

2. O.C. C. Coy. will arrange for No. 10 Platoon to move from its present position to STAFFORD TRENCH immediately north-west of QUEENS LANE and will submit sketch of the new position by 11a.m. 22nd July.

3. Acknowledge.

Sgd. S.W.F. Crofts,
2/Lieut.
Acting Adjutant, 2/6th London Regt.

Copies issued by runner ~~xx~~ at...........to:-
1. C.O.
2. O.C. A. Coy.
3. O.C. B. Coy.
4. O.C. C. Coy.
5. O.C. D. Coy.
6. 174th Inf. Bde.
7. File.
8./9. War Diary.

Appendix (N)

Secret

Order No. 15

(Ref. 57c SE & French Map)

Copy No. 10

22.7.17

1/ The Bn. will be relieved by the 5th LONDON REGT. by daylight July 23rd. The Bn on relief will move to YPRES & take over Camp now occupied by 5th LONDON REGT. & be in Divisional Reserve.

2/ Coys. will be relieved in the following order. –

Hdqtrs, C B D A; & B Coy. will not move out until the Coy relieving D Coy. has passed the junction of SHERWOOD AVENUE & DERBY RESERVE.

3/ ROUTE. On relief Coys will move by section at 50 yds. distance VIA –

Hdqtrs, B. D. A. – SHERWOOD AVENUE

C. Coy. (All platoons) – SHAFTESBURY AVENUE to light railway control point No. 15 (9.w. C. 59.) where they will entrain & detrain at CANTEEN SIDING P30. a.

Four trains will be available from 4 pm onwards & will move off as soon as they are loaded. 2/Lieut. SHOWELL will act as Entraining Officer & report to Staff Captain at 2.30 pm at Brigade H.Q.

4/ GUIDES. The Coys will detail a guide per platoon & the R.S.M. one for Bn Hdqtrs to report to Brigade H.Q. by 12 noon

Orders No. 15 Cont. 2.

5/ The greatest precaution will be exercised to prevent observation by the enemy & OC C & D Coys. will station trench police at all necessary points to prevent exposure of all ranks incoming & outgoing. Rifles will be carried at the trail. Trench police will march out with the last platoon of their Coys.

6 Relief will be reported to Bn. HdQrs by sending the word MESSINES

7 Lewis Guns & Ammunition & Trench equipment will be carried by incoming unit. Medical Stores, Officers Mess & Signalling Stores will be dumped at Bn. HdQrs and will be collected by T.O. after dark. All petrol tins for water will be dumped at Bn HdQrs before 12 noon & will be handed over to incoming unit

8 All Trench Stores, Very Lights, & S.O.S. Rifle Grenades, Maps, Aeroplane Photographs, defence schemes & standing orders will be handed over receipts in duplicate obtained & sent to Bn. HdQrs. by 6 pm. Particular care will be taken in handing over details of work in progress.

9/ 1 NCO. per Coy. will report to 2/Lieut WATSON at Bn. HdQrs. at 7am. with details of Coy strength & proceed to YTRES as an advance party

Orders No. 15 cont. 3.

10. Details at NEUVILLE will proceed under 2/Lieut. FOULDS to YTRES on the afternoon of July 23rd and to arrive before 4 pm.

11. TRANSPORT & Q.M. STORES will move to YTRES on 23rd July & take over Transport Lines from 5th LONDON REGT. Arrangements to be made by the Transport Officer who will report completion of move to Bn H.Q. at YTRES. Baggage waggons will report to T.O. on R.O.A. at 10 am 23rd July.

12. Acknowledge.

(Sgd.) J. R. F. Crofts,
2/Lieut.
A/Adj. 2/6 London Regt.

Copies issued by runner at - - - to:—

1. C.O.
2. O.C. A Coy.
3. O.C. B Coy.
4. O.C. C Coy.
5. O.C. D Coy.
6. 174th Inf Bde.
7. 5th London Regt.
8. Q.M. & T.O.
9. File
10/11. War Diary

Appendix N. OPERATION ORDER NO. 10.

Copy No. 9.....

2/5th Bn. THE LONDON REGT. 27/7/17

1. The Battalion will be relieved in divisional reserve by the 4th South African Infantry Regt. on the 28th July. Relief will be completed by 11a.m. On relief Coys. will take up positions in the neighbourhood of the Football Ground and await orders. These positions will be indicated by 2/Lieut. Showell [illegible] N.C.O. which each Coy. will detail to report to him at [illegible] a.m. On completion of relief the Battalion will move to BERTINCOURT and take over the billets vacated by the 4th S. African Infantry Regt.

2. The starting point will be the road opposite divisional baths. Companies will pass starting point in the following order.-

A. Coy.
B. Coy.
C. Coy.
D. Coy.

The Band will march at the head of the leading Company, and a distance of 100 yds. will be maintained between Coys. Headquarter personnel will march with Coys.

3. ROUTE. [illegible] - P 14 central - BERTINCOURT.

4. ADVANCE PARTY. An advance party consisting of 1 N.C.O. per Coy. and 1 N.C.O. for Bn. Hdqtrs. under 2/Lieut. Tew will parade at [illegible].15 a.m. 28th July and report to Town Major BERTINCOURT at P.7.b.51. at 10 a.m.

over

5. Companies will report in occupation of new quarters by runner to Bn. Orderly Room at BERTINCOURT.

6. Band Kits will be dumped at Q.M. Stores at [illegible] a.m. 28th July.

7. All stores other than those carried in the authorised loads for 1st. Line Transport must be dumped at Q.M. stores before [illegible] a.m. 28th July.

8. Unexpended portion of days rations and rations for the 29th July will be carried.

9. Orders for Transport have been issued to Transport Officer separately.

10. Officers Mess Kit (limited to one basket and one box per mess) will be carried in Officer's Mess cart and must be loaded by 10 a.m. Medical stores will be loaded by the same hour.

11. Acknowledge.

Sgd. S. W. F. Crofts,
2/Lieut.
Acting Adjutant, [illegible] Bn. London Regt.

Copies to.-
1. C.O.
2. O.C. A. Coy.
3. O.C. B. Coy.
4. O.C. C. Coy.
5. O.C. D. Coy.
6. ~~XXXX~~ 1[illegible]th Inf. Bde.
7. Q.M. & T.O.
8. File
9/10. War diary.
11. Adj., 4th S. African Inf. Regt.

Secret

IV Corps No. *G.S. 55/1*

3rd Division.
9th Division.
58th Division.
59th Division.

III Corps.)
VI Corps.)
Third Army.) for information.
Intelligence.)
D.A. & Q.M.G.)

1. The following nomenclature for the various Divisional, Brigade, and Battalion areas of the Divisions in the line will in future be adopted in all reports :-

(a) Divisional Areas will be known as "Sectors".
58th Division Area "Right Sector".
3rd Division Area "Left Sector".

(b) Brigade Areas will be known as "Sections" and will be named as following :-

Right Bde.	Area	of	Right	Divn.	BEAUCAMP	Section.
Centre "	"	"	"	"	TRESCAULT	"
Left "	"	"	"	"	HAVRINCOURT	"
Right Bde.	Area	of	Left	Divn.	HERMIES	"
Centre "	"	"	"	"	LOUVERVAL	"
Left "	"	"	"	"	MORCHIES	"

2. In all reports the Section in which the occurrence took place should be mentioned as well as the map reference.

H. De Prée

H.Q., IV Corps,
25th July, 1917.
ECK.

Brigadier-General,
General Staff, IV Corps.

6th Bn

Appendix O

<u>SECRET.</u> OPERATION ORDER NO.17 Copy No.9.....

2/6th BN. THE LONDON REGT. 28/7/17.

(Ref. Map Sheet 57c & 51c, 1/40000

---

1. The Bn. will move into quarters at BERNVILLE proceeding by.-
   (a) Bus to BAPAUME.
   (b) Train to BEAUMETZ
   (c) By march route from BEAUMETZ to BERNVILLE.

(a) The Bn. will fall in in line on the YTRES - BERTINCOURT road with its right flank resting on road junction at P.7.d.99. at 1.30 p.m., 29/7/17. Markers will meet the R.S.M. at the above road junction at 1.15 p.m.(with particulars of the strength of their Coys. - Officers and other ranks.) and Coys. will move off to the assembly point in the following order.-

Headquarters (under 2/Lieut. Tew)
A. Coy.
B. Coy.
C. Coy.
D. Coy.

at 1 minute intervals, commencing at 1.20 p.m.
As soon as the Bn. is in position, it will be told off from right to left in parties of 28 under an Officer.

(b) <u>ENTRAINING.</u>

The Bn. will travel by coaching stock train Serial No. 3, from BAPAUME to BEAUMETZ, approximate time of departure 8 p.m., approximate duration of journey 4 hours.

Coys. will be formed up in line on the station and N.C.O's. and men will be told off into parties of 8 each.

The Lewis Guns will be carried on this train

over.

in covered goods waggons, but Lewis Gun limbers will be taken on Train No.1, leaving at 12 noon in accordance with instructions issued to Transport Officer.

2/Lieut. Showell will act as Entraining Officer. He will report to Lieut. Wimble at BAPAUME at 2.45 a.m. He will proceed by train No.4.

(c) DETRAINING. The Bn. will detrain at BEAUMETZ.

2/Lieut. A.H. Tew will act as Detraining Officer and will report to Lieut. Harrison-Jones, immediately on arrival at BEAUMETZ.

MARCH ROUTE. The Bn. will move off in the follwoing order.-

Headquarters (including Q.M. Staff) under 2/Lieut. Foulds.

A. Coy.
B. Coy.
C. Coy.
D. Coy.

2. Full water bottles and the unexpended portion of the days rations for the 29th will be carried. Rations for the 30th will be issued in the new area.

3. The Transport will proceed by march route to BAPAUME, and by Trains No. 1 and 3, leaving at 12 noon and 6 p.m. respectively, to SAULTY, thence by road to BERNVILLE, in accordance with detailed instructions issued to the Transport Officer.

4. MEDICAL. The Medical Officer will travel by Train No. 1

over.

Operation Order No. 17. cont. 3.

leaving BAPAUME at 12 noon.

5. Medical Stores will be loaded up by 4 a.m., and the Medical cart will leave BERTINCOURT with the Transport column under Sgt. Price.

6. Acknowledge.

Sgd. S.N.F. Crofts,
2/Lieut.
Acting Adjutant, 2/6th Bn. London Regt.

Copies to.-
1. C.O.
2. O.C. A. Coy.
3. O.C. B. Coy.
4. O.C. C. Coy.
5. O.C. D. Coy.
6. 174th Inf. Bde.
7. Q.M. & T.O.
8. File.
9/10. War diary.

PARTS OF 51B, 57C & 57B ◇ SCALE 1:40000 ◇ Branch "I" Sect. MAP No 50
22-7-17
Corps Boundary
Agache R.
Lagnicourt Sect.
Boursies
Louverval
Doignies
Demicourt
Hermies
Canal du Nord
British Front
Havrincourt
Havrincourt Wood
Flesquières
Ribécourt
Trescault
Beaucamp
Graincourt-lès-Havrincourt
Bois de l'Orival
Anneux
Cantaing
Fontaine-Notre-Dame
Marcoing
Canal de l'Escaut
Corps Boundary

2/6 Bath

2/6th London Regt

August 1917

Index..........

SUBJECT.

No.	Contents.	Date.
	70/2926—2950.	

(49,674). Wt.42,605—128. 2000. 4/20. Gp.164. A.&E.W.
(51,507). „ 6005—137. 500. 5/20. „ „

Instructions regarding War Diaries and Intelligence Summaries are contained in F. S. Regs., Part II. and the Staff Manual respectively. Title pages will be prepared in manuscript.

WAR DIARY ~~or INTELLIGENCE SUMMARY.~~ of 2/16th Lon. Regt.

(*Erase heading not required.*)

Army Form C. 2118.

Vol 8

Place	Date	Hour	Summary of Events and Information	Remarks and references to Appendices
BERNEVILLE	Augt 10th to Augt 24th		Training at BERNEVILLE. Bde scheme 16th August on O.9 trenches FICHEUX-WAILLY Divisional scheme 21st August area as above	
	A. 24th		Bde moved to POPERINGHE. Train from ARRAS 1.54pm to GODEWAERSVELDE. Arrived POPERINGHE 1am night 24/5th	See app A.3.
	27th		To REIGERSBURG by train at 5pm. occupying New Camp No1 New camp No2.	
	28th		To CANAL BANK at 8.15pm by track Arrived 9pm Bn Hd Qrs at C25b1015 Sheet 28 NW in support to 7th London Regt.	
	29/31		At CANAL BANK	

[illegible] Lt A/Adj.

SECRET. Operation Order No. 1[illegible] C py No.
SECRET. 2/5th Battalion. London Regiment.
23/8/1917.

1. The Battalion will move to the new area tomorrow.
2. The Battalion less C Coy will parade in the WAILLY Road facing S. at [illegible].10am and march to ARRAS. Markers will meet R.S.M. at Bn. Orderly Room at [illegible] am.
3. Order of March. A. B. & D Coys at 200 yds distance.
4. Route. WARLUS - DAINVILLE - ARRAS. and via RUE ST. CLAIRE, BOULEVARD CRES EL XXXXX - XXXXPEL PLACE ST HUGO to LES HALLES. (All available cover is to be used for screening troops from enemy observation.
5. Rendezvous. Troops will rest at LES HALLES until required for entraining in station 100 yards away.
6. Train. Entraining station XXXXX ARRAS, line 11. Detraining station GODEWAERSVELDE. The Battalion less C Coy as above will proceed by train No. 6 serial No. 7 due to depart at 1,54 pm and to arrive at destination 9.54 pm. Each company will detail an picket at all stops under an officer to prevent men leaving the train.
7. Detraining. On arrival at detraining station. six regimental police under police sergeant will relieve a similar number of the 2/5th Bn. London Regiment and remain on duty until the Brigade group has completed detraining and left the station.
8 On march from detraining point 200 yards will be maintained between companies.
9. Transport. (except C Coy cooker) will leave BERNEVILLE at 8,45am. Detailed instructions have been given to Transport Officer separately.
10. C Company will leave BERNEVILLE by route as in para 4 at 2.0 am the night of 24/25th and arrive at XXXXXXXXX LES HALLES, ARRAS by 4.34am. An Officer will report to Staff Captain at station at 4.10am with an entraining state in triplicate. The company will proceed by train No. 20, serial No, 12 departing at 5,54am due at detraining point 1.54 pm 25th instant. A picket will be detailed under an officer at all stops to prevent men leaving the train. C Company's cooker will leave at 12 midnight 24/25 Aug. under a N.C.O. to be detailed by Transport Officer.
11. Separate instructions for rationing have been issued to Quartermaster
12. Acknowledge.

(signed) S.W.F.Crofts. 2nd Lt.
A/Adjt. 2/5th Bn. The London Regiment.

Copies to;-
1. Commanding Officer.
2. O.C. A Coy.
3. O.C. B Coy.
4. O.C. C Coy.
5. O.C. D Coy.
6. H.Q. 174th Inf. Bde.
7. Second in command & Medical Officer.
8. Transport Officer & Quartermaster.
9. File.
10. War Diary.
11. War Diary.

SECRET. SECRET.

Operation Order No. 19
2/6th Battalion. London Regiment.

Copy No.

23/8/1917.

1. The Battalion will move to the new area tomorrow.
2. The Battalion less C Coy will parade in the WAILLY Rod facing S. at 10.10am and march to ARRAS. Markers will meet R.S.M. at Bn. Orderly Room at 10.0 am.
3. <u>Order of March.</u> A. B. & D Coys at 200 yds distance.
4. <u>Route.</u> WARLUS - DAINEVILLE - ARRAS. and vis RUE ST. CLAIRE, BOULEVARD CRESPEL ~~XXXXX~~ - ~~CRESPEL~~ PLACE ST HUGO to LES HALLES. (All available cover is to be used for screening troops from enemy observation.
5. <u>Rendezvous.</u> Troops will rest at LES HALLES until required for entraining in station 100 yards away.
6. <u>Train.</u> Entraining station ~~XXXXX~~ ARRAS, line 11. Detraining station GODEWAERSVELDE. The Battalion less C Coy as above will proceed by train No. 8 serial No. 7 due to depart at 1.54 pm and to arrive at destination 9.54 pm. Each company will detail an picket at all stops under an officer to prevent men leaving the train.
7. <u>Detraining.</u> On arrival at detraining station, six regimental police under police sergeant will relieve a similar number of the 2/5th Bn. London Regiment and remain on duty until the Brigade group has completed detraining and left the station.
8. On march from detraining point 200 yards will be maintained between companies.
9. <u>Transport.</u> (except C Coy cooker) will leave BERNEVILLE at 8.45am. Detailed instructions have been given to Transport Officer separately.
10. C Company will leave BERNEVILLE by route as in para 4 at 2.0 am the night of 24/25th and arrive at ~~XXXXXXXX~~ LES HALLES, ARRAS by 4.24am. An Officer will report to Staff Captain at staton at 4.10am with an entraining state in triplicate. The company will proceed by train No. 20, serial No, 12 departing at 5.54am due at detraining point 1.54pm 25th instant. A picket will be detailed under an officer at all stops to prevent men leavingthe train. C Company's cooker will leave at 12 midnight 24/25 Aug. under a N.C.O. to be detailed by Transport Officer.
11. Separate instructions for rationing have been issued to Quartermaster
12. Acknowledge.

(signed) S.W.F.Crofts. 2nd Lt.
A/Adjt. 2/6th Bn. The London Regiment.

Copies to:-
1. Commanding Officer.
2. O.C. A Coy.
3. O.C. B Coym
4. O.C. C Coy.
5. O.C. D Coy.
6. H.Q. 174th Inf. Bde.
7. Second in command & Medical Officer.
8. Transport Officer & Quartermaster.
9. File.
10. War Diary.
11. War Diary.

S E C R E T.

B.M./7/20/1.

5th London Regt.
6th London Regt.
7th London Regt.
8th London Regt.
198th M.Gun Coy.
174th. L.T.M.By.
Bde. Signal Officer.

Ref. maps.
Sheet 28. 1/40,000.
POELCAPELLE. 1/10,000.

---

1. As far as can be seen at present the Division will probably relieve the 48th Division in the line on the night Aug. 28/29.

2. In this case the Brigade will relieve the 144th Inf. Brigade (left Brigade of 48th Division) on the night Aug. 28/29. The 175th Inf. Brigade is to relieve the 143rd Inf. Brigade (right Brigade of 48th Division) on the same night.

3. The Brigade will take over the front as follows :-

In Line. 7th London Regt.
In Support 6th London Regt. on the line MOUSETRAP FARM - OBLONG FARM. (C.16.b. and d.).
In Reserve.
5th London Regt.) Resting and Training in
8th London Regt.) vicinity of REIGERSBURG H.6.b.

4. Probable moves in connection with the relief are as follows :-

Aug. 27. *Monday*
7th London Regt. to REIGERSBURG by march route.
6th " " " " by train from HOPOUTRE (near POPERINGHE).

Aug. 28. *Tuesday*
7th London Regt. into the line.
6th " " into support.
8th " " to REIGERSBURG by march route.
5th " " " " by train from HOPOUTRE.
198th M.Gun Coy.)" " " "
174th L.T.M.Bty.)" " "
Brigade H.Q. to CANAL BANK.

5. Reconnaissances will be carried out as follows :-
(a) Aug 26. *Sunday* C.O's. and all company commanders of 6th and 7th Battalions London Regt., O.C. 198th M.Gun Coy. and two other officers from 198th M.Gun Coy., O.C. 174th. L.T.M.By. and one other officer from 174th L.T.M.Bty. will reconnoitre the line.
(b) Aug.27. C.O's. and one officer per company of 5th and 8th Battalions London Regt. will reconnoitre the REIGERSBURG and routes leading forward to the Brigade front.
(c) In all reconnaissances all possible information is to be obtained as to routes and tracks forward. *Int. Officer*
(d) Further details as to rendezvous and transport will be notified.

6. Please acknowledge.-

Recd CNG 25/8/17

[signature]
Captain,
Brigade Major,
174th. Infantry Brigade.

24th August, 1917.

Copies to :- Staff Captain.
Brigade Intelligence Officer.
58th Division.

"C" Form (Original).

Army Form C. 2123.
(In books of 50's in duplicate.)

MESSAGES AND SIGNALS.

No. of Message [illegible]

Prefix [illegible] Code [illegible] Words [illegible]	Received	Sent, or sent out	Office Stamp.
£ s. d.	From [illegible]	At.......m.	H.Q. 27 AUG 1917 [illegible] OFFICE
Charges to collect	By [illegible]	To............	
Service Instructions.		By............	

Handed in at...................Office..........m. Received..........m.

TO 8th & 16th bns

*Sender's Number	Day of Month	In reply to Number	AAA
[illegible]	27/8/17		

Ref para 3 of instructions [illegible] of the [illegible] each man will carry 2 Mills Grenades [illegible] which are to be taken from mobile reserve. 8th & 16th X 8th bns will not carry 2 Mills grenades per man unless instructions are given to that effect later in which case the bombs can be drawn from Divl Grenade store at CANAL BANK I.2.A.19 and not from mobile reserve.

FROM [illegible] INF BDE

PLACE & TIME 9.50 P

* This line should be erased if not required.

Wt. 432—M437 500,000 Pads. H W V 5 16 Forms C. 2123.

"C" Form (Original).

Army Form C. 2123.
(In books of 50's in duplicate.)

MESSAGES AND SIGNALS.

No. of Message

Prefix	Code	Words	Received	Sent, or sent out	Office Stamp.
Charges to collect £ s. d.			From	At ... m	27 AUG 1917 OFFICE
Service Instructions.			By	To	
				By	

Handed in at ... Office ... m. Received ... m.

TO 5th & 6th bns.

*Sender's Number	Day of Month	In reply to Number	AAA
	27/8		

Ref bde order the limits on the march will maintain distance of 200 yds between coys.

FROM 17th H.F. Bde

PLACE & TIME

* This line should be erased if not required.

Wt. 432—M437 500,000 Pads. H W V 5 16 Forms C.2123.

Army Form C. 2123.
(In books of 50's in duplicate.)

"C" Form (Original).

MESSAGES AND SIGNALS.

No. of Message........

Prefix ... Code ... Words 27	Received From LCD By	Sent, or sent out At ... m. To ... By ...	Office Stamp. H.Q. SIGNALS 27 AUG 1917 OFFICE
£ s. d. Charges to collect			
Service Instructions.			

Handed in at LCD Office ... m. Received ... m.

TO 5th + 6th Bns

*Sender's Number	Day of Month	In reply to Number	AAA
	27th	—	

Ref para 10 of 0.0.39 this order is now in force aaa acknowledge aaa addressed all recipients of 0.0.39

FROM
PLACE & TIME 174 Inf Bde 12.30pm

* This line should be erased if not required.

Wt. 432—M437 500,000 Pads. H W V 5 16 Forms C.2123.

"C" Form (Original).

Army Form C. 2123.
(In books of 50's in duplicate.)

MESSAGES AND SIGNALS. No. of Message

Prefix DM Code [illegible] Words 32

Charges to collect £ s. d.

Service Instructions. 2 addresses

Received From Z Q D By Bucket

Sent, or sent out At m. To By

Office Stamp. SIGNALS 27 AUG 1917 LOF OFFICE

Handed in at Z Q D Office m. Received 10.12 m.

TO 5th & 6th Bns

*Sender's Number	Day of Month	In reply to Number	AAA
SCT 1169	27/8/17		

Packs	will	be	worn	by
men	going	into	the	line
aaa	Necessaries	will	be	left
behind	in	Haversack	at	MARSH'S
FARM	under	battalion	arrangements	

10.34 Am

FROM 17th Inf Bde

PLACE & TIME 10 Am

* This line should be erased if not required.

Wt. 432—M437 500,000 Pads. H W V 5 16 Forms C.2123.

6th Bn.

ADMINISTRATIVE INSTRUCTIONS

in connection with

174th. INFANTRY BRIGADE OPERATION ORDER NO.39.

---

1. 6th. London Regiment will take over accommodation in "B" Camp, REIGERSBURG at H.6.a. from 4th. Gloucester Regt.

Before taking over an Officer should be detailed to report to the Area Commandant, Lieut. SMITH, C/o 48th. Divisional Salvage Company at H.6.a.

7th. London Regt. will take accommodation in CANAL BANK vacated by a Battalion of 145th. Inf. Bde.

Battalion will march via REIGERSBURG where a halt will be made until exact location of accommodation in the CANAL BANK has been ascertained and reconnoitred.

2. When Battalions move from the present area, Q.M.Stores and Transport of Units will move as follows :-

Rear Brigade Headquarters to MARSH'S FARM at H.3.b.0.8.
Q.M.Stores of 5th. Bn. to MARSH'S FARM. (Take over from 6th.Gloucester Regt.)
Q.M.Stores of 6th. Bn. to MARSH'S FARM. (Take over from 4th.Gloucester Regt.)
Q.M.Stores of 7th. Bn. to MARSH'S FARM. (Take over from 7th.Worcestershire Regt.)
Q.M.Stores of 8th. Bn. to MARSH'S FARM. (Take over from 8th.Worcestershire Regt.)
Q.M.Stores of 198th.M.G.Coy to MARSH'S FARM. (Take over from 144th.M.G.Coy.)

Transport of 5th. 6th. 7th. and 8th. Battalions and 198th. Machine Gun Company will be at horse lines at H.4.b.7.0. and will move under instructions to be issued by the Brigade Transport Officer.

Bde. H.Q. Transport will be at MARSH'S FARM.

174th. L.T.M.Battery will move to REIGERSBURG Camp.

O.C. 174th. L.T.M.Battery should arrange for an Officer to interview the Area Commandant as early as possible re taking over accommodation.

3. Before moving forward of REIGERSBURG Camp all Units will be in possession of 2 Mills Grenades per man and 170 rounds S.A.A. per man to be carried on the man.

This will be drawn from the mobile reserve and demands for the exact amounts required to replace will be sent by Units at once to the Staff Captain.

See amendment

4. The Main Divisional Grenade Store is at CANAL BANK, I.2.a.1.9.

The Advanced Divisional Grenade Store is at CROSS ROADS FARM, C.22.c.3.7.

The Brigade Ammunition Store, (CALF RESERVE) is at C.16.c.7.7.

R.E. Dump is near ADMIRALS ROAD, C.21.b.8.7.

Water Dump is at C.22.a.0.5.

F. BRYANT,
Major,
Staff Captain.
174th. Infantry Brigade.

27/8/1917.

MOVEMENT TABLE TO ACCOMPANY 174th Inf. Brigade Order No.39.

Serial No.	Unit.	Date.	From.	To.	March or Train.	Remarks.
I	7th London Regt.	August 27.	BROWN CAMP.	To CANAL BANK via REIGERSBURG.	March	Leave camp 2.30 p.m. Route, [illegible] Mine, A.30.central – SLEEPER Road – BATH Road. If wet, VLAMERTINGHE – H.12.c.2.7. – H.12.a.1.3. – I.1.c.2535.
II	6th London Regt.	27	POPERINGHE.	REIGERSBURG	Train.	Train leaves POPERINGHE Station 5 p.m. Detrain at REIGERSBURG 6.40 p.m.
III	8th London Regt.	28	BROWN CAMP.	do.	March	As for Serial I.
IV	5th London Regt. 198th M.Gun Coy. 174th L.T.M.Bty.	28	POPERINGHE.	REIGERSBURG.	Train	As for Serial II.
	Bde. H.Q.		do.	CANAL BANK.		
V	7th London Regt.	night 28/29	REIGERSBURG.	Front Line.	March.	Relieve Battalion of 145th Inf. Brigade.
VI	6th London Regt.	do.	do.	Support Line.	March.	do.
VII	198th M.Gun Coy.	night 29/30	do.	Line.	March.	Relieve guns of 208th M.Gun Coy.

"A" Form.

Army Fo[illegible]
(In pads [illegible]

MESSAGES AND SIGNALS.

No. of Message..............

Prefix.......... Code.............m	Words.	Charge.	This message is on a/c of:	Recd. at ....m.
Office of Origin and Service Instructions.	Sent		.... Service.	Date..............
Runner	At.............m.			From ....
	To..............			
	By..............		(Signature of "Franking Officer.")	By..............

TO { 194th Bde Hd Qrs.

Sender's Number.	Day of Month.	In reply to Number.	AAA
* CM 10	Twenty eight		

WATERBOTTLES

From HQ.

Place

Time 10.35 pm

The above may be forwarded as now corrected. (Z) A G Ford

Commanding

.... Censor. | Signature of Addressor or person authorised to telegraph in his name.

* This line should be erased if not required.

(3198.) Wt. W 12952/M1394. 375,000 Pads. 1/17. H. W. & V., Ld. (E. 818.)

(In pads of 100.)

MESSAGES AND SIGNALS. No. of Message 9

Prefix.......... Code.......... m. | Words. | Charge. | This message is on a/c of: .... Service. | Recd. at .... m.

Office of Origin and Service Instructions.

Sent At..........m. To.......... By..........

(Signature of "Franking Officer.")

Date.......... From.......... By..........

TO ~~PANAMA~~ UNBOLT ~~[illegible]~~

Sender's Number.	Day of Month.	In reply to Number.	AAA
* GD526	28th	–	

Reference amendment to ~~[illegible]~~ GO39 ~~att~~ [illegible] para one for WEST CANAL BANK read EAST CANAL BANK

From UNCLE

Place

Time 8 [illegible]

The above may be forwarded as now corrected. (Z)

Censor. Signature of Addressor or person authorised to telegraph in his name.

* This line should be erased if not required.

(3796.) Wt. W 492/M1647. 650,000 Pads. 5/17. H.W. & V., Ld. (E. 1187.)

S E C R E T.   Copy No.........3.......

174th. Inf. Brigade Operation Order No:39.

Ref. sheet 28.   28th August, 1917.
1/40,000.

---

1. The Brigade will move to the forward Divisional area in accordance with Movement Table attached.

2. The Brigade will relieve troops of the 145th Inf. Brigade in the Left Sector of the Divisional Front on the night August 28/29. Dispositions of Battalions will be :-

Line - 7th London Regt.
Support - 6th London Regt.
Reserve - 5th and 8th Battalions London Regt.

Further instructions will be issued as to the details of this relief.

3. Brigade boundaries will be as shown on the attached tracing.x

4. 198th M.Gun Coy. will relieve guns of the 206th M.Gun Coy. in the Left Sector on the night August 29/30.

5. Command of the Sector passes to B.G.C. 174th Inf. Brigade on completion of the infantry reliefs. The 175th Inf. Brigade will be on our right, the 32nd Inf. Brigade (11th Division) on our left.

6. Completion of reliefs will be reported by wiring code word WATERBOTTLES to Brigade H.Q.

7. All maps, aeroplane photographs, dumps etc. will be taken over on relief. Receipts for stores taken over will be sent in duplicate to Brigade H.Q.

8. Briga--de H.Q. will/open at CANAL BANK, C.25.~~b.3.0.~~ d 25 60 at ~~an hour to be notified later.~~ 6pm 28th

9. Administrative Instructions in connection with the move are issued separately.

10. ~~The foregoing order is provisional and will be brought into force by a wire from Brigade H.Q.~~ Confirmed

11. Acknowledge. Ackd

Acknowledge 27/8/17

R M Barrington-Ward
Captain,
Brigade Major,
174th. Infantry Brigade.

Issued to Signal at...... a.m.

Copies to :-
1 G.O.C.
2 5th London Regt.
3 6th London Regt.
4 7th London Regt.
5 8th London Regt.
6 198th M.Gun Coy.
7 174th L.T.M.Bty.
8 Bde. Signal Officer.
9 Staff Captain.
10 Sta-ff Captain.
11 58th Divn. "G".
12 58th Divn. "Q".
13 511 Coy. A.S.C.
14 Bde. S.O.
15 S.S.O.
16 511 Field Coy. R.E.
17 32nd Inf. Bde.
18 144th Inf. Bde.
19 145th Inf. Bde.
20 173rd Inf. Bde.
21 175th Inf. Bde.
22 War Diary.
23 File.

x not attached

SECRET.

Amendments to 174th. Inf. Bde. Order No. 39.

1. Add to para 2:

7th London Regt. will be disposed as follows:-

2 companies in line. each disposed in depth
1 company in support in ALBERTA FARM and STEENBEEK
1 company in reserve in O.G. Line.

Battalion H.Q. ALBERTA

6th London Regt. will be in WEST. CANAL BANK
Battalion H.Q. CANAL BANK.

5th London Regt. REIGERSBURG
8th London Regt. DAMBRE CAMP.
198th M. Gun Coy. 8 guns in line,
remainder in REIGERSBURG
174th L.T.M. Bty. 2 guns RACECOURSE FARM
remainder in REIGERSBURG.

Reliefs will take place in accordance with arrangements made between Commanding Officers concerned. 7th London Regt. will relieve 4th Oxford and Bucks L. I. and 1st Bucks Battalion.

Route: Duckboard track – Bridge 2a – HILLTOP FARM – ALBERTA.

Head of the column to arrive at ALBERTA at 10 p.m.

O.C. 7th London Regt. will detail special party to gain touch with 32nd Inf. Bde. on our left and will report as soon as touch has been gained.

2. Cancel para. 8 and substitute:-

Brigade H.Q. will open at CANAL BANK C. 25. d. 25 60 at 6 p.m. August 28th.

3. Add new para.:-

O.C. 7th London Regt. will arrange for post in the vicinity of ALBERTA to look out for and repeat S.O.S. signals from the front. This post will be handed over on relief.

4. Reference MOVEMENT TABLE attached to Order 39: Cancel Serials III and VI. These units will move as ordered above.

R. M. Barrington-Ward
Captain,
Brigade Major,
174th. Infantry Brigade.

28th August. 1917.

Copies to:
All recipients of 174th Inf. Bde.
Order No. 39 (except 144th Inf Bde)
and to 48th Division
+ O.C. Left Group R.F.A.

174
58

2/6 London Rgt

September 1917

Index ....

SUBJECT.

No.	Contents.	Date.
	70/2901—2925.	

(49,674). Wt.42,605—128. 2000. 4/20. Gp.164. A.&E.W
(51,507). „ 6005—137. 500. 5/20. „ „

Instructions regarding War Diaries and Intelligence Summaries are contained in F. S. Regs., Part II. and the Staff Manual respectively. Title pages will be prepared in manuscript.

WAR DIARY

~~or~~

~~INTELLIGENCE~~ SUMMARY.

(*Erase heading not required.*)

of 2/6 London Regt

Army Form C. 2118.

Vol 9

(1)

Place	Date	Hour	Summary of Events and Information	Remarks and references to Appendices
YSER CANAL BANK	Sep 1.	10pm	Bn (less 2 platoons B Coy remaining at CANAL BANK) relieved 7th Bn LONDONS (less 2 platoons) in line N.E. of ST. JULIEN. Forward Coys (A & D) H.Q at MON DU HIBOU. C Coy at STEENBEEK and THE BUND B Coy (with 2 Platoons of 7th Bn under orders of O.C 'B' Coy) in O.G line Bn. H.Q. at ALBERTA. Relief reported complete at 1.20 am 2nd Sept. Casualties during relief 2nd Lieut SCANLAN and 2 O/R killed 4 O/R wounded	
ALBERTA	2		Casualties 1 O/R killed, 2 O/R wounded.	
	3		-do- 1 O/R killed 1 O/R wounded	
	4	1am	C Coy & B Coy less 2 platns relieved A Coy & D Coy less 2 platns in front line. A Coy to STEENBEEK & THE BUND. D Coy (less 2 platoons) and 2 platns of 7th LONDONS in O.G line with H.Q GATWICK COTTAGE. Casualties 9 O/R wounded during day, during relief nil	see appen No 1
	5.		Casualties 1 officer 2/Lt THORNTON killed. 18 O/R wounded. Bn (less 2 plns & 2 platns of 7th Bn) relieved by 8th Bn less 1 Platoon. Leading pln of 8th left CANAL 8pm. Bn on relief moved to CANAL BANK. 8th Bn suffered during relief. Our casualties 1 O/R wounded	see appendix No: 2 & 3
CANAL BANK	6		Night of 6/7 2 platoons of B Coy 47 O/R under Capt WEBB & 2/Lt H.V. HART raided the BLUNT SALIENT. (Maps supplied to NCOs. Appendix No 4) Orders for raid - (appendix No 5) attached. Report on raid (appendix No 6) also attached. Casualties: Capt WEBB missing, 2/Lt HART wounded 15 O/R wounded 6 wounded at duty, 7 missing. Military medal awarded No 531935 Rfn V.N. CHAMBERLAIN	See appendix 4. 5 6 & 6A
REIGERSBURG	8	10.45 pm	Bn moved to camp at REIGERSBURG vacated by 5th LONDONS Casualties 3 O/R wounded 1 O/R wounded at duty	
	10		Casualties 1 O/R wounded	

T2134. Wt. W708—776. 500000. 4/15. Sir J. C. & S.

Army Form C. 2118.

Instructions regarding War Diaries and Intelligence Summaries are contained in F. S. Regs., Part II. and the Staff Manual respectively. Title pages will be prepared in manuscript.

WAR DIARY

~~or~~

~~INTELLIGENCE SUMMARY.~~

(Erase heading not required.)

(2)

Place	Date	Hour	Summary of Events and Information	Remarks and references to Appendices
REIGERSBURG	Sept 11	5.30 pm	Bn. moved via BRIELEN to DAMBRE CAMP vacated by 2/1st LONDON. Bn HQ. at B 27 d 3 7 (Sheet 28 N W 1/20000)	
DAMBRE	12-15		Training for attack	
	16		-do- Casualty 1 O/R wounded	
	17		-do- Casualties 2 O/R wounded	
	18		Final practice of attack. Bn. moved to B camp REIGERSBURG.	appendix 7
REIGERSBURG	19		Administrative Instructions (App^x 8 & 9) & Instructions for forthcoming operations (App^x 10) issued	appendix 8, 9 & 10
			Stores, rations &c distributed & final preparations made	
	20		Leading Coy left camp at 1 am. Bn formed up in CANOE TRENCH behind KITCHENER'S WOOD at 4.45 am to 5.5 am, Zero 5.40 am. Bn strength 17 officers 376 O/R. Attack completely successful	See appendix 11
Nr ALBERTA			and all objectives taken & held. Report (appendix 11) attached. Casualties 2/Lt KER killed (A Coy)	
SPRINGFIELD			Lieut Col FOORD, Lieut HORRALL (O.C. 'B' Coy), 2/Lt RUSSELL (A Coy), 2/Lt KILLICK (C Coy) wounded	
HIBOU			O/R killed 17 (including A/CSM CARR 'A' Coy), wounded 83, wounded at duty 1, missing 3, missing	
ALBERTA			believed killed 2 (of the wounded 3 since died of wounds). Total casualties Officers 5 O/R 106	
			HURST FARM, CLUSTER HOUSES, CLIFTON HOUSE & OLIVE HOUSE captured. The 8th Bn took first objective, 5th Bn took ~~the~~ second & 6th took third objective	
	21		All counter attacks beaten off. Bn relieved night 21/22nd Sept by 11th Bn & moved to B Camp REIGERSBURG	

T2134. Wt. W708—776. 500000. 4/15. Sir J. C. & S.

Instructions regarding War Diaries and Intelligence Summaries are contained in F. S. Regs., Part II. and the Staff Manual respectively. Title pages will be prepared in manuscript.

WAR DIARY

~~or~~

~~INTELLIGENCE SUMMARY.~~

(Erase heading not required.)

Army Form C. 2118.

(3)

Place	Date	Hour	Summary of Events and Information	Remarks and references to Appendices
REIGERSBURG	22		Rear of Bn (C & D Coys) reached camp at 10 am. Major A.H.B. FOSTER in Command	[initials]
	23	5-30pm	Bn. moved to BRAKE CAMP. H.Q. at A30 d 19 (Sheet 28 1/20000)	[initials]
BRAKE CAMP	24/6		At rest, refitting & reorganising. On 26th Officers & O/R nucleus & reinforcements rejoined. 24th Major A.H.B. Foster attached to Divisional Staff. Major C.B. BENSON assumed command.	[initials]
~~Aud~~	27		Bn. moved to AUDENFORT by train via BRIELEN, POPERINGHE & ST OMER. In billets at 10 pm	[initials] See appendix 12.
AUDENFORT	28		Bn disposed in billets as follows. H.Q. AUDENFORT, A & B Coys LE POIRIER, C Coy at FOUQUESOLLES, D Coy at LA QUINGOIE	[initials]
	29/30		Training	[initials]

[signature] Lt A/Adj.

T2134. Wt. W708—776. 500000. 4/15. Sir J. C. & S.

Copy.

SECRET. ORDER No. 21. Appendix No 1 1.

1. A. Coy. will be relieved by C. Coy., and D. Coy less two platoons by B. Coy. less two platoons on the night of the 3/4th.

2. GUIDES. One guide per post from A. Coy. will report at C. Coy. Headquarters STEENBEEK at 1 a.m.
One guide from each of the 2 forward platoons of D. Coy, will report at Bn. Headquarters at 1.30 a.m.

3. ROUTES. Duckboard track. For B. Coy. via ALBERTA.

4. ORDER OF MARCH. Leading Platoon of C. Coy. will be ready to move at 1 a.m. Five minutes interval will be maintained between platoons.
Leading Platoon of B. Coy. will reach Bn. Headquarters at 1.30 a.m. Five minutes interval between platoons.

5. ORDERS & STORES. All special instructions and information of patrol routes and information obtained by patrols will be handed over. Bombs will be handed over as trench stores.

6. O.C. D. Coy. will arrange for the platoons at present in support and reserve to be interchanged and to be in new locations before 1 a.m. These two platoons will pass under the orders of O.C. B. Coy. on completion of relief. O.C. B. Coy. will bring up rations and water for the two rear platoons of D. Coy. at the time of relief.

7. On relief A. Coy. will take over the accommodation at the BUND and at STEENBEEK at present occupied by C. Coy. and will take over the S.O.S. post at the BUND. D. Coy. less two platoons will take over the trenches now held by B. Coy. less two platoons. The two platoons of UNCORK now under orders of O.C. B. Coy. will pass under the orders of O.C. D. Coy. on completion of relief.

8. ADVANCE PARTY. O.C. A. & D. Coys. will send 1 guide per platoon to reconnoitre accommodation at present occupied by C & B. Coys. to reach respective Coy. Headquarters by 10 p.m.

9. Completion of relief will be advised to Bn. Headquarters by sending the word "CAT".

Signed ....

2/Lt. & A/Adj.

Copies:-
No. 1 A& D.Coys.
2 C. Coy.
3.B. Coy.
4 File.

Appendix No 2 2

SECRET. WARNING ORDER. 5/9/17. UNBOLT.
YZ2

The Bn. will be relieved by the 2/8th Bn. on the night of the 5/6th September.

C. Coy. 2/6 th.	will be relieved by	A. Coy. 2/8 th
B. " "		C. " "
A. " "		D. " "
D. " "		B. " "

Each Company will detail 5 guides (one for each platoon and one for Company Headquarters) to be at the rendezvous mentioned below at the times stated:
C. Coy. at the crossing of the duckboard track and STEENBEEK (C11 b.64.) at 9.30 p.m.
B. Coy. (including two platoons of D. Coy.) at the same place (C.11.b.64) at 9.45 p.m.
A. Coy. at ALBERTA at 9.30 p.m.
D. Coy. at the crossing of the duckboard track and ADMIRALS ROAD at 9.30 p.m.

O.C. A. Coy. will detail an officer to be at C.11.b.64 at 9.30 p.m. He will be responsible that guides of C. & B. Coys. pick up their correct platoons in accordance with the following table.

No.				No.		
9	C. Coy.	2/6th	Meet	1	A. Coy.	2/8th.
10	"	"	"	2	"	"
11	"	"	"	3	"	"
12	"	"	"	4	"	"
13	D. Coy.	"	"	9	C.Coy.	"
15	"	"	"	10	"	"
7	B. Coy.	"	"	11	"	"
8	"	"	"	12	"	"
1	A. Coy.	"	"	13	D.Coy.	"
2.	"	"	"	14	"	"
3	"	"	"	15	"	"
4	"	"	"	16	"	"
X		2/7th	"	5	B. Coy.	"
14	D. Coy.	2/6th	"	6	"	"
X		2/7th	"	7	"	"
16	D. Coy.	2/6th	"	8		

On relief platoons will march out independently at 200 yards distance to a destination to be advised later.

Westward moving traffic will give way to Eastward moving traffic. This is to be impressed on all ranks.

Detailed instructions as to handing over trench stores will be issued later.

Empty petrol tins will be taken out.

Acknowledge.

Sgd. S. Crofts, 2/Lt.
A/Adj.

Appendix No 3

3

SECRET. YZ 3 5/9/17.

O.C. All Coys.

The Bn. less two Platoons and two platoons of 7th Regt. will be relieved tonight by the 8th London Regt. as laid down in warning Order No. YZ2 and will move on relief to CANAL BANK (E)and take over the accommodation vacated by the 7th London Regt. The two platoons of 7th London Regt. under the orders of O.C. D. Coy. will rejoin their Bn. at REIGERSBURG CAMP after relief.

TRENCH STORES. The usual receipts for trench stores will be forwarded to Bn. Headquarters by 4 p.m. 6th September.
(1) All unexpended S.A.A. brought into the line will be carried out on the man.
(2) The bombs brought in(and(those taken over) will be handed over in boxes in the posts.
(3) Petrol tins empty, will be taken out and dumped at the usual ration dump (junction of track 2 A and ADMIRALS ROAD). a limber will collect them at 2 a.m. O.C. D. Coy. will detaila loading party.
(4) Tools, Very Lights, S.O.S. rockets and flares will be handed over in posts.

COMPLETION OF RELIEF will be notified by sending the word MOON and occupation of new position by the word STAR.
Consolidated casualty returns, work reports, marching in states and burial reports will be rendered as soon as possible after relief.

Sgd. S. Crofts,
2/Lt.
A/Adj.

S E C R E T.   Box   Appendix No 5

6th London Regt.

RAID.

PLAN.

1. "B" Company will carry out a raid against the hostile points marked A and B on map attached.

Point C. - Assembly position of Raiding Party.

Point 1 - Starting off position of Right Party.
Point 2 - " " " Left "

Points D & E - Approximate point of entry to enemy's position of Right party.
Point F - Approximate point of entry to enemy's position of Left Party.

OBJECTS.

2. (a) Reconnoitre enemy's defences.
(b) To obtain identifications.
(c) To kill Germans.
(d) To take a few prisoners to supplement (b).

ZERO.

3. Date and hour of Zero will be given later.

COMPOSITION OF RAIDING PARTY.

4. Raiding party will be sub-divided as follows :-
Right Party to be known as HARE'S Party consisting of :-

Officer, 1 Sergt. (Plaistead)
1 N.C.O. and 5 men (Bombers)
1 N.C.O. and 5 men (Riflemen)
(Tozer) 1 N.C.O. and 5 men (Rifle Grenadiers)

Total - 1 Officer
4 N.C.O's.
15 men.

Sgt Ellis
Plaistead
Cpl Tozer
Cpl Wells
L/c Fowler

Left Party to be known as WEBB'S Party consisting of :-
1 Sergt. (Ellis)
Officer/and 2 Tapemen
1 N.C.O. and 5 men (Riflemen) - Cpl WELLS
1 N.C.O. and 5 men (Bombers)
1 N.C.O. and 5 men (Bombers)
1 N.C.O. and 2 men (Rifle Grenadiers)

1 N.C.O. and 3 men (Lewis Gunners)
(Fowler) 3 men (Rifle Grenadiers)

Total - 1 Officer
6 N.C.O's
25 men

Total Strength of Raiding Party -

2 Officers 2
10 N.C.O's 10
40 men 40

2 Off
10 NCOs
40 men
52

ADVANCE and ASSAULT

5. From ZERO the entire Raiding Party will move forward stealthily and get as close as possible to the hostile section to be raided. The Artillery will open fire at ZERO on a certain portion of the enemy's front and at ZERO plus 2 will form a box barrage round the area shown on attached map. The enemy's position will be entered as rapidly as possible. Two men of WEBB'S party (the second and third in the file) will run out a tape to the hostile position.
(Note. It must be firmly impressed on all ranks that under no circumstances must anyone stop to attend to casualties when going over. When returning however every effort should be made to bring back our killed and wounded).

All N.C.O's and men must be warned not to be disturbed in any way by our overhead barrage and machine gun fire, which at times may appear to them to be very close.

ACTION IN HOSTILE POSITION.

6. Any enemy discovered in hostile positions will be taken prisoners. They will be escorted back via the tapes as rapidly as possible. Concrete shelters will be dealt with in the manner detailed during training. Blocking groups will immediately proceed to the positions to which they are respectively detailed, halting and forming a block at the points shown on map attached.

The Raiders will move under orders of their leaders. They will thoroughly search all trenches, shelters and concreted buildings. If any leader decides that it is impracticable to obtain a prisoner or booty from a concreted building on first entering it should be bombed and a subsequent effort made to obtain these.

RETURN.

7. The signal for the return will be given at plus 15. The signal will consist of 2 clusters of 4 White Very's. Lights each to be sent up from the derelict tank at C.6.c.9277 2/Lieut. WATSON will be responsible for the necessary arrangements.

Leaders of parties will also blow a series of short blasts on their French horns.

Neither the ordinary whistles nor the word "RETIRE" must on any account be used. If heard it will be regarded as an enemy signal. Independently of the Very's Light signal to return, leaders will despatch one of their party to warn all the remaining men - particularly the bombing groups.

Leaders must take prompt steps to prevent congestion at any points or point. Similarly men must not huddle together on return owing to enemy Very lights and the possibility of machine gun fire.

Every endeavour should be made to return by ZERO plus 30, but full advantage should be taken of shell holes and other cover if necessary.

RALLYING POINT and ROLL CALL.

8. The Rallying Point will be at C.6.a.24. indicated by two white crosses. Numbers will be checked and booty collected. 2/Lieut. WATSON will undertake the above and will be responsible for the salvage arrangements generally. 2 N.C.O. and 8 men will be placed at his disposal by the O.C. "B" Coy. He will keep the Commanding Officer informed by runner as to the numbers returned and forward to him any details which might necessitate sending out of a search party.

DRESS and ARMS.

9. N.C.O's and men - Service Dress without badges, putties steel helmets (must be covered), and P.H. helmets.

Rifles with fixed swords. Rifles loaded, magazines charged with 4 rounds, safety catches back.

Orders regarding other details concerning S.A.A. and bombs to be carried have already been issued.

N.B. Indiscriminate bombing is absolutely forbidden and all leaders and N.C.O's will see that it is properly controlled.

Officers - Service dress, revolver, steel helmet, luminous watch (covered) electric torch French horns, and P.H. helmets.

GENERAL DETAILS.

10. Wire Cutters 3 pairs will be carried by each party.

Sandbags 3 will be taken by each party.

Identifications. All identity discs, shoulder badges, marks on helmets or clothing will be removed with the exception that each individual will have his name and number (NOT regiment) written on a label and tied to the button of the left breast pocket of his S.D. Jacket - label to be inside the pocket. No papers or correspondence must be taken. It is imperative that all ranks are carefully instructed that if captured by the enemy the only information he will give will be his rank and name.

/11. Countersign.

COUNTERSIGN. 11. The word WEBB will be employed if necessary. The reply will be HART.

GARRISON OF OUTPOSTS. 12. will be ready to cover the withdrawal of the raiding party should this be necessary.

STRETCHER BEARERS. 13. Stretcher bearers with stretchers will be stationed as under :-

(a) At C.6.d.6638 with Lewis Gun Section.
(b) The Rallying Point.
(c) C.6.c.7033.
(d) MON DU HIBOU.
(e) ALBERTA.

HEADQUARTERS. 14. Advanced Battalion H.Q. will be at THE BUND and will be in lamp communication with MON DU HIBOU.

A G. FOORD,
Lieut.-Colonel,
Commanding 6th London Regt.

6th September, 1917.

C.P. 42 SECRET. 8th September, 1917.

Appendix 6.

Headquarters

174th Infantry Brigade.

Reference your Q.D. 694 attached I have to report as follows:

(1) CASUALTIES.
(a) WEBB'S Party. Captain Webb missing, believed killed, Other ranks: missing four, wounded five, wounded at duty - one.
(b) HART'S Party. 2/Lieut. Hart wounded. Other ranks missing two, wounded three, wounded at duty three.

(2) IDENTIFICATIONS OBTAINED.
Nil.

(3) CAUSE OF FAILURE.
(a) WEBB'S PARTY leaders having become casualties at the commencement of the raid.
(b) HART'S PARTY shell holes were found to be strongly held much in advance of where reconnaissance reports had indicated. Also leader became casualty.

(4) STATE OF WIRE.
Well broken up - practically no obstacle.

(5) STATE OF THE GROUND.
Much cut up by shell holes - fairly dry with mud in the shell holes.

(6) POSITION OF OCCUPIED SHELL HOLES IN FRONT.
(a) WEBB'S Party.
Information vague but all agree, pits, shell holes or saps 15 - 20 yards W. of Northern corner of blunt salient.
(b) HART'S Party.
Shell holes about 40 yards in front of breast work covering the trench raiding party intended to enter.

(7) STRENGTH OF GERMANS IN THEM.
(a) about 10 men - stated all to have been killed.
(b) 30 - 40 men. Considerable casualties inflicted judging by cries and groans heard.

GENERAL. Both parties reached the assembly positions and left their standing off positions up to time without incident. Barrage started punctually and lifted as arranged. The box barrage was particularly good. Captain WEBB was apparently hit as he commenced to go forward, the leading Corporal was also temporarily knocked out but the men pushed on, bayoneted a machine gunner who was trying to work his gun from the parapet, bombed the mebus and fired on the enemy as they attempted to rush out of the Northern door and along the trench behind as shewn on sketch. Two of them also siezed the machine gun and brought it back to our side of the wire, but were unable to get it back to our lines as one man fell into a shell hole and lost touch and the other was apparently shot as he is missing.
The rear sections stopped to deal with two pits where the enemy was apparently trying to mount a M.G., to prevent the advance sections from being fired on in flank and state that they accounted for all the occupants with rifle fire and bombs. The recall signal then went up. This party did not come under M.G. fire.

(b) HARTS Party. Evidence goes to shew clearly that 2/Lieut. HART was hit before the barrage lifted but although unable to go forward he still endeavoured to direct operations and gave the signal for withdrawal by sounding his French horn. This party found the enemy in considerable numbers - estimated at 30 to 40 in shell holes about 40 yards in front of the trench. They bombed the enemy

over.

bombed the enemy and appear to have done good execution judging by the cries and groans heard. They were not however able to get through this enemy party and reach the trench. The action of this party undoubtedly had the effect of engaging the attention of strong advanced bodies of the enemy which would otherwise have been able to take our left party in flank. Machine gun fire at first from left front which however ceased abruptly after about 1 minute.

Sgd. ....

Lieut. Col.
comdg. 3/6th Bn. The London Regiment.

Bm/7/37/4
17 SEP 1917

6th London Regt.
198th M.Gun Coy.
164th Infantry Brigade (for information).

Please

Detail proportion of your officers concerned to meet Officer and N.C.O. of 1/8th Liverpool Regt. who reached WURST FARM and AVIATIK FARM in a recent attack, at 10 a.m. to-morrow at the Corps Model in A.30.c. All information possible should be obtained and anything of interest or importance reported to Bde. H.Q.

[illegible signature]
Captain,
Brigade Major,
174th. Infantry Brigade.

17th September, 1917.

Officers instructed verbally 17/9/17

Bde. advised [illegible]

Information

[illegible]

"A" Form.

Army Form C. 2121.
(In pads of 100.)

MESSAGES AND SIGNALS.

No. of Message..............

Prefix........... Code............ m	Words.	Charge.	This message is on a/c of:	Recd. at........ m.
Office of Origin and Service Instructions.	Sent		.... Service.	Date..............
	At.............m.			From..............
	To..............			
	By..............		(Signature of "Franking Officer.")	By................

TO { 6th London Regt
~~198th M.G. Coy~~
~~164th Inf. Bde~~

* Sender's Number.	Day of Month.	In reply to Number.	AAA
GD 848	17	-	

Reference this office No. Bm/7/37/11 of today ~~AAA~~ for model in A.30.c read model near 55th Div H.Q. in H1.a. ~~AAA~~ Addressed 6th London Regt 198th M.G. Coy to acknowledge repeated 164th Inf. Bde.

Bde advised

From 174th Inf Bde
Place
Time 6.20 pm

The above may be forwarded as now corrected. (Z) RmBW

Censor. Signature of Addressor or person authorised to telegraph in his name.

* This line should be erased if not required.

(3796.) Wt. W 492/M1647. 650,000 Pads. 5/17. H.W. & V., Ld. (E. 1187.)

Secret

Ref. Map
POELCAPPELLE
Edition 2.

Headquarters
174th Inf Bde

Reference your No Bm/7/37/11 dated.
17/9/17 –
Captain Browne & 4 Company Comdrs. proceeded to H 1 a & met an Officer of 1/8th Liverpool Regt at 10 a.m. today
Of the information gained the following is of importance:–

(a) DEAR HD commands CLUSTER HOUSES with Machine Guns.

(b) CLIFTON HD and WURST FM buildings are very adjacent to one another.

(c) There were concrete shelters at WURST FM 6' deep with about 18" above ground level. Slits for Machine Guns on N. & S. sides.
The farm house itself was in ruins.

INSTRUCTIONS for operations. 10.

23. The following maps only will be taken into the attack:

Sec. map (1/5,000) showing objectives of individuals.

Barrage maps F2 and H2 1/10000

POELCAPELLE 1/10000 (unmarked)

Pigeon maps 1/20000

Sheet 28 N.W. 1/20000 (unmarked)

No map will contain details of barrages or of complete battalion or brigade objectives.

24. ACKNOWLEDGE.

Signed:- S.E.P. Crofts, 2/Lieut

Acting Adjutant, 2/8th Bn. London Regt.

Copies issued by runner at.....to:

1. Commanding Officer.
2. O.C. A. Coy.
3. O.C. B. Coy.
4. O.C. C. Coy.
5. O.C. D. Coy.
6. ~~Quartermaster and Transport Officer.~~ 2/8th Bn. London Regt.
7. 174th Infantry Brigade.
8. File.

9/10. War Diary.

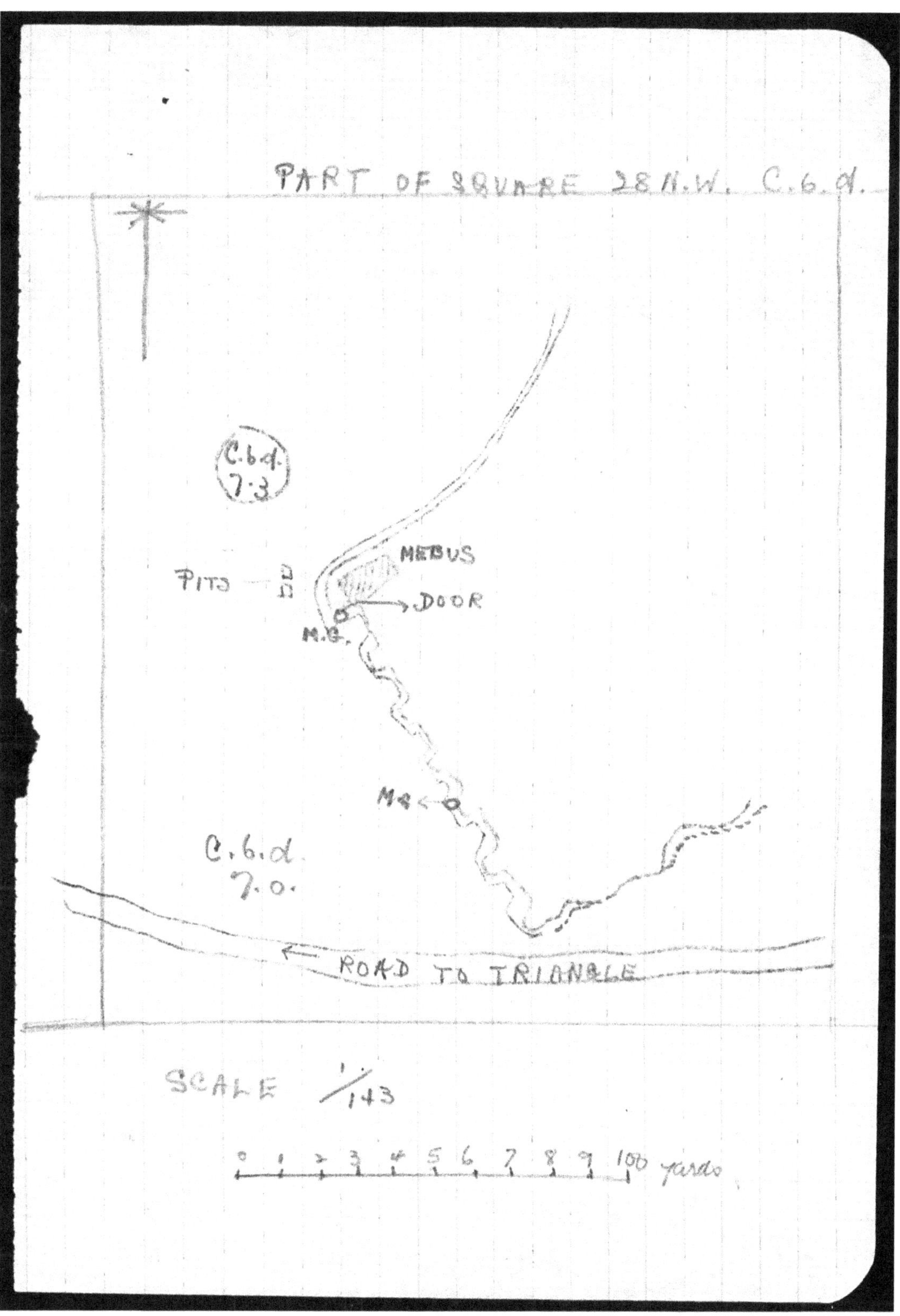
PART OF SQUARE 28 N.W. C.6.d.
C.6.d.
7.3
MEBUS
PITS
DOOR
M.G.
MG
C.6.d
7.0.
ROAD TO TRIANGLE
SCALE 1/143
0 1 2 3 4 5 6 7 8 9 100 yards

(d) The concrete shelters at CLIFTON HO.
did not contain Machine Gun on 31/7/17

(e) DOOM Trench has good concrete shelters
but trench was obliterated & wire was
found to be good on 31/7/17.

(f). Dead ground to N. in vicinity of
VALE HO were enemy massed for
counter attack could not be seen from
WURST FM.

(g) Heavy Machine Gun fire was experienced from VON TIRPITZ FM. on
31/7/17

General Our troops attacked roughly
from S to N on 31/7/17.
Ground was dry in vicinity of
WURST FM, grass long, many &
large shell holes.

A. G. Hoord Lieut Col
Comdg 2/6th London Regt

18/8/17

SECRET.

Copy No. 2.

13 Company, E Battalion,
TANK CORPS.

Order No. 3.

13/6/743

Reference
POELCAPELLE MAP 1/10000
Edition 2.

1. The following additional Tanks will take part in the forthcoming operations with the 174th Infantry Brigade.

E.7 EXPLOSIVE	- 2/Lieut.	Hughes T.C.Y.
E16 ELIMINATOR	"	Ball J.A.
E3 ECLIPSE	"	Maitland V.K.

2. These Tanks will operate against the prearranged objectives in conjunction with those already detailed, as follows.

E19 ERADICATOR)
E16 ELIMINATOR) Objective CLIFTON HOUSE.

E17 EXTERMINATOR)
E3 ECLIPSE) Objective WURST FARM.

E18 EXTIRPATOR)
E7 EXPLOSIVE) Objective CLUSTER HOUSE.

Headquarters
13 Coy. "E" Bn. Tank Corps.
Issued at Y p.m.
18/9/17.

Signed:- William Briggs, Major.
comdg. 13 Coy., "E" Bn. Tank Corps.

SECRET. appendix No 7 ORDER NO. 22 Copy No. 10 ... 7

18/9/17.

2/5th Bn. LONDON REGT.

(Ref. Sheet 28 N.W. 1/20000).

1. The Battalion will move to-day to [illegible] and occupy "Y" Camp - ~~[illegible]~~ H6 a 83

2. The Battalion will assemble by Companies at conclusion of todays exercise and march by Platoons at 200 yards distance in the following order:

A. Coy.
C. Coy.
D. Coy.
B. Coy.

3. ROUTE.- [illegible] Road.

4. An advance party consisting of 1 N.C.O. per Coy. and 1 for Battalion Headquarters under 2/Lieut. [illegible] will take over the new camp at 2 p.m. from Camp Commandant, [illegible].

5. Half the Pioneers will remain in the present camp under 2/Lieut. [illegible] to act as loading party and to clean up; the other half will move to the new camp with the baggage wagons and act as unloading party.

6. 2/Lieut. [illegible] will hand over tentage at present camp to Camp Commandant and obtain receipts and a clean camp state and hand these in to Battalion Headquarters.

Quartermasters Stores will remain at [illegible] FARM and Transport lines remain as at present.

7. Officers' kits to be dumped by cookers at 12.30 p.m.

8. Mess Cart to be loaded by 1.30 p.m.

over.

Order No.31. -2-

9. Lewis Gun ammunition not carried on the men to be dumped by cookers under Lewis Gun Officer.

10. Sandbags containing kits, and greatcoats in bundles to be dumped by cookers.

11. Acknowledge.

Signed:- G.T.F. Crofts, 2/Lieut.
Acting Adjutant, 2/6 th Bn. London Regt

Copies issued at.......by runner to:-

1. Commanding Officer.
2. O.C. A. Coy.
3. O.C. B. Coy.
4. O.C. C. Coy.
5. O.C. D. Coy.
6. Quartermaster & Transport Officer.
7. 174th Infantry Brigade.
8. File.

9/10. War Diary.

18

SECRET. ADMINISTRATIVE INSTRUCTIONS Copy No....10. 8

Appendix 8

IN CONNECTION WITH ORDER NO. A1

1. **DRESS.**

(a) Battle-order with pack instead of haversack.
Pack to contain only rations, iron rations, cardigan, waterproof sheet, Tommy Cooker and bombs as detailed.

(b) S.A.A. Each man will carry 170 rounds of S.A.A. except bombers and rifle-grenadiers who will carry 100 rounds and Lewis Gunners, Signallers, Scouts, Snipers and Runners who will carry 50.

(c) BOMBS. Each man, except bombers and rifle-grenadiers will carry 1 bomb in his pack (50% carry Mills No. 5 and 50% Mills No. 23) and each man will carry one ground flare.
Bombers will carry 6 Mills bombs and 2 P. Bombs in buckets.
Rifle-grenadiers will carry 3 No. 23's and 3 No.24's (in a S.A.A. bandolier) and 2 No. 27 smoke grenades.

(d) TOOLS. Every other man will carry a shovel or a pick (90% shovels, 10% picks) except those men detailed for constructing strong points who will each carry a tool.

(e) SANDBAGS. Every man will take 2 sandbags, one to be carried round each brace.

(f) VERY LIGHTS 1", white red and green and S.O.S. rockets will be issued to each Company as follows:-

White 80
Red 8
Green 8
S.O.S.12

over.

Administrative Instructions.

7. MAPS AND PAPERS.

No maps showing details of Headquarters, objectives, barrages or dumps; no letters or papers likely to give information to the enemy, should be taken into action. No envelopes or letters giving the man's name and address will be carried.

8. CARE OF ARMS. All men will carry the oil can in pocket (in addition to oil bottle in butt-trap), extra flannelette for for cleaning, and every man will take his breech cover with him and have a small piece of sacking or bagging to tie loosely over the muzzle.

Extra flannelette and oil will be carried by each team of Lewis Gunners and a small piece of sandbag or similar material will be tied loose over the fore end radiator casing to prevent mud getting into the barrel.

Rifles, Lewis Guns and Ammunition must be kept clean at all costs and be ready for use at any moment.

9. PERSONAL PROPERTY & SPARE KIT.

Companies have been issued with Sandbags, one for each man going into the line. All spare kit and personal property should be put into the sandbag, which is to be tied up and marked with the man's number, name, section, platoon and company. Sandbags should be tied together by sections.

Overcoats will be collected and fastened together in bundles of sections.

over.

<u>Administrative Instructions.</u> -4-

10. The packs of all men will be painted with the distinctive colour of their Company as follows:-

A. Coy.	Red.
B. Coy.	Blue.
C. Coy.	Yellow.
D. Coy.	Black.

11. Should a man be taken prisoner, the only information he is to give is his name and number, not the name of his Battalion or the number of his Division.

Signed:- S.J.P. Crofts, 2/Lieut.
Acting Adjutant, 2/6th Bn. London Regt.

Copies issued by runner at..........to:-
1. Commanding Officer.
2. O.C. A. Coy.
3. O.C. B. Coy.
4. O.C. C. Coy.
5. O.C. D. Coy.
6. Quartermaster & Transport Officer.
7. 174th Infantry Brigade.
8. File.
9/10. War Diary.

appendix 9

ADMINISTRATIVE INSTRUCTIONS NO. 2 — Copy No. 10 9

IN CONNECTION WITH OPERATION ORDER NO. A1 — 19/9/17.

---

12. WIRE CUTTERS. Long handled Wire Cutters are available and will be distributed as follows:-

A. Coy.	3
B. "	2
C. "	2
D. "	2

The full normal establishment of wire cutters will also be carried.

13. ROCKET MESSAGE CARRIERS. These will be issued one per Company Approximate maximum range is 1000 yards when fired at an angle of 45°. They should be directed to fall at SPRINGFIELD where constant watch will be ~~manned~~ kept for them.

14. PIGEONS. Will be issued as follows:
Pigeons

A. Coy.	2
C. Coy.	2
D. Coy.	2

Pigeon maps will be also distributed on which information can be marked.

15. PRISONERS OF WAR. A temporary collecting station will be established at HILLTOP FARM C.21.d.58.

An escort must be provided for prisoners as far as this station where they will be handed over to the A.P.M's. representative and a receipt obtained. The escort is not to exceed 10% of the number of prisoners, but this percentage may be reduced where the batch is a large one.

over.

-3-

ADMINISTRATIVE INSTRUCTIONS.

Arms and ammunition only will be taken from prisoners, except in the case of Officer prisoners, when all documents will be taken from them and carried down by the escort to [illegible] FARM and handed over against receipt. As far as possible all prisoners should be made to carry wounded men.

10. STRAGGLERS. There will 3 Straggler Posts and one Main Collecting Station at the following places.

Posts at C.10.d.06
C.17.c.24
C.23.a.67

Main Collecting Station at [illegible] FARM C.18.b.82.

Signed: E.?.?. Crofts, 2/Lieut.
Acting Adjutant, 2/5th Bn. London Regt.

Copies issued to:-
1. Commanding Officer.
2. O.C. A. Coy.
3. O.C. B. Coy.
4. O.C. C. Coy.
5. O.C. D. Coy.
6. Quartermaster & Transport Officer.
7. 174th Infantry Brigade.
8. File.
9/10 War Diary.

Order No A1 Appendix 10

SECRET.

INSTRUCTIONS FOR THE FORTHCOMING OPERATIONS.

Copy No. 10. 10

19/9/17.

(Ref. maps Sheet 28 N.W. 1/20000, and POELCAPPELLE Edn. 2 1/10000).

---

1. The attack on the enemy is to be resumed on a day and at an hour t o be notified.

The boundaries and objectives of the Division have been marked on a map circulated to Company Commanders. The final objective of the day's operations is the capture and consolidation of the BLUE line.

2. The attack will be made in three bounds

First bound - To DOTTED BLUE line where barrage pauses until Zero plus 1 hour 25 minutes.

Second bound -To BROWN LINE where there will be a pause of 16 minutes.

Third bound - To BLUE LINE.

3. The 55th Division is attacking on the Right and the 51st Division on the left.

4. (a) The attack on the 58th Division front will be carried out by the 174th Infantry Brigade.

(b) The 173rd Brigade on the right will simultaneously carry out an attack against WINNIPEG.

(c) The 174th Brigade will form up for the attack on Y/Z night; troops to be in posit_ion by Zero minus one hour thirty minutes.

OVER.

INSTRUCTIONS for Operations. -2-

4. (a)(i) The 8th Bn. will form up behind present front line) Hqtrs.
(ii) The 5th Bn. will form up behind the 8th Bn.) MON du HIBOU

(iii) The 6th Bn. will be disposed along the line of [illegible] TRENCH west of KITCHENER WOOD with its left resting on [illegible] in readiness to move forward. Headquarters ALBERTA.

(iv) The 7th Bn. will be in Brigade reserve in CALIFORNIA DRIVE, Headquarters - CALIFORNIA RESERVE.

(v) The [illegible] M.G. Coy. will be disposed
4 guns in rear of 8th London Bn.
4 guns in rear of 5th " "
4 guns at [illegible] to move in rear of 6th Londons.
4 guns at the [illegible] (Brigade Reserve) Headquarters ALBERTA.

(vi) 174th L.T.M. Battery will be disposed
4 guns [illegible].
4 guns [illegible] TRENCH. Headquarters [illegible].

5. The 174th Brigade attack will be on a one Battalion frontage.

(a) Objectives of all three battalions have been issued to Company Commanders.

(b) Definite, complete and distinct Platoons and Sections have been detailed to capture all known enemy strong points and Mebus.

(c) The Battalion in its advance will be prepared to encounter and drive back hostile counter-attacks or to complete, if the situation requires it, the capture of objectives allotted to the Battalion in front of them.

over.

INSTRUCTIONS for Operations. (8)

5. (d) The capture and consolidation of the high ground about WURST FARM is of special importance.

(e) Guns of the 198th M.G. Coy. move to position as soon as mopping-up permits.

The guns within and adjacent to the Battalions objectives will be disposed as follows:

2 guns WURST FARM.
2 guns [illegible] HOUSES.

---

2 guns VON TIRPITZ FARM.
2 guns D.1.d. central.

One from each pair will move if a more advantageous position presents itself.

TWO guns will move to the Battalion area and be placed to fire East in the direction of AVIATIK FARM and [illegible] HOUSE.

The remaining guns will be in depth back to the [illegible].

(f) 176th L.T.M. Battery will send 4 guns to strong point in LANGEMARCK Line C.12.b.8595 to C.6.d.8020 as soon as fighting there has ceased. These guns will deal with and break up hostile counter-attacks and enfilade the southern continuation of the LANGEMARCK LINE and bombard any centre of resistance holding up our troops. Two guns will move forward to [illegible] when the BROWN line has been captured.

6. The attack is to be preceded by an intense hurricane bombardment of all available artillery (field and heavy) for 24 hours before Zero.

7. The attack will be made under cover of

(a) a creeping barrage.
(b) a standing barrage.
(c) a distant Heavy Artillery barrage.

OVER.

2. RATIONS.

Every man will carry into action rations for two days in addition to the ordinary iron ration. Every man will receive chocolate, a tin of sardines and a sandwich.

3. WATER.

Every man will go into action with one full water bottle. A proportion of extra bottles will be issued to Companies for distribution to bring the number up to 3 bottles between 2 men.

4. TOMMY COOKERS.

Special cookers to burn from 1½ to 2 hours will be issued.

5. REGIMENTAL AID POSTS. The R.A.P. will be at ALBERTA and the R.A.P's. of the 7th and 8th Battalions at the [illegible].

All stretcher bearers in each Company (including the four reserve men) will be unarmed and wear armlets.

6. LABELS.

The following labels will be drawn from Brigade dump at CANAL BANK [illegible] on the morning of [illegible] October and distributed to Companies as shown:

CLUSTER HOUSE	2	A Coy.
OLIVE HOUSE	1	A
WURST FARM	2	C
CLIFTON HOUSE	1	C

over.

INSTRUCTIONS for Operations. (4).

7.contd. (d) A machine Gun barrage provided by 4[illegible] guns of the 206th, 214th and 215th M.G. Coys.

Details of the barrage (and times) are shown on the maps which have been circulated.

8. The special task of the Battalion is to pass through the 8th and 5th Battalions and capture, consolidate and garrison the area between the BROWN and BLUE lines. [illegible] That is to gain and maintain a footing on the high ground. The order of battle will be

A. Coy.
C. Coy.
B. Coy.

with D. Coy. in rear of A & C Coys. Each Coy. will work with three platoons and hold one in reserve, and will garrison the area it occupies..

B. Coy. will be the reserve Coy. of the Battalion, but will act at whatever point may be necessary without awaiting orders from Battalion Headquarters.. Areas allotted to Companies and Platoons are shown on maps already issued.

9. Strong points will be constructed at

WURST FARM by C. Coy.
[illegible] HOUSE A. Coy.
[illegible] HOUSE C. Coy.

each built for all round defence and to hold a garrison of one platoon. They will be made as inconspicuous as possible.

over.

INSTRUCTIONS for OPERATIONS. -4-

9 contd. The 5th Battalion will construct strong points at

[illegible]

[illegible] FARM

[illegible] FARM

D.1.d.57.

10. As soon as possible after the attack the Brigade dispositions will be reformed so as to have

(a) 3 Battalions east of [illegible] - SPRINGFIELD ROAD.

(b) 1 Battalion in ALBERTA area.

(c) 1 Battalion in O.G. Lines.

The Brigade will probably be relieved on the night of Z plus 1/2plus 2,

11. Battalion Headquarters will open at ALBERTA at zero minus one hour thirty minutes.

12. TANKS of No. 13 Company will co-operate with the Bn./as follows:-

2 Tanks via WINNIPEG cross roads to H of [illegible] HOUSE. then North to N of CLIFTON HOUSE. OBJECTIVE: CLIFTON HOUSE.

2 Tanks to move via WINNIPEG to objective [illegible] FARM

2 tanks to move via WINNIPEG to objective [illegible] HOUSE.

All ranks will be warned that they are on no account to wait for tanks. If a Tank gets ahead of the infantry it is the duty of the infantry to push on and support it. No request by a Tank for assistance in the forming of a strong point in advance of the

over.

INSTRUCTIONS for operations. -6-

[illegible] line, or overcoming hostile resistance is to be refused or neglected.

Signals between Tanks and Infantry have been communicated to all concerned.

13. A contact aeroplane will fly over the objectives at
Zero plus one hour.
Zero plus 2 hours 30 minutes.
Zero plus 4 hours and when ordered by Corps Headquarters.

Infantry will be ready to light red flares at these hours but will not do so unless called for by the aeroplane sounding its KLAXON horn or dropping WHITE lights.

14. LINE COMMUNICATION.

There will be an exchange (telegraph and telephone) at HIBOU.

The Brigade forward station at SPRINGFIELD will move to [illegible] VIEW (small triangle)(at D.1.c.20) after first objective has been taken and consolidated.

Should the Battalion Headquarters move forward of SPRINGFIELD the advance party will lay and maintain a line from the new Headquarters to [illegible] VIEW as soon as practicable after the capture of the second objective.

15. A Brigade central visual station will be established at C.17.a.45 prepared to read from
MON DU HIBOU, [illegible] VIEW, [illegible], and CLUSTER HOUSES.

This Battalion will man the last-named station as soon as possible

16. [illegible].

over.

16. RELAY RUNNER POSTS.

Runner posts will be established by the Brigade Signal Officer at the following points, and are available for use by any unit. They will be marked with a blue flag bearing a white number as under:-

No. 1 OLD WINDSOR.
No. 2 C.17.a.4.5.
No. 3 ALBERTA
No. 4 ST. JULIEN (connecting with 173rd Brigade Runner system from CHEDDAR VILLA).
No. 5 about C.12.c.5.9.
No. 6 SPRINGFIELD.

A Runner Post will be established by the 8th London Regt. at [illegible] VIEW to connect with R.P. No. 6 and by the 6th London Regt. at their Forward Headquarters if and when formed.

Runner messages from MON DU HIBOU will be forwarded by the senders as far as R.P.No.3 at ALBERTA.

17. COUNTER-ATTACK. (a) All ranks must be taught and must accustom themselves to regard an enemy counter-attack as a normal phase of the present battle.

(b) The enemy must always counter-attack at a disadvantage and has only a remote chance of success provided that all ranks

(i) Are expecting and looking-out for it coolly and know their duties and the plan arranged for repelling it.

(ii) Have made cover for themselves.

(iii) Have their arms (rifles, Lewis Guns) serviceable and are placed so that they can use them to the best advantage.

OVER.

(c) The enemy usually launches an immediate counter-attack (with his reserve companies) and a [illegible] later counter-attack (with his reserve battalions).

The fight is not won when one counter-attack is beaten off and everyone must be ready and arrangements made to meet another and another if they develop.

Troops are to be reformed as soon as objective has been captured and other troops have passed through.

(d) Companies will be disposed in depth. Supporting troops will be ready to carry out a counter-attack and will do so without waiting for orders from the rear. The knowledge that our leading troops are in difficulties or part of our ground lost is an urgent reason for counter-attacking at once.

14. INFORMATION. (a) Information from front to rear must be as full and frequent as circumstances permit. The question every officer and N.C.O. has to ask himself continually is whether his commander is fully informed as to the situation.

Without information those in rear can do little or nothing to help those in front.

(b) Report maps have been issued to Companies.

(c) Every means of communication must be used or tried; telegraph, pigeon, visual, power-buzzer.

(d) Much help comes from the air reconnaissance provided: leading troops will light their flares when called upon to do so by the aeroplane. This is of great importance.

15. (a) The word RETIRE will not be used, understood or obeyed by any officer, N.C.O. or man of this Brigade.

OVER.

INSTRUCTIONS for operations. -3-

19. (b) Anyone using this word is to be shot or bayonetted forthwith.

20. Details of the artillery and machine gun barrages covering the attack have been issued. When the protective barrage is about to commence to move forward again, fire will become intense previous to restarting. When, therefore, this fire becomes intense, it will be taken by the Infantry as a signal that the barrage will shortly move on, and they should get as close to it as possible before it moves.

21. A Protective 'plane will also fly continuously over the front during daylight on Z day from Zero onwards. Its mission will be to detect the approach of enemy counterattacks.

Whenever this 'plane observes hostile parties of 100 men or over moving to counter-attack it will drop WHITE PARACHUTE LIGHTS over that portion of the front threatened.

Whenever this 'plane has been able to observe definitely the results of any enemy counter-attack it will drop a short message stating results, at [illegible], which will be marked on the ground by white strips forming the letter "[illegible]".

The action of this 'plane will be carefully explained to all ranks.

22. Important messages will always be sent by several alternative routes.

Negative information and information regarding troops other than their own must not be neglected by units on their reports.

OVER.

Ref map
POELCAPPELLE

NOTES AS TO TANKS.

1. Nos. 13 and 15 Coys. "E" Battn. Tank Corps are co-operating with this Brigade in the a_ttack.

2. No. 13 Coy. (O.C. Major MORGAN, H.Q. CANAL BANK) supplies three tanks as follows to co-operate with 6th London Regt.

1 Tank (female) moves via WINNIPEG cross roads to H of OLIVE HOUSE, then NORTH to N of CLIFTON HOUSE. Objective, CLIFTON HOUSE.

1 Tank (male) to move via WINNIPEG to objective WURST FARM.

1 Tank (female) to move via WINNIPEG to objective CLUSTER HOUSES.

These tanks on arrival at above named destinations will assist infantry to consolidate and form strong points.

The leading tank is timed to reach WINNIPEG at Zero plus 1 hr. 30 mins and CLUSTER HOUSES at Zero plus 2 hours 50 minutes.

The remaining two tanks will follow at 5 minute intervals. O.C. No. 4 section, from which these tanks are provided, will move forward with O.C. 6th London Regt. to SPRINGFIELD on the Infantry Battn. H.Q. moving.

3. No. 15 Coy. (O.C. Major MONTGOMERY, H.Q. at CANAL BANK), are supplying nine tanks to co-operate with 5th and 8th Battns London Regt.

No. 12 section (O.C. - H.Q. at MON DU HIBOU from Zero) supplies five tanks to co-operate with 8th London Regt. as follows:

(a) 1 Male and 1 female (Name EMPEROR and EMPRESS) under Lt. A.G.GRIFFITHS and 2 Lt. H.L.DAWSON respectively. Objectives: The PROMENADE C.6.d.9.0 and MARINE VIEW D.1.c.2.0. Route, St. JULIEN - TRIANGLE FARM.

(b) 1 Male and 2 females (Names ELLES, ENCHANTRESS and EASTERN) under 2/Lts. F.DAWSON, LLEWELLYN DAVIES, and M.L. ATKINSON respectively. Objectives, GENCA and HUBNER FARMS. Route as for (a) thence via the PROMENADE.

These tanks arrive at Starting point (C.6.c.8.5) at Zero minus 15 mins, and leave it under orders of Coy Commander.

No. 11 Section (O.C. - H.Q. at MON DU HIBOU from Zero) supplies four tanks to co-operate with 5th London Regt as follows:

1 female (name EGYPT) under 2/Lt. R.BARRINGER. Objective ARBRE.

1 female (name EAGER) under 2/Lt. H.P.BUDGE. Objective VON TIRPITZ FARM.

1 male and 1 female (names, ETNA and ENERGETIC) under 2/Lt. G.TESTI and Lt. L.H.BATTERSBY respectively. Objective, STROPPE FARM.

These four tanks arrive at starting point C.6.c.5.1 at zero and leave under orders of Coy Commander.

4. When tanks have completed the tasks allotted them and are no longer required to assist the infantry in consolidation they will return independently to the canal area Tankodrome by the route they came by. There will be no intermediate rallying point.

5. Tanks ditched in the enemy's lines will be held as strong points by their own crews. They will not be handed over to the infantry unless specific orders to do so are issued by the Tank Commander concerned.

6. The following signals will be used between Tanks and Infantry :-

RED)
WHITE) Disc. Enemy in concrete posts.
RED)

A

OPERATION REPORT

from 1.30 a.m. 20/9/17 to 5 a.m. 22/9/17

A Coy left Reigersburg Camp at 1.30 a.m. 20/9/17. arriving at assembly trench at 5 a.m.

The night was dark & tracks very slippery rain having fallen during the night, so progress was exceedingly slow. The men rested in the assembly trench until ZERO HOUR 5.40 a.m.

At ZERO HOUR the company formed up in the open & advanced along the FLEMINGS WOOD MONDOMBOY ROAD 100x in the rear of C Coy.

After proceeding about 200x the Coys in front halted, & we took cover in the shell holes by side of road. After a halt of 15 minutes we moved on again crossing the Steenbeek about 6 a.m. A light barrage of 5.9s was playing on the Steenbeek at

of this area but we managed to cross without a casualty.
After crossing the Steenbeek the Coy moved off to the right of the road about 50x to avoid shells which were falling on & near the road. Three tanks were observed to be in difficulties about C5 b 40·20.
Approaching the TRIANGLE the shelling was much heavier & it was here the first casualties occurred. 2/Lt Russell was wounded & his platoon Sgt took command of the platoon.
We continued to advance very slowly towards the Blue dotted line. Three tanks were observed to be in difficulties about C6 b 40·05.
On reaching ~~RE~~ MARINE VIEW the coy got into artillery formation forming up closely behind D Coy who could easily be recognised by the distinguishing marks on the pack.
The first batch of prisoners (abt 50

joined us here. They looked very scared & their appearance had an encouraging effect on our men.

The effect of our barrage was seen to the best advantage from this point. Following closely behind D Coy. we continued to advance very slowly. The going was very heavy, huge ~~shellholes everywhere~~ shellholes everywhere. The MARINE VIEW DEAR HOUSE ROAD could not be recognised but direction was kept by following DIMPLE TRENCH.

This trench was blown in practically throughout its whole length, but brushwood was observed at intervals enabling us to follow the line of the trench.

We came under machine gun & rifle fire after passing the ARBRE & snipers were busy on our right flank. When D Coy had taken their objectives we pushed right

through them getting to within 50x of the barrage.
Numbers of the enemy were seen to be retiring in the direction of Derry House and most of them were caught by our heavy artillery which was bombarding the whole position from 50x behind the 18 pdr barrage.
When the barrage lifted I moved the left half company 50x half left & rushed a large tower shaped mebus which I took to be ~~Cluster~~ part of CLUSTER HOUSES. This mebus was badly knocked about by our shell fire & offered very little protection.
The right rear company then pushed on to a concrete shelter about D 70 80·70. The enemy had vacated this shelter & were lying out in shell holes about 150x E of this. They were immediately tackled by rifle & Lewis gun fire upon which they retired, & were shot down by our guns. A number of them were later taken prisoners & sent back

to the rear. The final objective

OLIVE HOUSE was then occupied under heavy rifle & machine gun fire & immediately consolidated. The company was very disorganised at the time but our protective barrage in front of the BLUE LINE enabled us to straighten things out & by the ~~time~~ the protective barrage closed down I had the company distributed as follows. 1 Platoon at OLIVE HOUSE. 2 Sections about D7d 90.70. + ~~also~~ 1 platoon about D7d 80.75. (Strongpoint)
Each post was consolidated for all round defence.
One VICKERS Gun was brought up to Strongpoint by half a section of the 198th M.G. Coy.
~~Sniping~~ Snipers were very busy during consolidation. They were dealt with when consolidation was

6

complete. At least 20 snipers were put out of action during the day. [struck out]

Flares were lit at each post when called on by our contact plane. During the afternoon enemy planes flew low over our posts firing their machine guns.

A weak counter attack was attempted against Olive House during the afternoon. It was broken up by our rifle & Lewis gun fire. No S.O.S rocket was put up for this counter attack.

The day passed quietly as far as shelling is concerned.

Some of our own shells fell short at OLIVE HOUSE.

The night passed without incident except that 3 [struck out] Boche gave themselves up at OLIVE HOUSE.

At dawn on the morning of

the 21st our artillery opened a heavy bombardment in front of our positions. Nothing unusual followed this.
There was great aerial activity during the day by both sides. E.A. firing at our positions as they passed over.
About 6.15pm the enemy opened a bombardment on positions on the right near SCHULER FARM.
Our artillery replied almost immediately. Owing to the amount of smoke which spread over these positions nothing could be seen of infantry actions.

At 1 a.m 22nd inst we were relieved by B Coy 11th LONDONS who took over ammunition bombs etc which we had carried up to the line & taken from casualties during the night of 20/21st.

8

No casualties occurred on our way back. When crossing ADMIRALS ROAD a few gas shells dropped near us. But respirators were on for about 5 minutes.

Arrived back at REIGERSBURG CAMP about 5 a.m.

Total Casualties during the operation

~~1 officer killed~~ Killed. Wounded
1 Off. 8 OR 1 Off. 20 O.R.

R W Anderson 2/Lt
O.C. A Coy.
2/6. C.L.R.

(1) Report of Operations 20th to 21/22 Sept

'B' Company

When we reached Canoe Trench at about 5 am. 20th inst, certain points in the enemy territory were being heavily bombarded & this lasted until 5.40 am (Zero) when a most complete barrage was put down by our artillery on the Hun lines. 'B' Coy led by Lieut E. E. Worrall, then proceeded along the FLEMINGS WOOD - GRAVENSTAFEL ROAD in an easterly direction until it reached a point 40x before coming to the little cemetery on the rt-hand side of the road. Here the enemy barrage which had just started was met - most of the shells dropping on either side of the road. The Company proceeded, encountering 4 Tanks apparently disabled or unable to make progress along the road, which had suffered severely from shell fire. With difficulty the Coy managed to pass the Tanks as they were clearly targets, but not before a few casualties had occurred,

(2)

and it was here that O.C. Company was knocked down by the bursting of a shell some 3 yards from where he was walking. He was helped up, and continued to lead the Company. By this time the enemy barrage had become quite hot and it was only by cool + skilful leading that the journey forward could be negotiated; and, in addition, some snipers and M.Gs became active. Lieut. Worrall was one of the first of several to get sniped, and had to be left to the tender care of two Bosches who dressed his wounds. During the temporary halt a small party of Germans were seen advancing from shell hole to shell hole on our left taking "pot shots" at our men, but they were promptly dealt with. Quite a long string of some 70 Huns were seen coming from HUBNER TRENCH across to our lines, without arms, prepared to surrender. The 8th Battalion took them over.

The Company had temporarily become

(3)

somewhat dispersed – due to the halt occasioned by the O.C. Company being put out of action, the heavy barrage, and the snipers, and it was with some difficulty that they were rallied; but eventually they were got together & proceeded until a Mebus at about D 7 a 4/7 was encountered and taken.

The Company then made for GENOA and HUBNER FARMS. The latter place was found to be a dressing station, several wounded & unwounded Huns being within, and 2 M.G.s pointing out of the exit. The M.G.s were left because of their weight. A party of 5 other ranks of B Company under an officer of the 5th Battalion were left to deal with the situation while the remainder of the Company proceeded from the two points in the direction of VON TIRPITZ FARM. It was most difficult to make any progress or distinguish any landmarks because of the thorough artillery preparation – barely a square yard having been left unshelled. A M.G. was seen but it was too heavy to carry any distance.

(4) A number of tear shells from our own guns landed within a few yards, some in the same shell pole through which we passed causing irritation. From what I gather the range generally of these shells was decidedly short, few if any intended for the enemy getting beyond our line.

Eventually we reached the line "B" Coy had to occupy, gauged to be correct from the position of VON TIRPITZ FARM (in ruins) and what was taken to be WURST FARM. As an extra precaution a party was sent to get into touch with "C" Coy on our right flank. It moved round via CLUSTER HOUSES, OLIVE HOUSE, WURST FARM until it reached a spot which was taken to be where CLIFTON HOUSE stood. This party also served the purpose of getting into touch with "C" Coy before consolidation started. An officer was also sent to get into touch with the 5th Battalion on our left. Satisfactory reports having been received consolidation was commenced and 3 Lewis Gun & 2 rifle

(5) posts were established. A machine gun post was also made in the between our second & third posts by the M.G. Coy.

YALE HOUSE could not be found & must have been reduced to ruins by shell fire.

At 2.30 pm small groups of Germans were seen to be coming from the direction of WINCHESTER FARM and ALBATROSS FARM. There seems to be no organised form of attack, but they appeared to be making for a hedge (about D8 a 8/10) with the idea of forming up. Before they could do so however they were picked off to a good extent by rifle fire. A sufficient number did in time reach the hedge to make an organised attack possible. Masses of men were also seen some 2000 yards away and they started to come forward to the same spot in the form of a stream. The S.O.S was sent up from Coy HQ (D7b 6/5) but no response from the artillery was made until fully 15 minutes afterwards. The barrage then came down on the last few men seen to make for the hedge, completely enveloping them, and making it impossible for them to go back. Many were seen to deliberate amongst themselves walking backwards + forwards, first towards our line + then to where the the shells were falling, + they evidently decided that it was useless to go back, so they came on and joined their comrades at the hedge. Presumably on a command being given those who had congregated at this point came towards our line in extended order and ~~after~~ when they had advanced to within 400 yards, machine gun, Lewis gun + rifle fire was opened on them. The result was that the attack was completely repulsed, the ~~[illegible]~~ waves being thinned out almost to a man. Quite a few afterwards were sniped.

By this time our ammunition was running low and an urgent request for more was sent to BHQ

(7) with a report of the situation. In order to thicken the line to meet a further attack a platoon was sent from "D" Coy under 2/Lt Heaton. Arrangements were also made for the troops in support (3 platoons of D Coy and of a similar number from the 7th Battn) to be ready to beat off the enemy with fixed bayonets should they succeed to break through our front line. At dusk men were seen to mass about 2 miles away and another counter-attack ~~would~~ during the night seemed certain. The enemy artillery was very quiet, which gave rise to a suspicion that a bombing raid would be launched by them. Nothing happened however, but they were busy during the night getting away their dead & wounded & moving men up to occupy a line close to ours. In the morning it was found that they had come up & were consolidating about 100x in front of our line.

(8) The Company kept them occupied with rifle fire whenever a head was shewn, & where they were seen to be, an occasional rifle bomb was directed.

Aeroplanes were particularly active, flying very low trying to examine our positions. I should have mentioned that during the morning following the advance 'planes were equally busy. Their interest seemed to be somewhat centred around the Mebus (O.7.b. 6/5), for besides continually circling around it at a low altitude an observer was seen to look over the side & gaze intently at it all the time his plane was over. It was for this reason principally that it was decided to have our counter-attack waves near this point, directly the Bosche shewed any signs of progress.

On the 21st at about 7 pm the enemy put down a very heavy barrage on our right & very shortly after on our lines as well. This barrage lasted quite 2 hours and although no S.O.S went up from the positions

(9) held by the 2/6 London Battn, ~~the~~ our artillery kindly responded on our behalf so effectively that it made another counter attack on us impossible. Both barrages (ours & the enemy's) ceased about 9 pm. It was during these that 'B' Company runners – Burgess & Leader did such excellent work. We had a few casualties & I think one of my "shorts" was responsible for them.

At 10 pm information was received that we were about to be relieved & guides were sent to SPRINGFIELD to conduct the relieving Company of the 7th London Regt. Before, however, these had time to return ~~we~~ were relieved – so presumably the 7th had started off before the guides found their way to SPRINGFIELD

All orders regarding stores were complied with and 'B' Company moved out about 3.30 am returning via HIBOU, & ALBERTA to RIGERSBURG CAMP. The men much

(10) the thoughtfulness which prompted the arrangement whereby they were able to undertake most of the journey back to Camp by train.

I should like to mention in conclusion how helpful the Company distinguishing colour was.

We went into the attack 80 strong and our casualties were

1	Officer	wounded.
4	O.R.	killed
2	"	missing (believed killed)
1	"	missing
13	"	wounded
1	"	" (at duty
1	"	shell shock

A. E. Scott
2/Lieut
OC "B" Coy

24.9.17

C 1

Report on Recent Operations

The Attack on Clifton House [illegible] Farm. C. Company

The Company left the Assembly Trenches a few minutes after Zero behind B & D Coys. No trouble was experienced until the Steenbeek was reached when the enemy barrage was encountered. At intervals along the road Tanks were found struggling through the mud. These attracted the fire of the enemy and their extension along the road made progress difficult. After the arrival at Hubner Farm little or no opposition was encountered. The great difficulty was the changing of direction. This was successfully done by the aid of the compass and our own barrage.

All the way up to [illegible] Farm the going was very heavy. The ground had been churned up by our artillery, and water logged shellholes had become full of mud.

McGeown the N.C.O in charge of No. 11

Platoon ~~repeated that~~ Lewis Gun Section reported that two guns had been buried in the barrage.

When the left half Company had occupied Clifton House and had started to dig its strong point the right half Company under C.S.M. Palonkar had also occupied Murat Farm.

The strong points are situated as follows

D7 b 95 covering Clifton House
D7 b 81 covering Murat Farm

At the same time A Company took up its position in Loam Trench covering our right flank, and B Company on our left covering our left flank.

The objective had only been reached a few minutes when a ~~the~~ Machine Gun Section of the 198th M.G.C. under Lieut. J. F. G. Smith came up and immediately placed out five guns firing ~~in all~~ to our right, left and front. The energy of Lieut J. F. G. Smith was especially noticeable.

About 5pm. parties of the enemy were observed approaching our position. Every man was at his post and opened fire. The attack was of such a sort that controlled fire was not possible, but each man carefully selected his target and large numbers of enemy were seen to fall. He could not approach within 100 yds of our lines.

The night passed quietly enough but about 6.30 a.m., after an attack by the left Battalion of the Division on our left, parties of the enemy were seen coming from some wooded ground at D 8 b 6 4 and going to earth in the fields in front. This was immediately reported. The assembly continued for some time. Captain C. G. Godfrey and later an R.F.A. Officer came up and the area was pointed out to them. Some enemy endeavoured to reach the trench at D 8 a 28 00 but they were sniped by our men.

At 5 pm. Heavy Artillery bombarded the area round D 8 b 10,00. Later about 5.30 pm our barrage came down and smothered the whole area over which movement had been seen. This drove some men forward but they were picked off by our riflemen. The attack lasted until dusk, and the enemy had again been denied approach.

Throughout the night our artillery continued firing occasional shots. The enemy sent over Trench Mortar shells.

The enemy snipers were active making approach to our post difficult from the rear. In spite of this 323543 Pte. Fudge carried important messages, showing great keeness in carrying out his duty.

The Company was relieved at 5.30 a.m. on Saturday morning 22/9/17. by 2/11 Battn London Regt.

The Barrage put down by the Artillery was excellent, altho' shells, High Explosive Shrapnel and Gas, sometimes fell short on our post and local supports endangering the men holding them.

Contact Aeroplanes passed over our positions at scheduled time and were communicated with by ground flares.

Plenty of S.A.A. was sent up from the rear, although the absence of Very Lights was unfortunate.

The Tanks were not a success and I do not think that they would have been able to manoeuvre had they reached their objective owing to the fact that the ground was soft having been churned up by our shelling.

Two Lewis Gun No1 did not report, but they have since been reported wounded.

V. L. Keddson 2nd Lieut.
O.C. C Coy.

D

[illegible] D

Report of Attack and occupation of BLUE LINE 21/22 Sept

At [illegible] D by 2/Lt CAROL [illegible] [illegible] of [illegible] platoons. [illegible] [illegible] [illegible] the barrage [illegible] they had to [illegible] almost to catch up. [illegible] half [illegible] FLEMING'S HEAD [illegible] [illegible] organise & clean up. [illegible] [illegible] that H.E.s were falling around ALBERTA. [illegible] then proceeded and all went well [illegible] where [illegible] stopped very heavy H.E. At least 4 Tanks were [illegible] stuck along road of march. In spite of previous warnings, there was a tendency for men to [illegible] behind Tanks. Tanks required no help. As mentioned above the barrage seemed too rapid, consequently we ~~[illegible]~~ were held up behind BLUE DOTTED LINE as LRB had not yet reached all objectives. ~~[illegible]~~ Between BLUE DOT LINE and BROWN [illegible] was naturally some confusion [illegible] [illegible] and Coys. (The [illegible] [illegible] more than [illegible] [illegible] I suppose

(2)

that [illegible] have [illegible] correspondingly on [illegible]

as of a [illegible] is not always [illegible] ~~[illegible]~~ [illegible]

[illegible] ~~[illegible]~~. D. 7. a. [illegible] 90 the first

[illegible] of prisoners was encountered. They

were [illegible] scared but quite [illegible] [illegible]

[illegible] this point the road was [illegible]

[illegible] and [illegible] [illegible] WURST FM as [illegible]

[illegible] [illegible] [illegible]

[illegible] [illegible] in the [illegible] of a

[illegible]. [illegible] was only [illegible] up

[illegible] [illegible] which I make [illegible] to [illegible]

[illegible] 10.05. [illegible] McCrott and I arranged

a plan of attack & had just got the

L. Gs firing when the Boche "kamerades".

One Boche [illegible] [illegible] [illegible] a [illegible]

detonators (very like our [illegible] detonators) in

a purse. Most of them had only tobacco

paper or cigarettes. I passed the Boche

[illegible] [illegible] [illegible] not take it along

[illegible] [illegible]. We [illegible]

up [illegible] a series of [illegible] and [illegible]

[illegible] [illegible] could make [illegible] along

line allotted to us.

[illegible] as [illegible] to the [illegible]

WURST FM from WEST

smashed to pieces, but [illegible] the [illegible] [illegible] rocks [illegible] the most [illegible] [illegible]. Both the [illegible] [illegible] have splendid positions commanding the valleys on both sides of the ridge. The supposed [illegible] [illegible] 5 [illegible] 4 has been lent to B (C?) [illegible] is in position [illegible] message [illegible]

Air Craft. Marked increase in aerial activity has been evident yesterday & today on both sides. Boche planes have flown very low over our positions; it seems to be a case of "live & let live" in the air in this sector.

MAP READING. This is simple enough for general location, but is most difficult for accurate locations. DIMPLE TR. & [illegible] the beginning of DOON TR is quite defined, remarkably so considering what this area must have gone thro'. Of course it is broken in [illegible] sides of trench almost touching in places, and but is quite a salient feature of landscape.

(4)

Towards the evening of 20th, the artillery fire of enemy became rather harassing. It was noticed that our shrapnel bursts at a much smaller angle than the Boche's, in some cases his shrapnel appeared to burst practically straight downwards. During the night 20/21st our artillery fired a number of rounds short both H.E., Shrapnel, & Gas. One gas shell fell in the adjoining shell hole to my Coy H.Q. & was lachrymatory; gas shells were also sent over by the enemy so as to fall south of our men at MARINE VIEW, the wind blowing the gas back over our troops. The gas had the effect of causing a difficulty in breathing, had neither mustard or pineapple smell, but soon blew away.

GAS SHELLS

STATE OF GROUND.

The ground on PASSCHENDAELE RIDGE is very churned up by shell fire but it is possible to dig 6 feet down and the ground is still dry at the bottom. The soil crumbles a great deal & is consequently easy for digging, but there are occasional patches of clay.

21/9/17 It was reported to me by an officer of the 2/11 Bn that his Bns relief was to be complete by 8.30 pm 21st inst. Accordingly I issued instructions to the Coy that all Bombs were to be collected, dumped and a receipt obtained on relief. Very, SOS lights & all tools were to be taken back, but L. Gunners were only to take back 50% magazines filled (i.e. all mags: but every other one filled). Also all surplus SAA to be handed over & receipt obtained. At 6.0 pm (approx) the enemy started an intense bombardment of our lines which lasted until 9.0 pm (approx.) Our artillery replied most effectively. No Casualties occurred in this Coy during the bombardment which speaks well for the men's digging in.
No relief arrived during the night, so about 6.0 am I went forward to the Coy of 2/11 which had taken over from A Coy 2/6

(6)

The O.C. this 2/4th Bn Coy. could give me no help re relief, so I went down to JANET Fm to HQ 2/4 Bn. Their Adjt gave me an officer & 20 OR which I brought up to my Coy area & found that the Coy had been withdrawn under Capt Browne's orders. I gave the officer all information I could and made my way back to 174 Inf Bde HQ CANAL BANK with my C.S.M. & servant.

J.C.A. Wilkinson 2/Lt
O.C. D. Coy.

Appendix 12

12

SECRET.

OPERATION ORDER NO. 23

Copy No...9..
26/9/17.

2/6th Bn. THE LONDON REGIMENT.

1. The Battalion will move to the new area tomorrow, 27/9/17.

2. Companies will parade at 8.15 a.m. and march off in the following order:

A. Coy.
B. Coy.
C. Coy.
D. Coy.

at 200 yards distance.

3. Leading Company will pass starting point (point in sleeper track 200 yards S.E. of cross-roads at A.30.d.19.) at 8.45 a.m. following the 5th Battalion.

4. Paradex States shewing exact number entraining will be rendered to Battalion Orderly Room at 7.45 a.m. and a note of the actual numbers on parade will be handed to the Assistant Adjutant at starting point. 2/Lieut. A.H. TEW will furnish parade state for Headquarters and note of actual numbers.

5. ROUTE. SLEEPER track W. of VLAMERTINGHE and VLAMERTINGHE - BRIELEN ROAD.

6. The Battalion will arrive at BRIELEN Station at 10 a.m. andleave by first train at 11.30 a.m. Capt. H.H. BROWNE will act as entraining officer. Brigade entraining officer is Lieut. HARRISON-JONES.

7. Battalion will detrain at AUDRUICQ and march to billets at AUDENFORT.

8. DRESS. Full marching order with helmets.
Packs will be dumped on arrival at AUDRUICQ station under a guard furnished by A.Coy. whence they will be carried by lorry to destination.

9. LEWIS GUNS. will be carried to BRIELEN. Lewis Gun magazines will be taken by limber. Guns and magazines will be stacked in covered vans on the train. The Lewis Gun Officer will be responsible for loading magazines into limber and into covered wagons.

10. WATER. Water bottles will be filled immediately after breakfast before leaving camp and the water will not be used without orders.

11. TOMMY COOKERS. A supply has been issued to Companies for heating food on the journey. These are not to be used until ordered.

12. RATIONS. Unexpended portion of the day's rations will be carrie Rations for the 28th will be issued in the new area.

13. MESS CART. Mess boxes to be ready packed and stacked outisde Mess at 8 a.m.

14. DISCIPLINE. No man will leave the train without permission. A.C. & D. Coys. will furnish picquets at all stops to see that these orders are enforced.

15. ACKNOWLEDGE.

Signed:- S.W.F. CRofts, 2/Lieut
Acting Adjutant, 2/6th Bn. The London Reg.

GREEN)
GREEN) Disc. Enemy clear of concrete post.
GREEN)

RED)
RED) Disc. Tank broken down.
RED)

Infantry requiring the help of a tank will wave their steel helmets on top of their rifles.

7. Position of tanks on situation maps sent in will be marked as follows :-

▲ —— Tank in action.

△ —— Tank out of action.

The Battalion letter and number of tank should be added.

The position of all derelict tanks will be reported through Brigade H.Qrs.

8. Infantry are on no account to wait the arrival of tanks. On the other hand, if a tank has pushed on ahead of the Infantry and seized an enemy Strong Point, it must be immediately supported by the nearest Infantry.

This must be impressed on all ranks.

Captain,
Brigade Major,
174th. Infantry Brigade.

18th September, 1917.

Copy to :-

5th London Regt.
6th London Regt.
7th London Regt.
8th London Regt.
198th M.Gun Coy.
174th L.T.M.Bty.
Brigade Signal Officer.

Tanks

Appendix No 11

11

REPORT ON OPERATIONS OF THE 20th, 21st & 22nd September 1917.

2/8th BN. THE LONDON REGIMENT (RIFLES).

The Battalion left B Camp, REIGERSBURG, at 2 a.m. on Thursday, the 20th September. The night was cloudy and dark; there was no moon. Rain had fallen and the ground was heavy and slippery and progress necessarily slow.

The assembly point, CANOE TRENCH Westward from BOSCASTLE ESTAMINET (Sheet 28 N.W. 1/20000, C.10.d.0881) was reached by the leading Company at 4.45 a.m.; the last Company arrived at 5.5 a.m. The leading two Companies were put into position in the trench and the rear two Companies formed up and lay down in the open in continuation of the line. The roll was called and no casualties reported. It is perhaps worthy of remark that there was a general request for an issue of rum.

The barrage opened punctually at zero hour 5.40 a.m. and the head of the column left theposition of assembly in column of route of half platoons in fours at 40 paces distance and one hundred paces between Companies and moved along the FLEMINGS WOOD - GRAVENSTAFEL ROAD. The advance proceeded without incident up to the STEENBEEK where a light enemy barragewas passed through without casualties. At this point the column the left the road to avoid the shells which were falling on it. Three tanks were noticied to be in difficulties about C.5.b.13. As the TRIANGLE (C.6.d.21.) was approached shelling became more heavy, 5.9's and shrapnel, and the first casualties were suffered. Progress now became slower until MARINE VIEW was reached when the Battalion swung into Artillery formation, D & B Companies leading covered by A & C Companies.(see Appendix No. 1). The coloured distinguishing patches on the packs of the men were of the utmost assistance to Company Commanders in the necessary organization. Three tanks were observed in difficulties at about C.6.b.2905. The first batch of prisoners - about 50 in number - passed the Battalion here.

The advance of the Battalion from this point onwards to the BROWN LINE was slow, owing to heavy going and the huge shell-holes everywhere. The MARINE VIEW - DEER HOUSE ROAD could not be recognised but direction was kept by following DIMPLE TRENCH, which although practically destroyed was distinguished by brushwood revetments at various points. Some congestion and confusion arose between the BLUE DOTTED LINE and the BROWN LINE but the distinguishing marks on the packs enabled the men to be speedily sorted out.

Heavy machine gun and rifle fire, especially from the right flank, was encountered about ARBRE and several casualties were suffered from snipers. Direction from this point forwards would have been difficult but for the fact that the remains of WURST FARM in the shape of a shattered tower were easily distinguishable.

The Battalion reached the BROWN LINE well up to time and the little necessary re-organisation was carried out under cover of the protector barrage. The right flank Company was temporarily checked at a MEBUS at D.[illegible].1005. In accordance with the prearranged system of attack covering fire was given by the Lewis Guns; the troops advanced and the garrison speedily surrendered.

On the protector lifting the whole line pushed forward keeping well up to the barrage and, as a consequence, suffered only slight casualties and little opposition from isolated groups which was easily dealt with. The leading Companies reached their objectives without additional incident, reconnoitred, dug-in, and consolidated. The left flank Company at once sent out an officer to establish liaison with the 5th Battalion.

During the advance up to this point 3 or 4 German machine guns were passed but left for the Machine Gun Company to deal with as prearranged.

The rear Companies - A & C - passed through the leading Companies without dificulty and got to within 50 yards of the barrage. Numbers of the enemy were seen to be withdrawing in the direction of DEER HOUSE and were caught by our heavy artillery which was searching the ground behind the 18 pounder barrage.

On the right Company reaching CLUSTER HOUSES the mebus at D.7.d.5[illegible] were found to be badly damaged by our gun fire and the garrison in surrounding shell holes; they were dealt with by rifle greanade and Lewis gun upon which they withdrew and were shot down by our men or taken prisoner and sent back. The final objective - OLIVE HOUSE - was then occupied and consolidated under heavy rifle and machine gun fire. Under cover of our protective barrage in front of BLUE LINE the Company was re-organised and positions consolidated for all round defence, considerable trouble being experienced from enemy sniping.

The left flank Company proceeded with little opposition to its objectives - CLIFTON HOUSE and WURST FARM -which were taken and strong points dug, covering both places, at D.7.b.95 and D.7.b.31 The 1[illegible]th Machine Gun Company with 5 guns arrived soon after the objectives had been reached and the guns were placed in dominating positions.

The dispositions were now as shown in Appendix No, 2.

Flares were lighted at each forward post when called for by contact 'planes.

A weak counter attack against OLIVE HOUSE during the afternoon was broken up by rifle and Lewis Gun Fire from that post.

At [illegible].30 p.m. groups of enemy were seen to be coming from the direction of WINCHESTER and ALBATROSS FARMS towards our left front. They were broken up by our rifle and machine gun fire. Larger bodies were seen some [illegible] yards away to be advancing. The S. O. S. put up from Company Headquarters (D.7.b.[illegible].5.) was replied to with good effect by our artillery, completely enveloping the enemy and making it impossible for them to go back. They advanced to within 400 yards in waves where Machine gun, ~~and~~ Lewis gun, and rifle fire were opened and the waves thinned out and broken, the survivors being sniped.

About 6 p.m. a small party of enemy approaching CLIFTON HOUSE was dispersed with heavy casualties: the foremost attackers not getting nearer than 150 yards from our position.

In order to thicken our line, one platoon from the Company in reserve was sent forward to the left flank and the remaining 3 platoons and a similar number of the 7th Battalion were ordered to stand by.

At dusk men were seen massing about 2 miles away and another counter attack seemed evident, but nothing happened on the whole front the night being quiet. During the night supplies of water and ammunition were sent forward to the whole line.

At dawn on the 21st it was found that the enemy had pushed forward posts to within 100 yards of our lines on the left flank.

Our artillery opened a heavy barrage at dawn without resulting action on the part of the enemy.

Considerable aerial activity on both sides took place during the 21st September the enemy planes flying very low and firing their machine guns on the captured area. Shelling was intermittent but nothing of importance happened during the day. Continuous sniping went on from our posts with good results and consolidation proceeded.

At 6.15 p.m. the enemy opened a heavy barrage all along the line extending to the divisions right and left of us dotting the whole of captured area and lines of communication from the rear, which lasted until about 9 p.m. The S. O. S. signal was was seen to be put up but not on our Battalion front. Our Artillery replied immediately and the barrage was exceptionally good. Apparently a counter attack was developing on the right but owing to the smoke no observation of infantry action was possible, but it was made certain that no enemy movement was taking place on our front.

Relief took place during the night and though some difficulty was experienced owing to relieving Battalion not arriving at rendezvous arranged for guides all positions were handed over and the whole Battalion reached camp in REIGERSBURG by 10 a.m. with only 3 casualties.

COMMUNICATIONS.

Communications were maintained with forward Companies by runner through relay posts at SPRINGFIELD and HIBOU and by lamp and pigeon. The lamp which was established at CLUSTER HOUSES was in operation within half an hour of the occupation of that point and proved of great use. Runners did good work and pigeons were also used but other means of communication failed. The power-buzzer at SPRINGFIELD was out of order up to 5 p.m. on the 20th September when the Battalion Headquarters moved to MON DU HIBOU, but came into action after that hour. The establishment of a line both to ARBRE and MARINE VIEW was attempted but casualties and lack of accomodation prevented this from being carried out.

The smoke of the barrage prevented discs from being seen. Smoke rockets were not used and the available dog at SPRINGFIELD was used but this method proved slow, It is suggested that had each Company been equipped with a LUCAS LAMP better results would have been obtained.

CO-OPERATION WITH OTHER ARMS.

(a) ARTILLERY.

The work of the artillery was beyond all praise. The shooting was most accurate and our troops who followed barrage closely suffered few casualties from it. No gaps were observed and the pace was found quite suitable to the ground. Some complaints of short shooting were received during the 20th September from our right and centre front Companies; this was quickly corrected and the final barrage on the evening of the 21st was particularly good and all ranks were greatly impressed by the power and accuracy of our artillery fire.

As soon as information could be got back, all ground occupied by the enemy was most thoroughly searched.

Liaison officers moved to forward positions early in the operations but it is questionable whether it is advisable for them to get ahead of their communications.

(b) TANKS.

Those tanks detailed to take part in the attack in the area allotted to this Battalion apparently did not reach their objectives and none were seen.

(c) MACHINE GUNS.

The overhead machine gun barrage was most effective and encouraged the advancing troops. The gunners did work of great merit.

The guns told off to accompany the infantry arrived well up to time and were ready to be placed as soon as objectives had been secured by the infantry. The selection of positions for the greatest fire effect could not have been better and the guns were handled with great coolness skill and effect during enemy counter attacks and their presence gave a sense of great confidence and security to the Infantry. Co-operation was good and ammunition sent up to the infantry was shared with the gunners.

(d) AIRCRAFT.

The work of aeroplanes previous to and during the early stages of the battle was very successful and up to midday on the 20th September enemy aeroplanes gave no trouble. After that hour our planes were apparently partially withdrawn and considerable trouble was experienced during the remainder of the day and on the 21st from low flying E. A. which spotted the position of our posts and used their machine guns on the garrisons (fortunately with little effect).

Representations were made to the Brigade about this and lat our planes came out again in force with a corresponding decrea in enemy activity.

CO-OPERATION OF INFANTRY ARMS.

Both rifles and Lewis guns were used with great effect and

obvious results during the attack and the subsequent maintenance of the position, but little use was found for the bomb or rifle grenade, probably owing to the very thorough artillery preparation. Also the nature of the soil prevented full effect being obtained from percussion rifle grenades.

GAS.

No trouble was noted from enemy gas except by right flank Company during advance through MARINE DRIVE (Box Respirators worn temporarily) and by one Company during relief at ADMIRALS ROAD. - No casualities suffered. A few gas shells fell on forward positions.

SUPPLIES.

The pack pony convoy proved of great value in brining up ammunition and water and the carrying parties from the 173rd Brigade did good work and were successful in getting it forward from WINNIPEG FARM and from MON DU HIBOU to front line and support Companies,

RATIONS.

Rations were adequate and the additional ration of sandwiches chocolate and sardines were greatly appreciated. The additional water bottles were of the utmost value.

ENEMY MORAL.

The enemy semmed greatly demoralized by our artillery and the speed with which the infantry followed the barrage and surrendered freely. All Company Commanders are of opinion that could additional troops have been pushed through little resistance would have been experienced from the demoralized enemy. All prisoners taken appeared to belong to the 176th and 183th R. I. R.

R.A.M.C.

The R.A.M.C. arrangements were good and wounded quickly evacuated. It is suggested, however, that even better results might have been achieved had large dumps of stretchers been made at convenient points such as the TRIANGLE and SPRINGFIELD.

The work of all Battalion [illegible]

was beyond praise.

CASUALTIES.

Casualties were light and a considerable number due to enemy snipers.

DISTINGUISHING MARKS.

The coloured patches on the packs distinguishing Companies were of great assistance in leap frogging and in re-organization and suggestions have been made that they should be worn also on the arms.

GROUND.

Direction was kept by Compass Bearings by following the barrage and by working on recognisable points on the high ground.

PRISONERS AND BOOTY.

Large numbers of prisoners were passed back; actually between 50 and 60 from the area captured by the Battalion.

Four heavy machine guns were passed over and left for the Machine Gun Company as arranged.

Captain.

Commanding 2/8th Bn. London Regiment.

6A

APPENDIX. 6 A.

REPORT NO. 2 ON RAID ON BLUNT SALIENT.

It can be considered definite that the MEBUS raided was at point C.6.d.76.18. but some doubt exists as to whether its position is in front or behind the main HUBNER TRENCH.

Two statements with regard to this are well supported.
(a) That the MEBUS attacked was much nearer than they were told it would be, and
(b) There was a slope or bank in front of the MEBUS which may have been the breastwork.

Only two MEBUSES were seen definitely the second, 25 to 30 yards South of the one already mentioned.

The MEBUS attacked was about 10 ft. square but reliability can not be attached to this statement as opinions differ.
The roof appeared to be 2 or 3 feet above the top of the slope.
There were no loopholes or slits in the MEBUS but one door low down, about 3 ft. high, facing N.W.

A trench surround d the MEBUS the parados being the wall of the MEBUS. The accompanying sketch gives a better description That part of the trench on the N.W. side of the MEBUS appeared to continue N.W. and some Germans were seen to leave the MEBUS and run up this trench when it was attacked.
This trench is probably the continuation of HUBNER trench running N.W.

The trench was shallow, width unknown, and it did not appear to be revettedin any way. It was badly damaged by shelling fire.

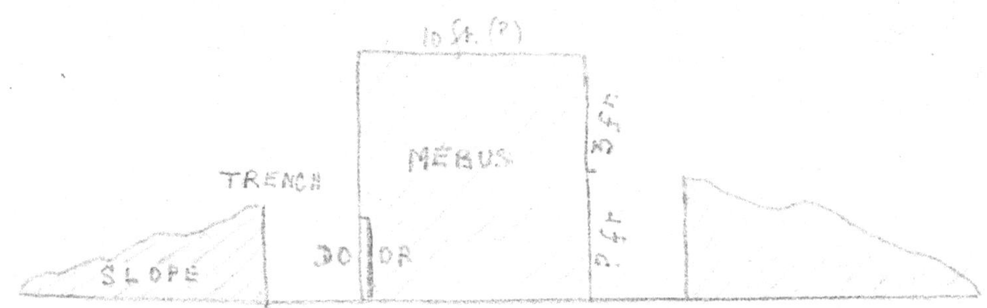

Appendix No 4 4

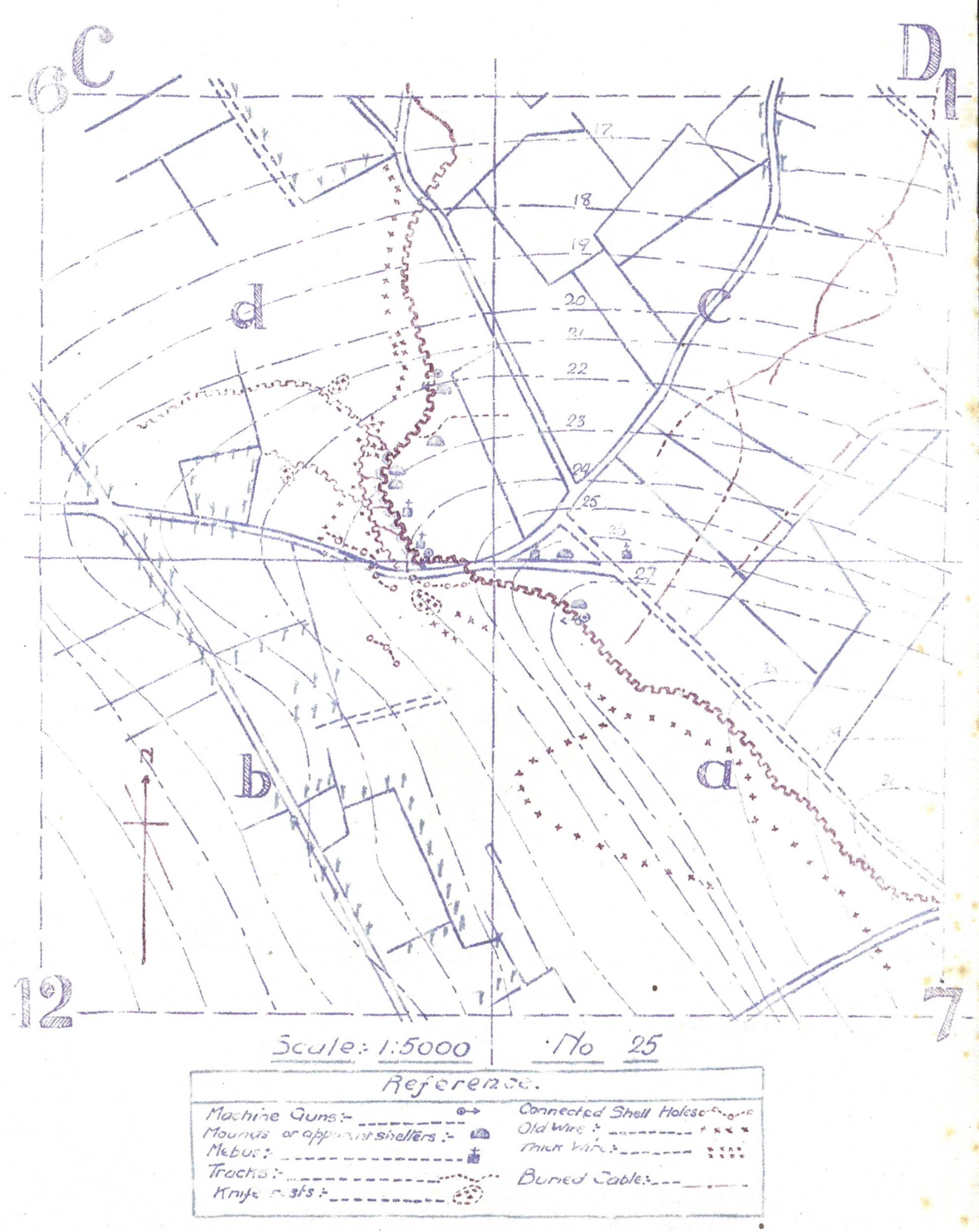

2/6 London

October

1917

Index..

5.A.
to
13.A.

SUBJECT.

3RD DIV.

No.	Contents.	Date.
	7TH INF. BDE., 2ND BATTN. The S. LANCASHIRE RT. WAR DIARY, JAN. - SEPT., 1915	

(56,425). Wt.24,741—161. 2000. 11/20. Gp.164. A.&E.W.

8

Instructions regarding War Diaries and Intelligence Summaries are contained in F. S. Regs., Part II. and the Staff Manual respectively. Title pages will be prepared in manuscript.

WAR DIARY
or
INTELLIGENCE SUMMARY.
(Erase heading not required.)

Army Form C. 2118.

2/6 London Regt

Vol 10

Place	Date	Hour	Summary of Events and Information	Remarks and references to Appendices
	Oct.			
AUDENFORT	1st to 20th		Bn. Training. Lt. Col. Benson leave 10th Oct. Major A.W. BROWNE (appointed 2nd in command 28/9/17) assumed command in his absence.	[initials]
POPERINGHE	20th		Bn. moved to POPERINGHE to billets in the town by march route to AUDRUICQ thence by train to HOPOUTRE & by march route to POPERINGHE.	[initials]
do.	21/23rd		Training at POPERINGHE Lt Col Benson returned from leave 21st Oct & assumed command	[initials]
SIEGE CAMP	24th		Bn. moved by march route to SIEGE CAMP. Tpt & QM details in same camp.	[initials] APPENDIX No 1
CANAL BANK	25th		Bn moved by march route to CANAL BANK WEST leaving Tpt & QM details at SIEGE CAMP	[initials] APPENDIX No 2
KEMPTON PARK	26th		Bn moved to KEMPTON PARK (in huts) 1 O/Rank wounded.	[initials] APPX No 3
	27th		Bn. at KEMPTON PARK.	[initials]
KEMPTON PARK and Line	28th		Lt Col. Benson established advanced Bde HQ at VARNA FARM as O.C. Outpost line (with Capt GODFREY and LIEUT. CROFTS). Major BROWNE assumed command of Bn. Bn moved at 3pm to relieve 7th Bn LONDON REGT. ~~[illegible]~~ in line. Bn HQ at V21.c 71 POELCAPELLE SHEET (1/10,000). Relief complete by 10pm (reported at 1.30 am 29th thro' failure of communications). Casualties 10 O/Ranks wounded	[initials] APPX No 4
	29th		Bn holding line E. of POELCAPELLE from Quad E. of TRACAS FARM to HELLESHOUSE. LIEUT. COL. BENSON returned and assumed command of Bn at 7 pm. B Coy detailed to attack NOBLES FARM at 10 pm. copy orders attached on morning 30th suffered severely during 29th. A. Coy therefore detailed in their place. Casualties. 8 O/R killed 18 O/R wounded, 1 wounded at duty, 2 missing	[initials] APPX No 5

Army Form C. 2118.

Instructions regarding War Diaries and Intelligence Summaries are contained in F. S. Regs., Part II. and the Staff Manual respectively. Title pages will be prepared in manuscript.

WAR DIARY
or
INTELLIGENCE SUMMARY.
(Erase heading not required.)

Place	Date	Hour	Summary of Events and Information	Remarks and references to Appendices
			(2)	
In line	Octobr 30th		At zero 5.50 am the 2/8th Bn LONDON REGT attacked MORAY HOUSE, HINTON FARM, PAPA FARM and CAMERON HOUSE, and A Coy of this Bn, less one platoon, under Captain ANDERSON M.C. and 2Lt FOULDS attacked NOBLES FARM & trench S.E. of it. The attack was completely successful and all objectives were taken consolidated and held in spite of very bad going & the difficulty of moving through the mud. The 8th Bn on our right were unable to reach their objectives owing to the state of the ground. The appended maps (Appendix 6 & 7) show (a) dispositions of Bn at zero and (b) dispositions after attack.	Appx Nos 6 & 7
			The Bn (& the 2/8th Bn) relieved by 2/5th Bn. Relief complete 10 pm. Bn marched to KEMPTON PARK & proceeded thence by bus (B Coy) to SIEGE CAMP.	Appx No 8.
			Casualties 2Lt FOULDS killed & 2Lt SPARK missing. 19 O/Ranks killed 48 O/R wounded 13 O/R missing. Wounded at duty 47 O/Ranks.	[illegible]
SIEGE CAMP	31		Cleaning & refitting.	[illegible]

[illegible] Lieut
A/Adjutant

S E C R E T.

58th Divn.
G.S.1149.

Fifth Army,
S.G. 784/8.
9th October, 1917.

QUESTIONS TO ASK DIVISIONS ENGAGED IN RECENT BATTLES.

1. Pace of Barrage.

What was it and was it suitable ?

2. Was there serious opposition crossing "NO MAN'S LAND." ?
If so, of what nature ?
Hostile barrage - M.G's - Rifle fire or bombs ?
When did the hostile barrage come down.

3. Forming defensive flank.
Any special points or lessons to be deduced
from action of flank Divisions ?

4. Any extra water carried on man, and if so, how ?
Arrangements for reserve of water.

5. Was the issue of maps, plans Oblique photos sufficient ?

6. Keeping direction.
Use of compasses.
Smoke from barrage - any difficulties ?

7. Was there any M.G. fire from positions some distance in
rear of the enemy's trench line (front or support) ?

8. Communications how maintained forward of our old front line ?
Any use made of dogs or message carrying rockets ?

9. In attacks on a concreted M.G. emplacement, at what distance
from the emplacement did the troops come under M.G. fire ?

10. Did M.G's fire from the emplacement or from outside, i.e.
on top of the shell-holes at the sides ?
How many M.G's to each emplacement ?

11. Does the enemy still hold isolated shell-holes, and if so were
the mopping-up parties satisfactorily organised and led in
order to deal with them ?

12. As much detail as can be got is required regarding hostile
counter-attacks, e.g.

(a) How many ?
(b) Strength of each ?
(c) Time of each after Zero ?
(d) Formations adopted by enemy ?
(e) Any indications of a pending counter attack -
men dribbling forward or collecting in certain areas ?
Instances where our reserve troops acted on their
own initiative in assisting to repel a counter-attack ?

13. Have they been properly served as regards :-

(a) Ammunition of all natures.
(b) R.E.Stores.
(c) Supplies and Transport.
(d) Ordnance Stores including tentage.
(e) Remounts.
(f) Veterinary services.
(g) Postal services (detailed remarks required).

14. Have they any legitimate criticisms to offer on :-

 (a) Railway services.
 (b) Bus arrangements.
 (c) Roads.

15. Can they put forward any requirements which will help to alleviate the work or discomfort of the Officers and Soldiers in the actual fighting area. Any suggestion as to shelters, food, water, equipment, pack gear, transport, clothing, etc., are urgently required.

16. Have you any suggestions to make as regards the improvement of Liaison between Artillery - both Field and Heavy - and Infantry.

17. What arrangements were made as regards the Infantry making known their positions to the Artillery ?
 Were F.O.Os. helped in this respect ?

18. Did you see any distant hostile M.G. firing during the advance ? If so, when and where ? Could they have been stopped by Artillery fire ?
 Where was the barrage at the time ?

19. <u>AIRCRAFT</u>.

 (a) Were flares used and was the supply sufficient. ?

 (b) Were reports by aircraft helpful ?

 (c) Was the counter-attack aeroplane helpful ?

 (d) Was any inconvenience caused by hostile aircraft ?

58th Divn.
G.S. 1149.

S E C R E T.

B.M./519.

5th London Regt.
6th London Regt.
7th London Regt.
8th London Regt.
198th M.Gun Coy.
174th L.T.M.Bty.
Bde. Signal Officer.

Please reply shortly to the questions attached as far as your experience goes, and forward them to Brigade H.Q. by 5 p.m. 14th inst.

Captain,
Brigade Major,
174th. Infantry Brigade.

12th October, 1917.

Headquarters
174th Infantry Brigade.

Reference your B.M./519, I herewith enclose report as instructed thereon.

[signature]
Lieut.
Asst. Adjutant.
for Lieut. Colonel,
Comdg. 7th Bn. London Regt.

14/10/17

G.S. 1149.

(1) 50 yards in 4 minutes. This pace was found suitable to the ground over which this Battalion attacked.

(2) Yes. M.G. from flanks. Enemy barrage opened 11 minutes after Zero – but was weak in back areas

(3) The right flank was open & was defended by strong point. (Strength 1 Platoon & 1 M.G.)

(4) (a) Two additional water bottles to every three men – it is suggested that every man shall be equipped with two water-bottles owing to the difficulty of replenishing isolated posts.
(b) Taken forward at night by pack-pony transport in petrol tins.

(5) The issue of maps & plans was sufficient. Oblique photos did not sufficiently cover area allotted.

(6) Direction was kept by means of locating
(a) Local features, from maps & plans.
(b) Compass direction, supervised by officers on either flank of leading companies.
(c) Direction of our barrage was found to assist greatly.
(d) No difficulty from smoke of barrage — as wind was blowing towards enemy.

(7) Yes — Long range indirect fire from enemy's reserve positions.

(8) (a) Visual, i.e. lamp.
(b) Runner relay posts.
Message dog & pigeons were used by Advanced Bn. H.Q. in cases of special emergency.
Signal rockets were not used.

(9) Owing to configuration of ground, at comparatively short range varying from 100 to 300 yds.

(10) (a) In most cases from shell hole position either in front or to flanks of concrete emplacement.

(b) Owing to the continuous withdrawal of enemy it is impossible to estimate.

(11) Yes.
Mopping up was carried out during the advance – Set barrage materially reduced the necessity for special mopping up parties behind the enemy organized line.

(12) (a) Three
(b) First two were local & quite small. 3rd Estimated strength 2000.
(c) Troops were seen massing at 2:30pm – nine hours after Zero.
(d) Small columns – about 400 yds. from our posts – leading columns formed into waves

(13) (a) Yes
(b) Yes
(c) Yes

(14) No criticisms.

(15) Food. Bread ration is unsuitable on account of its becoming crumbled, wet & uneatable. Biscuit ration only with a preserved meat ration is recommended.

(15 cont.) An additional ration of chocolate & raisins was greatly appreciated by the troops, as it was easily carried & consumed.
A liberal tobacco ration before going into battle is desirable.

<u>Water.</u> See para. 4.

<u>Equipment.</u> The amount of material the man is required to carry into the attack has a tendency to considerably reduce his fighting efficiency on reaching his objective & it appears worthy of consideration that lightly equipped (i.e. rifle, bayonet, bandolier & box respirator) men under an officer of the Battalion attacking be provided for the purpose of relief in this respect by carrying as much as is possible of the material required for consolidating & holding the ground gained.

<u>Clothing.</u> The waterproof cape appears to have many & distinct advantages over the waterproof sheet.

(16) NO.

(17) Disposition maps were passed to Liaison Offrs with Bn. Hdqrs. as soon as received which enabled F.O.O^s to move to more forward positions.

(18) ——

(19) (a) Yes, & sufficient were supplied.
(b) Information from this source did not reach Bn. Hdqrs.
(c) ——
(d) Yes. R.A. located positions of posts & flying low fired M.G. on them (no observation.)

H M Browne
Major,
for Lieut. Colonel,
Comdg 7/6 Bn London Rgt.

14/10/17

APPENDIX I

2/6th Bn London Regt. Copy No. 10

Secret Order No. 24 23/7/17

(Map Reference Sheet 28 NW 1/20,000)

1. The Bn. will move to SIEGE CAMP, on the 24th.

2. Brigade starting point is at cross roads B.3.c.20.95. Head of the Bn will pass this point at 12.35 pm.

3. Starting point of the Bn will be A Coy. Headquarters. Companies will pass the starting point in the following order:–

A. Coy
D. "
C. "
B. "

at ~~intervals~~ distances of 200 yards. A Coy will pass this point at 12.20 pm.

4. ROUTE will be Switch road N. cross-roads B.3.c.20.95 – ELVERDINGHE ROAD A.12.d.2.8. – HOSPITAL CORNER B.20.b.3.7.

5. DRESS Full marching order

6. RATIONS Each man will carry the unexpended portion of the days ration.

7. Lewis Gun limbers will be loaded at 9 a.m. under Lewis Gun Officer.

continued

Order No. 24. 2.

8\. Officers' Kits will be stacked at Quartermasters Stores by 10 am.
Orderly Room boxes etc., will be ready for loading at 10.30 am.
Officers Mess boxes will be at Bn. Headquarters at 11.30 am.

9\. ADVANCE PARTY consisting of 4 C.Q.M.S., 1 NCO for Quartermasters Stores & 1 NCO for Bn. Headquarters will report to 2/Lieut. A. MORROW at 9.30 am.

10\. Further orders re loading parties, etc., will be issued later.

11\. ACKNOWLEDGE.

[signature]

2/Lieut & A/Adjt.
2/16 Bn. London Regt.

Copies to:–

1. Commanding Officer
2. 2nd in Command
3. OC A Coy.
4. OC B Coy.
5. OC C Coy.
6. OC D Coy.
7. 174th Inf. Bde.
8. File
9/10. War Diary
11. Quartermaster
12. Transport Officer

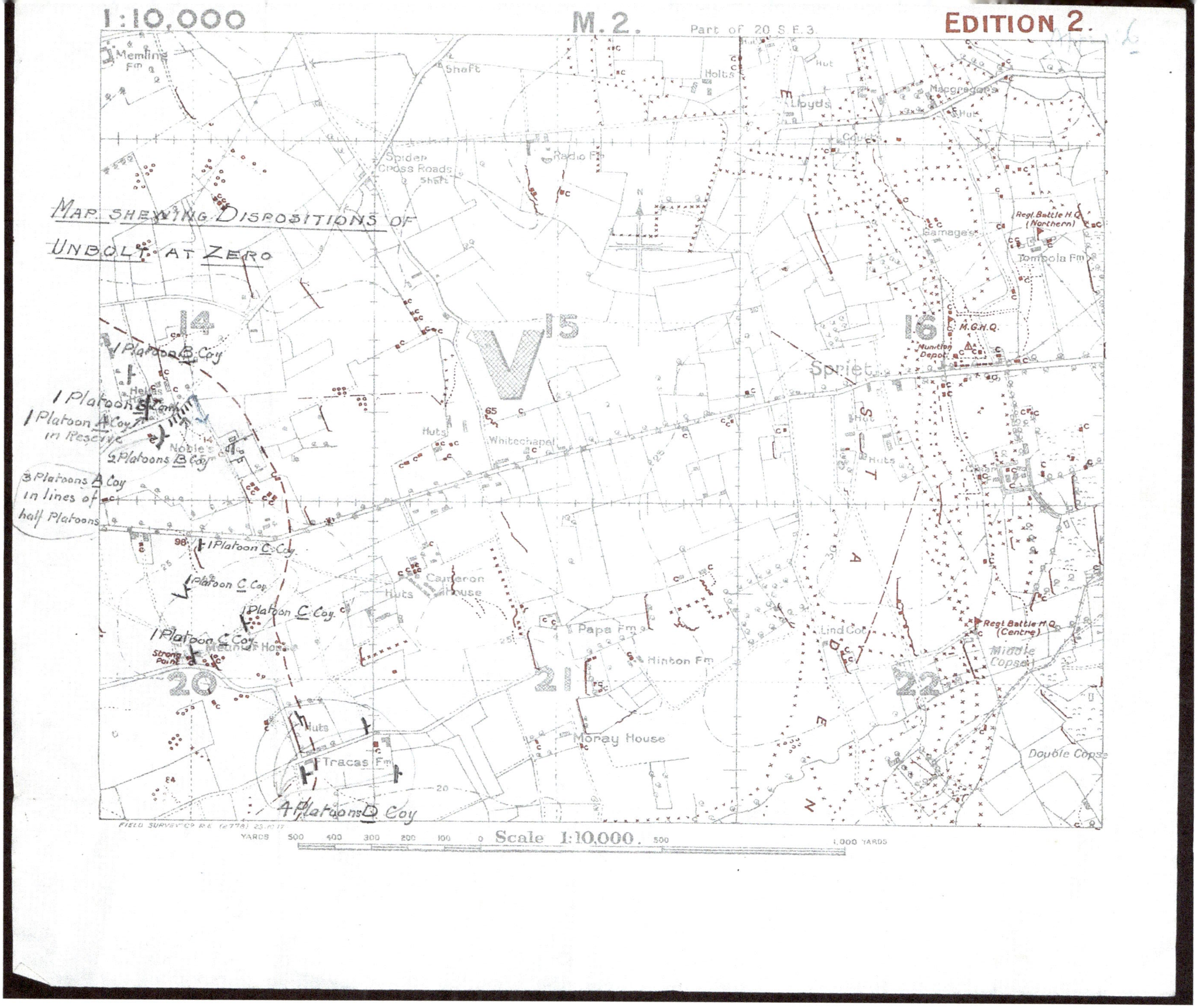

1:10,000 M.2. Part of 20 S.E.3. EDITION 2.

MAP SHEWING DISPOSITIONS OF UNBOLT AT ZERO

Memling Fm
Shaft
Holts
Hut
Lloyds
Macgregor's
Hut
Spider Cross Roads Shaft
Radio Fm
Regt. Battle H.Q. (Northern)
Gamage's
Tombola Fm
14
15
16
V
M.G.H.Q.
Munition Depot
Spriet
S T A D E N
1 Platoon B Coy
Helles
1 Platoon B Coy
1 Platoon A Coy in Reserve
Noble's
2 Platoons B Coy
3 Platoons A Coy in lines of half Platoons
Huts
65
Whitechapel
Huts
Hut
1 Platoon C Coy
1 Platoon C Coy
Cameron House
Huts
1 Platoon C Coy
1 Platoon C Coy
Strong Point
Papa Fm
Hinton Fm
Lind Cot
Regt. Battle H.Q. (Centre)
Middle Copse
20
21
22
Huts
Tracas Fm
Moray House
Double Copse
4 Platoons D Coy

Scale 1:10,000.
YARDS 500 400 300 200 100 0 500 1,000 YARDS

Message Form.

....................Division.

Map reference or mark own position on Map at back.

1. I am at...

2. I am at.......... ....and am consolidating.

3. I am at..and have consolidated.

4. Am held up at ....by M.G. at...

5. I need :—Ammunition.
   Bombs.
   Rifle Grenades.
   Water.
   Very lights.
   Stokes shells.

6. Enemy forming up for counter-attack at..

7. Enemy withdrawing at...

8. I am in touch with................................on Right / Left at...

9. I am not in touch on Right. / Left.

10. I estimate my present strength at..rifles.

11. Hostile {Battery / Machine Gun / Trench Mortar} active at......................................

Time................................a.m. (p.m.)

Date...

Name...

Platoon.................. Company.......... ....

Battalion............. ....

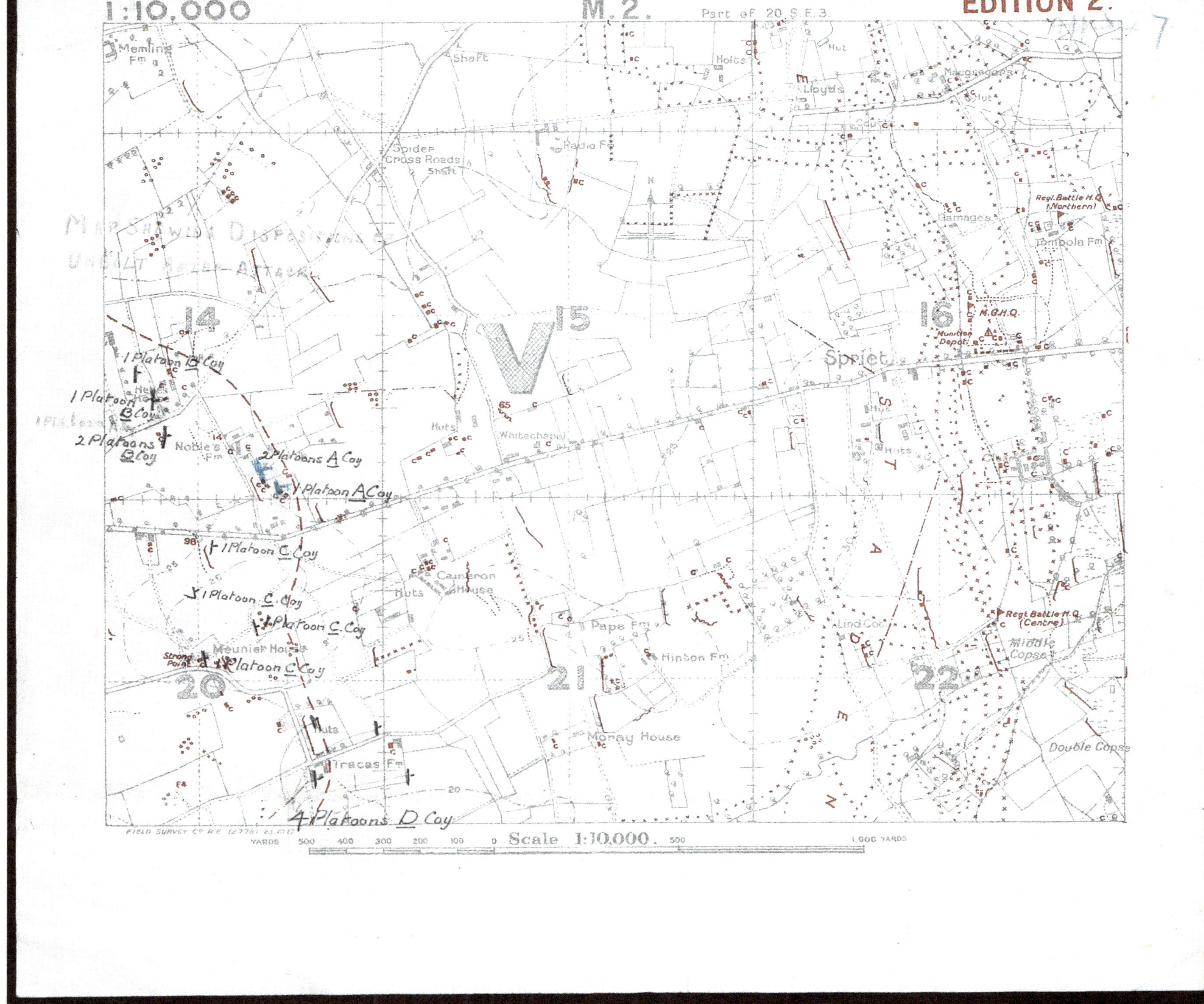
1:10,000
M.2.
Part of 20.S.E.3.
EDITION 2.
Memling Fm
Shaft
Holts
Hut
Lloyds
Macgregors
Radio Fm
Spider Cross Roads
Shaft
Damages
Regt. Battle H.Q. (Northern)
Tombola Fm
14
V
15
16
M.G.H.Q.
Munition Depot
Spriet
1 Platoon B Coy
1 Platoon B Coy
2 Platoons B Coy
Noble's Fm
2 Platoons A Coy
1 Platoon A Coy
Huts
Whitechapel
Hut
Huts
S
T
A
N
D
E
1 Platoon C Coy
1 Platoon C Coy
1 Platoon C Coy
1 Platoon C Coy
Cameron House
Huts
Papa Fm
Hinton Fm
Lind Cot
Regt. Battle H.Q. (Centre)
Middle Copse
Strong Point
Meunier House
20
21
22
Huts
Tracas Fm
Moray House
Double Copse
4 Platoons D Coy
Field Survey Co R.E.
Yards 500 400 300 200 100 0 Scale 1:10,000. 500 1,000 Yards
Map showing dispositions of ... before attack

Message Form.

....................Division.

Map reference or mark own position on Map at back.

1. I am at...

2. I am at......... ....and am consolidating.

3. I am at...and have consolidated.

4. Am held up at ....by M.G. at ....

5. I need :—Ammunition.
   Bombs.
   Rifle Grenades.
   Water.
   Very lights.
   Stokes shells.

6. Enemy forming up for counter-attack at...

7. Enemy withdrawing at...

8. I am in touch with..............................on Right / Left at.......................................

9. I am not in touch on Right. / Left.

10. I estimate my present strength at...rifles.

11. Hostile {Battery / Machine Gun / Trench Mortar} active at....................................

Time.............................a.m. (p.m.)

Date..

Name...

Platoon.................. Company.......... ....

Battalion............. ....

APPENDIX 2

Order No 25 Copy No FILE

2/6th Bn. London Regt 25/10/17

Secret

1 The Bn. will move to the Canal Bank this afternoon.

Companies will move independantly Platoons at 100 yards distance.

A Coy. will lead (followed by B C + D) 1st Platoon leaving Siege Camp at 2 0 pm An advance party will meet them on arrival about C.25.a.3.8.

2 ROUTE DAWSON'S CORNER – BRIELEN

3 Dinners 12.30 pm.

4 Dress Battle Order

5 Officers valises + mess boxes will be stacked near Headquarters Officers Mess Cookhouse at 1 pm.

6 Unexpended portion of the days rations will be carried.

7 . Acknowledge

2/Lieut

25/10/17 [illegible] Adjutant

Appendix 3

OC Details
2/6th Bn

SECRET

1. The Battalion will move to Kimpton Park forthwith.
2. Capt E. G. Godfrey & 2nd Lt Goulds will report at Kimpton Park as soon as possible for duty during the tour. The Quartermaster will report at Kimpton Park as soon as possible. It is possible to ride right up to Kimpton Park.
3. Cookers and watercarts will move to Kimpton Park at once, to provide Battalion with tea.
4. 1500 ~~yds~~ sandbags (3 per man) must be sent to Kimpton Park. If the 150 shovels have not arrived ~~with~~ when the Battalion moves, they will be

sent on afterwards.

5. Tommy cookers (1 per man) will be sent to Kempton Park.

6. Rations for as far forward as possible will be sent to Kempton Park i.e. for 28th inst. These will arrive tonight.

7. 300 waterbottles filled will be sent to Kempton Park.

8. Lewis guns with parts & SAA to be sent up also.

9. Two extra runners and 2 extra signallers are required to report to Kempton Park at once.

10. More food and drinks are required for HQ and Coy messes.

11. It is possible for transport to bring supplies to Kempton Park.

12. Transport is required to carry back to you, great coats, officers valises and mess boxes. This material will be dumped in Billet 158 i.e. 3 to the right of the railway. A certain number of details in charge of Cpl Yeo will also report to you.

13. Thick trench candles are required for H.Q.

14 The Bn will probably go into the line tomorrow

C B Bucknall Lt Col

26/10/1917

SECRET

Reference Operation Order 1/28/10/17

For "The line is from second E in HELLES to MEUNIER FM"

Read "The line is from second E in HELLES to NOBLES FM"

Lucid +
Asst Adjt

28/10/17

SECRET APPENDIX 4

Operation Order No 27
by Copy NO 6
Lt Col C.B. Benson DSO 28 10 17

The Battalion will relieve UNCORK in the line this afternoon. Companies will move off by platoons at 200x distance. First platoon leaving at 3 0 pm in following order
D Coy. B Coy. C Coy. A Coy.

ROUTE For D Coy C Coy & leading 2 platoons of A Coy duckboard track to PHEASANT FARM and thence to GLOUCESTER FARM where they will be met by guides
For B Coy & rear 2 platoons of A Coy duckboard track to V19 a 7 1 where they will be met by guides
Bn HQ is at V19 a 7 1

Guides will be as follows:-

D Coy	GLOUCESTER FM	5.0 pm
C	"	5 30 pm
B	at Bn HQ	5.0 pm

Leading 2 platoons of A Coy will be met at GLOUCESTER FM at 6 0 pm and rear 2 platoons A Coy will lead

straight on to Bn. H.Q. where they will be met by guides.
Bn H.Q. details will follow Abey.

The line is from 2nd C in HELLES to NOBLES FM not now held V.14.C.8.3 V.20 a 8.8. MEUNIER HOUSES TRACCAS FM any metres 400 x East. On the right of the Battalion is the 63rd Division with which touch cannot be obtained owing to swamp in LEKKERBOTTERBEEK. 57th Division on left hold RIQUETTE FM.

193 M.G. Coy – HELLES HOUSE
MEUNIER HOUSES TRACCAS FARM.

Reliefs to be reported to Bn H.Q. as soon as complete. Code word KEMPTON.

Lieut. +
Asst. Adjt.

Issued to

No. 1 Commanding Officer
2 A Coy
3 B "
4 C "
5 D
6 Colonel C.B. Benson D.S.O.

Ref. Map SPRIET 1/10000
APPENDIX 5

OC. A coy

1 As B coy has suffered somewhat heavily you will with your company take NOBLES FARM and the M. buses to S.E of it tomorrow.

2 It is understood that you are well acquainted with the situation and plan of attack; to ensure this I give a resume below in the following paras.

3 Situation and Plan

(a) Zero is 5 30 am 30th inst.

(b) Assembly
You will form up facing EAST and N of the road POECAPPELLE - SPIDER CROSS ROADS namely right flank at V.14 C 80.45 and left flank V.14 C 80.65 You will be in position one and a half hours before ZERO. B coy will take over this post when you move off to close with the barrage.

(C) Direction of Attack SE via Road Junction at V.14 D.00.60 to NOBLES FARM and mebuses S.E. of it

(d) Formation
Lines of half platoons in file

(e) Objectives
NOBLES FARM. (one platoon)
Mebuses SE of NOBLES FARM. (one platoon)

(2)

One platoon to take NOBLES FARM which will have a box barrage on it by sending 2 sections against it from the NE and 2 sections pass W of the farm and attack the farm N.E.

A second platoon in similar formation will pass W of the farm and be detailed to capture the rebuses S.E. of it

NOTE Study the Barrage map carefully as all this practically comes in the box.

A third platoon advancing originally behind the two leading platoons will after NOBLES FARM is captured form and consolidate a strong point at V.14.D 8.4

The fourth Platoon will advance from the place of assembly ~~at~~ and ~~V 14 D 25.90~~ make a strong point at V 14 D 25.90

NOTE You need not send more than 2 sections for this post if you so desire.

F Co operation "C" Coy will send 2 sections along the POELCAPPELLE - SPRIET Road to form a liason post with UNBIND at V 15 C 1.0. This has been instructed to co-operate with your platoon attaching the mebuses if necessary.

(9) "B" Coy will reoccupy their original posts taken over by you today at ZERO minus 1½ hours.

4 Dress + Ammunition Flares &c

NO packs. Iron ration in pockets. 16 Drums in Lewis Guns 120 rounds S.A.A. per man. You will take over Bombs FLARES 'P' Bombs from O.C. "B" Coy

(If possible change tunics with a man before the attack, as I wish you dressed as the men if possible).

NOTE You can draw tape from B. Coy

5 When NOBLES FARM is taken and if it is fit for a VICKERS GUN ask for one to be sent up from HELLES.

6 You will report when in assembly position by CODE word "GALLANT"

7 Communication. You will endeavour to establish Visual communication with B. Coy at HELLES. To enable you

to do this you will take 2 signallers from B. Coy. and 2 discs or luc lamp. Communication is to be maintained also by pigeon and runner as necessary

8 Acknowledge by bearer (duplicated)

29/10/16

Lt Col.
UNBOLT

TIME 8.48 pm.

GOOD LUCK to you and your men from us all. We have great confidence in you.

Appendix 8

SECRET Copy No 6.

OPERATION ORDER

1. Relief. The Battn will probably be relieved by [illegible]NDER troops

2. ~~[illegible] [illegible] [illegible] contact to relieving~~ [illegible] to the HQ of the Coy to be relieved. Coy Commanders must provide a guide for each post and OC B Coy will arrange all necessary guides for A Coy. The hour of relief is uncertain but Coy Commanders should have their guides ready at C H Q from 5.0 pm onwards.

2a. Commanders of posts etc will communicate all particulars of importance especially regarding the enemy to the relieving units.

3. Stores. OsC A Coy B C & D Coys will hand over all trench stores, all unexpended water and other trench stores with the exception of Very light pistols and will obtain receipts for everything handed over.

4. Withdrawal. Each platoon when relieved will move off independently to KEMPTON PARK where it will be met by transport and conveyed to SIEGE CAMP.

5. Report. Company Commanders will report to Battn HQ when their Companies are completely relieved. OsC A & B Coys will report personally. OsC C & D Coys will report by lamp and also by runner.

The order will be for complete relief to MICE

(c) Casualties Coy Commanders will make ~~a return to HQ~~ a list of wounded left behind so that steps may be taken to have them brought in. All posts notify OC MG & E ~~the locality~~ where wounded have been left and the locality of any particular area where wounded are known to be should be specially noted.

for R. [illegible]
Capt & Asst Adjt

30.10.17

Issued to:-

1 Commanding Officer
2 OC A Coy
3 OC B
4 OC C
5 OC D
6 UNDER
7 File
8 } War Diary
9

Instructions regarding War Diaries and Intelligence Summaries are contained in F. S. Regs., Part II. and the Staff Manual respectively. Title pages will be prepared in manuscript.

WAR DIARY 4/2/6 London
or
INTELLIGENCE SUMMARY.
(*Erase heading not required.*)

Army Form C. 2118.

Vol 11

Place	Date	Hour	Summary of Events and Information	Remarks and references to Appendices
	1917			
SIEGE CAMP	November 1to6		Cleaning and refitting	RLS
KEMPTON PARK	6		The Battn moved to KEMPTON PARK vacated by 2/9th Bn LONDON Regt to supply working parties. Lt Col BENSON left for HOUTKERQUE. Major BROWNE assumed command. Casualty. 1 OR killed	RLS APPENDIX No 1 RLS
	7		Battn supplied working parties. Lt Colonel BENSON returned and assumed command	RLS
	8.		"A" Coy relieved a Coy of the 2/9th Bn LONDON REGT in PHEASANT TRENCH. Relief reported complete 2.30 p.m.	RLS APPENDIX No 2
	9		Cleaning and inspecting of Coys	RLS
In the LINE	10		Battn relieves 2/7th Bn London Regt in front HELLES HOUSE – NOBLES FARM – MEUNIER HOUSE – TRACAS FARM. Relief complete 7.50 p.m. A Coy relieved by 1 Coy of 2/5th LONDON REGT at 2.30 p.m. Casualties 1 OR wounded. 4 OR missing. Details to SIEGE CAMP	APPENDIX No 3 RLS RLS
	11		Battn holding line. Casualties 1 O.R. killed.	RLS
	12		Battn relieved by 2/5th London Regt. Relief complete by 7 p.m. 1 Officer (2/Lt Hodges A Coy) wounded at duty. 2 O.R. killed. 5 O.R. wounded 5 O.R. missing. Battn marched to	APPENDICES Nos 4 ~~& 5~~ RLS
CANAL BANK	12		CANAL BANK to dug-outs on WEST BANK	
	13		Cleaning and refitting	RLS

T2134. Wt. W708–776. 500000. 4/15. Sir J. C. & S.

Army Form C. 2118.

Instructions regarding War Diaries and Intelligence Summaries are contained in F. S. Regs., Part II. and the Staff Manual respectively. Title pages will be prepared in manuscript.

WAR DIARY
or
INTELLIGENCE SUMMARY.
(Erase heading not required.)

Place	Date	Hour	Summary of Events and Information	Remarks and references to Appendices
CANAL BANK	November 14.		Battn moved to BRAKE CAMP by march route via BRIELEN-VLAMERTINGHE-SEEGER	APPENDIX No6 RLS
BRAKE CAMP	14		TRACK. DETAILS rejoined Battn	
PROVEN AREA	15		Bn moved to PETWORTH CAMP PROVEN, under orders of 173rd Bde, by march route.	APPENDIX No7 RLS
	16		Cleaning & refitting.	RLS
	17		Battn moved under orders of 173rd Bde to WYLDER, Herzeele area by march to	
WYLDER			PROVEN, thence by train to HERZEELE thence by march to WYLDER, to accomodation	APPENDIX No8 RLS
			vacated by 20th LANCS FUSILIERS. NUCLEUS rejoined Battn	
	18 to 25		Cleaning refitting and training.	RLS
PROVEN AREA	25		Battn moved to PADDINGTON CAMP PROVEN, by march route via HOUTKERQUE.	APPENDIX No9 RLS
			and took over from 2/2nd Bn London Regt. Transport by road to COULEMBY	
COULEMBY	26		Battn marched to Proven, entrained there for WITZERNES, thence by march route	APPENDIX No10. RLS
			to COULEMBY Transport rejoined Battn	
QUESQUES	27		Battn moved by march route to QUESQUES. 2 Coys billeted in LE VERVAL	APPENDIX No11
	28		Lt COL BENSON proceeded to 18th CORPS course Major BROWNE assumes command	RLS
	to 30		Training and refitting	RLS

R Boyle Lt
Acting Adjutant

T2134. Wt. W708—776. 500000. 4/15. Sir J. C. & S.

Order for move from SEICE CAMP TO KEMPTON PARK

APPENDIX 1

SECRET. Copy No.1....

Reference: Map Sheet 28 N.W. 1/20000.

ORDER NO. 29
2/6th BN. THE LONDON REGT.

6/11/17.

A1

1. The Battalion will move to KEMPTON PARK today and take over Quarters from 2/9th Bn, The London Regt.

2. STARTING POINT.
The starting point will be the entrance to the camp,

3. ORDER OF MARCH.
Order of march will be
C, Coy.
D. Coy.
A. Coy.
B. Coy.
200 yards between Companies.
100 yards between Platoons.
All headquarters personnel will parade and march with their Companies.

4. The leading platoon will pass the stating point at 1.30p.m.
Dinners will be at 12 noon.

5. ROUTE.
BRIELEN . ESSEX FARM - BURNT FARM - ALGERIAN COTTAGE.

6. HALTS.
Halts will be observed at the usual clock hours.

7. DRESS.
Full marching order, overcoats in packs.

8. ADVANCE PARTY.
An Advance Party of the 4 Compay Quartermaster-Sergeants and 1 N.C.O. from Bn. Headquarters will proceed, under 2/Lieut. L.G. Watson, at 10 a.m.

9. LEWIS GUNS.
All Lewis Gun magazines etc. will be loaded on limbers at 11 a.m. 4 Lewis Gunners per Company will report to Lieut. A.C. Coltman at 10 a.m. for this purpose.

10. KIT.
Men will pack their personal kit in sandbags (which were issued on 25th October for the purpose) which will be marked with name, number, section, platoon and Company; and fastened together in bundles of sections. These will be stacked in the Guard Room by noon.

11. MESS BOXES.
Mess boxes will be stacked at the entrance to the camp by 2 p.m.

12. CAMP.
The camp will be left clean and tidy, and all rubbish burnt. Company Commanders will render a certificate to this effect, to Bn. Headquarters by 1 p.m. The Bn. Orderly Officer will inspect all vacated accommodation and report to O.C. Details.

13. WATCHES.
Watches will be synchronised from Battalion signals at 12 noon.

continued.

14. Quartermaster's Stores, Transport Lines and Details will remain in the present camps.

15. ACKNOWLEDGE.

Lieut.
Acting Adjutant.
2/6th Bn. The London Regiment.

Copies issued by runner at...... to:-

1. Commanding Officer.
2. Major H.M. Browne.
3. O.C. A. Coy.
4. O.C. B. Coy.
5. O.C. C. Coy.
6. O.C. D. Coy.
7. O.C. Headquarter Details.
8. Quartermaster & Transport Officer.
9. 174th Infantry Brigade.
10. Medical Officer.
11. File.
12/13 War Diary.

"A" Coy MOVE TO PHEASANT TRENCH.

2/6th Battn London Regt.

SECRET. OPERATION ORDER 7/11/17.

Ref Map Sheet No 30.

28. N.W. APPENDIX 2

(1) "A" Coy. 2/6th London Regt will relieve one Coy. of 2/9th London Regt in PHEASANT TRENCH to-morrow (8th inst)

(2) Relief will be complete by 2-30 p.m O/C Coy will arrange to have dinners before moving off & will move off in time to complete relief before hour stated.

(3) Usual receipts for trench stores etc will be given & duplicates forwarded to this office within four hours of relief.

(4) One Very pistol will be carried.

(5) Completion of relief will be reported to this Office by runner. The code word for this will be "BUNKERED".

(6) Any deficiency of trench stores, S.O.S. etc will be reported to this Office at once

(7) Dress – Battle order – Overcoats & blankets will be tied in bundles of sections & stacked in one of the Coy. huts by 10 a.m. "A" Coy. Q.M.S. will be responsible that these are taken down on ration limbers & stacked at Siege Camp.

(8) Men will carry the unexpended portion of the day's rations with the exception of tea & sugar. Hot tea will be sent up & daily rations will be cooked & sent up.

(9) Water bottles will be filled before moving off.

(10) Acknowledge.

(signed) R. Wylie.
Acting Adjutant.

RELIEF OF 2/7th by 2/6th. SECRET.
UNBOLT. ORDER No 1. Nov: 9th 1917.
APPENDIX 3.

(1) UNBOLT will relieve UNCORK on night 10/11 inst.

(2) "A" Coy UNBOLT will relieve "B" Coy UNCORK and will be reserve company having 2 platoons at GLOSTER FARM & 2 platoons at BREWERY.
"B" Coy UNBOLT will relieve "D" Coy UNCORK and take up positions explained verbally.
"C" Coy UNBOLT will relieve "C" Coy UNCORK and take up positions explained verbally.
"D" Coy UNBOLT will relieve "A" Coy UNCORK and take up positions explained verbally.

(3) Dispositions.
"B" Coy Right front.
"C" " Centre.
"D" " Left front.
"A" " Reserve.

(4) Guides. One per post will meet "B", "C" & 2 platoons "A" at GLOSTER FARM. Headquarters will proceed without guides. One guide per post will meet "D" Coy & 2 platoons "A" Coy at NORFOLK HOUSE.

(5) Route. B, C & 2 platoons A via S track to GLOSTER FM. H.Q. D & 2 platoons A Coy "N" track via NORFOLK HOUSE.

(6) March & Distances.
300x between platoons 400x between Companies. "D" Coy will pass KEMPTON PARK ROADS.

(leading platoon) at 2.45 p.m.
"B" Coy. Head of leading platoon will pass KEMPTON FORK ROADS at 2.55 pm
"C" Coy. will follow "B" Coy.
"A" Coy when relieved will proceed to their posts but will wait for "D" Coy to pass on "N" track and "C" Coy on "S" track & will then follow.
In case of halts companies & platoons must not close up.

(7) Trench Stores, Rations & Ammunition – All companies will take rations up to midnight 12th & an iron ration. They will also take the following:

1 extra water bottle per man
12 filled petrol tins per coy.
15 flares (ground)
1 T. Cooker per man
3 Sand bags per man.
120 rounds S.A.A. per man.

In addition coys will take:–

"A" Coy. 20. Magazines per L.G.
4. S.O.S.
30 Very Lights.
3 Watson Fans.

"B" Coy 12. Magazines per L.G.
6. S.O.S.
20 Very Lights.
4 Watson Fans.

"C" Coy   10 Magazines per L.G.
4 S.O.S.
20 Very Lights
3 Watson Fans.

"D" Coy   10 Magazines per L.G.
4 S.O.S.
40 Very Lights.
3 Watson Fans.

The following are the stores that will be handed over from UNICORN Coy those used to-night. A receipt is to be given for these stores. The coys shown under are those of UNICORN.

	"A"	"B"	"C"	"D"	"H.Q."
S.A.A.	12000.	10000	–	[illegible]	30000.
Webley	–	–	–	150	–
L.G. drums (filled)	129	30	138	96.	17.
Bombs No 5.	108.	176	362	120.	–
" 23	23	28.	–	130	–
" 24	18.	17.	–	–	–
S.O.S. old type	28.	13	9.	50	116.
" new "	5	5	5	2.	19.
Very Lights	11	31	48	100	230.
Shovels.	7.	14.	–	30.	37.

The old S.O.S. rockets are to be put on one side & precautions taken against their being used.

(7) The [illegible] arrangement for relief will be made on going out of the line and same guides provided at same places & having

4.30 pm unless otherwise ordered.

(9) Communication will be carried out by Runners from MEUNIER to NORFOLK HOUSE & from BREWERY to NORFOLK HOUSE if possible.

(10) R.A.P. is on 5th duckboard track near PHEASANT TRENCH. There are also dressing stations at RUDOLPH FM & MINTY FM. and relay posts of R.A.M.C. bearers at NORFOLK HOUSE & PHEASANT FM. The MO will proceed to his R.A.P. from KEMPTON PARK at 1.30 pm.

(11) Disposition maps will be sent in to Bn H.Q at the earliest possible moment.

(12) Relief complete will be reported going in & coming out by key word "BUNKERED" followed by letter of company e.g. "BUNKERED" "D".

(13) On relief the Bn. will proceed to CANAL BANK. Platoons will move off under orders of their Company Commanders without further orders when they have been correctly relieved.

(14) One patrol at least will be sent out by each front line company on night of 11th/12th and 12/13 according to orders already issued. Any gain of ground is to be immediately reported to Bn. H.Q. Important posts that may be found empty & which have been indicated to Company Commanders

will be immediately occupied by one platoon reinforced if necessary by an extra Lewis Gun without awaiting orders from Bn. H.Q.

(15) <u>Sanitation.</u> Proper attention must be paid to this. Burial parties to be sent out from front & support companies when necessary each night.

(16) <u>Trench Stores</u> including those taken in will be handed over to relieving battalion & receipts taken or forwd. Empty petrol tins will be taken out but full ones left as trench stores. S.A.A. & G. [illegible] taken over will be handed over as trench stores but those taken in by companies will be brought out.

(17) Patrol reports must be made out according to specimen & all information given clearly & concisely.

(18) Company OP's are to be established at TRAPPIS MEBUS, MEUNIER HOUSE in proximity & at K.11.C.3.5. of NOBLE'S FM. & at any other place that is eminently suitable. Positive information regarding any retrograde movement of the enemy is to be immediately reported. Negative reports under the heading "Nothing observed" & routine reports

from these O.P's are to be furnished to H.Q by 7 a.m & 7 p.m daily.

(19) Identification of enemy between SPRIET ROAD & LIKKERBOTERBEEK particularly important.

(20) These instructions are not to be taken forward of Company H.Q

(21) Acknowledge.

(signed) C.R. Brown
Lt Col.

9/11/17. UNBUILT

Copies to

No 1. UNCLE
2. "A" Coy.
3. "B" "
4. "C" "
5. "D" "
6. UNCORK
7. FILE

Relief of 2/6th by 2/5th Bn in the line

Order No 4   Copy No 8

UNBOLT   SECRET

appendix 4

1) Relief The Battn will be relieved by UNDER on night 12/13th

2) Guides will be provided by Company Commanders as under.
One for each post handed over to them by UNCORK & one for their Company H.Q.
Guides provided by D Co & the left two platoons of A Co will report to 2/Lt [illegible] ALLDEN on the 12th inst at 4.30 p.m. at Battn H.Q.
Guides provided by C & B Coys & the rt. two platoons of A Co will report to 2/Lt D VICK at 4.30 p.m. at GLOSTER FARM
Each guide besides knowing the way to his post must be

will point out readily the exact location of the post & the number of the platoon of UNBOLT by which it is at present occupied.

3) Companies of UNBOLT will be relieved by companies of UNDER as follows

D Co UNBOLT by B Co UNDER
C " " A "
B " " C "
A " " D "

4) Commanders of Posts etc will communicate all particulars of importance concerning the movements of the enemy to the officer or N.C.O. in command of the incoming unit

5) Stores. Officers i/c units of UNBOLT will hand over to officers

the units of UNDER all trench stores except Very ~~by~~ pistols & all drums of Lewis Gun ammunition in serviceable condition whether brought into the line by them or not, but will bring out a number of serviceable magazines equal to the number brought in by them.

Receipts will be obtained for everything handed over

6) Reports. O.C. Companies will report relief complete to Battn H.Q. by lamp, power buzzer, or runner by sending the name of their company & the code word "BUNKERED

O.C. A & D Co will also report personally.

7) Withdrawal. Platoons immediately they are relieved will move

off to [illegible] & Bdge [illegible]
by the following route
2 Platoons of D Co & the two
left platoons of A Co by the
NORTHERN [illegible]
[illegible] PLEASANT
FARM & AT HSE CAVE
TRENCH & ~~[struck]~~ BOUNDRY
ROAD where the duckboard
track ends then to the left
along the road & [illegible]
[illegible] to [illegible] (ZOUAVE
FM) & so to Bdge 4
Bn HQ & two rt platoons
of A via SOUTHERN track
to KEMPTON PK & thence by
rd to BDGE 4

8) Reports On arrival at Bdge 4
Company Commanders will
report their companies [illegible]
& give details of any casualties

– Move from Canal Bank to BRAKE CAMP

Secret — Order No. 3 — Copy No. 10

2/6 Bn London Regt — 13/7/17

APPENDIX 6

1 The Bn will move from CANAL BANK to BRAKE CAMP by march route.

2. STARTING POINT Bridge 4.

3. ORDER OF MARCH Bn. will move in the following order

B Coy
C "
D "
A "

200 yds will be maintained between Coys
100 yds between platoons

4 Leading Platoon will pass the starting point at 10 30 am.

Marching out state will be handed to the Adjutant

5. ROUTE BRIELEN – VLAMERTINGHE, thence via sleeper track to BRAKE CAMP

6. HALTS will be observed at the usual clock hours

7. DRESS – Full marching order with greatcoats in packs

8. RATIONS – Unexpended portion of the days rations will be carried

9. ADVANCE PARTY detailed as under, will parade under the L. ALDEN at Bridge 4 at 8 30 am.

4 C.Q.M.S

1 one NCO or senior Rifleman from each Coy

L/C Rogers from Bn Headquarters

Cont

2

10 Blankets will be rolled in complete bundles of 10 & stacked in [illegible] by 9 am. For this purpose R.A.P. Coy & C.C. Coys will work together.

11 Officers' kits will be packed in their quarters ready for removal by 9 am

12 Mess boxes will be stacked in D. Coy lines at 9 am

13 All buildings will be left in a clean sanitary condition & the usual certificate will be obtained from the Camp Commandant by the Orderly Officer

14 Loading parties will be detailed by the Sergeant Major & will work under the direction of the Orderly Officer

15 Company Commanders will report the amount of their company supplies [illegible] to stores

16 DETAILS. Personnel of Details Camp will move so as to be in position at BRAKE CAMP by 1 pm and personnel who have rejoined Coys from Details Camp. R.E. Details will send a runner to report to [illegible] at BRAKE CAMP at 10 am. Company will hand in Parade State showing numbers from each Coy & from Headquarters who will require accommodation.

(Sd) J A H IDRIS
Lieut
Actg Adjutant
[illegible]

17 ACKNOWLEDGE

1. C.O.
2. OC A Coy
3. OC B Coy
4. OC C Coy
5. OC D Coy
6. [illegible]
7. R. Details Camp
8. [illegible]
9. QM & TO
10. [illegible]
11. [illegible]
12. File
13. Orderly Officer

9) Feet of all men will be rubbed & oiled under the supervision of company officers before they retire to rest

10) Lt J. VICK & 2/Lt L. ALLDEN are responsible for a seen thing the guides at NORFOLK Ho. & GLOSTER FARM respectively & will ensure that guides are correctly told off for their several posts & handed over to the platoons & sections of UNDER detailed for these posts

11) Acknowledge

19/11/17

[illegible]
[illegible]

Copy No 1 to A Co. Copy No 5 to UNDER
" " 2 " B " 6 " 2/Lt VICK
" " 3 " C " 7 " 2/Lt ALLDEN
4 " D " 8 File

MOVE FROM BRAKE CAMP TO PETTWORTH CAMP., PROVEN

Reference [illegible]
Map Sheets [illegible]
27.A.SE.

ORDER NO. [illegible]
2/4th Bn. The London Regt.

14/11/17.

APPENDIX 7

Orderly Officer.......2/Lieut. [illegible].
Breakfast 7 a.m.
Sick Parade 7.45 a.m.

1. The Battalion will move to [illegible] CAMP, PROVEN Area tomorrow the 15th inst.

2. STARTING POINT will be junction of MILITARY Road and [illegible] Road in [illegible].

3. ORDER OF MARCH will be
   [illegible] Coy.
   [illegible] Coy.
   [illegible] Coy.
   [illegible] Coy.

   The Bn. will march by Companies at 100 yards distance. The leading Company will maintain a distance of [illegible] yards in rear of the preceding Bn. (2/2nd Bn. London Regt.)
   Particular attention will paid to march discipline.

4. The leading Company will pass the starting point at 10.11am.

5. ROUTE. MILITARY Road to [illegible] CORNER ([illegible]) - [illegible] (Sheet 27) to No. 2 Area PROVEN.

6. HALTS will be observed at the usual clock hours without further orders.
   The Band will march off with the leading Company and fall back in front of next Company in rear at each halt.
   Bn. Headquarters will march in rear of Battalion.

7. DRESS. Full marching order, greatcoats in packs.

8. ADVANCE PARTY of the 4 Coy. Quartermaster Sergeants, one N.C.O. detailed by O.i/c [illegible] Details, and 1 N.C.O. and 12 men to be detailed by O.C. A. Coy. will parade under 2/Lieut. [illegible] on the road outside Bn. Headquarters at 7 a.m. and will proceed by the first lorry to act as Advance party and unloading party.

9. REAR PARTY of 1 N.C.O. and 10 men to be detailed by O.C. B. Coy. will remain behind to clean up the camp. A certificate will be obtained from the Camp Adjutant that the camp has been left in a clean and tidy condition. The Orderly Officer will remain in charge of this party. It will report at Quartermaster's Stores at 7 a.m. to load limbers. O.C. B. Coy. will detail a relief for this party between the hours of 8 a.m. and 8.45 a.m. to enable them to obtain breakfast.

10. LEWIS GUNS. Lewis Guns, magazines etc., will be loaded on the limbers at 8 a.m. outside Quartermaster's Stores. 4 Lewis Gunners per Company will report to L/Cpl. Hurley there at [illegible] a.m. for this purpose.

11. TRANSPORT will move with unit, 200 yards in rear of column. Cookers will move with Transport. Dinners will be cooked on the way and served on arrival.

12. BLANKETS will be tightly rolled in complete bundles of 10, tied in at least two places and labelled. This must be done under strict supervision, so that as little as possible Transport may be required for same. They will be stacked by 7 a.m. in a hut which will be detailed to Coy. Orderly Sergeants by the Regtl. Sergeant Major.

13. [illegible], [illegible] and ORDERLY ROOM [illegible] will be ready in quarters at 8 a.m.

(sd.) [illegible], Lieut.
Acting Adjutant.
2/4th Bn. The London Regt.

Copies issued:-
See over.

16th Bn. The London Regt.

Orderly Officer's Report

.... 1917.

My tour of duty commenced at

During my tour of duty:

I attended all parades in [illegible]

I visited the [illegible], everything was correct with the exception that

I inspected the [illegible] at everything was clean, with the exception

I made a tour of the camp at and inspected Stores, Latrines, Cantins, incinerators, [illegible], Ablution places, & Drainage, & found everything clean & in order with the exception that

A fire bucket full of clean water was in each building.

I was present at Guard mounting at

I turned out the guard by day at

by night at

I inspected the prisoners & [illegible] them [illegible] they made no complaint

I found the sentries alert & acquainted with their duties.

I inspected the Fire Piquet at and found all in order.

I was present at Staff parade at the Battalion was reported present with the exception of

I saw that all lights were out at with the exception of

Nothing unusual occurred during my tour of duty with the exception that

No. Sergt. Bn. Orderly Sergeant

No. Cpl. Bn. Orderly Corporal

carried out their duties to my satisfaction.

SECRET. Move from PETTWORTH CAMP to HERZEELE AREA. Copy No......

MOVEMENT ORDER NO. 31

Reference Map Sheet HAZEBROUCK 5A 1/100000

2/8th BN. THE LONDON REGIMENT.

13/11/17.

APPENDIX 8

1. The Battalion will move to the HERZEELE Area tomorrow and take over from the 20th Lancs. Fusiliers.

2. STARTING POINT will be the entrance to the camp.

3. ORDER OF MARCH will be

D, Coy.
A. Coy.
B. Coy.
C, Coy.

100 yards between Companies.

All Headquarters personnel will parade and march in rear of C. Coy.

4. The leading Company will pass the starting point at a time to be notified later.

5. ROUTE. PROVEN, thence by train to HERZEELE, thence to destination.

6. DRESS. Full marching order, overcoats in packs,

7. BLANKETS. One blanket per man will be rolled on pack.
One blanket per man will be tightly rolled in Complete bundles of ten, labelled and stacked at Camp at 8-30 a.m.

8. LOADING PARTY of 1 N.C.O. and 20 men will be detailed by O.C. C. Coy. These will report to the Quartermaster at the Camp entrance at 6 a.m. They will be relieved by a party to be detailed by O.C. C. Coy. between the hours of 7 a.m. and 7-45 a.m. so that they may obtain breakfast.

9. UNLOADING PARTY of 1 N.C.O. and 10 men will proceed to destination by the first available lorry at 6 a.m. Breakfast for this party will be at 5-45 a.m. They will be detailed by O.C. D. Coy.

10, ADVANCE PARTY of the 4 Company Quartermaster Sergeants, 1 N.C.O. from Bn. Headquarters, 1 N.C.O. from Transport Section have proceeded to destination to day.

11. LEWIS GUNS. All Lewis Guns, magazines etc, will be loaded on limbers at 8 a.m. 4 Lewis Gunners per Company will report to Lieut. J.H.W. Idris at that hour for this purpose.

12. MESS BOXES, ORDERLY ROOM BOXES etc. will be stacked at the entrance to the camp by 8-30 a.m. (Officers will carry a haversack ration).

13. OFFICERS KITS will be ready stacked at the entrance of the camp by 8-30 a.m. These must be well packed and be at the place appointed punctually.

13a 14. CAMP will be left clean and tidy and all rubbish burnt. Company Commanders will render a certficate to this effect to Bn. Headquarters by 12 m. The Orderly Officer will obtain a certificate from the Area Commandant that the camp has been left in a satisfactory condition and will hand same to Bn. Headquarters on arrival at destination.

14 15. TRANSPORT OFFICER & QUARTERMASTER have received detailed instructions.

16 ACKNOWLEDGE.

(sd) R. Wylie,
Lieut.
Acting Adjutant,
2/8th Bn. The London Regt.

(Copies issued - see over)

14. ~~O.C. Coy. will detail one Corporal and three men to act as guard and loading party at Quartermasters Stores to-morrow. Dress and rations as above. This guard will report to the Quartermaster at 7 a.m. The N.C.O. in charge will detail one man to report at School, [illegible] at 7 a.m. on the morning of the 28th inst. in order to guide 2 motor lorries detailed for this unit to the Quartermasters Stores. When these have been loaded the guard will proceed on lorries and rejoin Unit.~~ Delete

15. Billets, Tents and Huts etc. are to be left absolutely clean. O.C. Coys. will report to the Bn. Orderly Room by 8 a.m. that this has been done. 2/Lieut. Fox will obtain certificate from Area Commandant that the Camp has been left clean, which certificate must reach this office by 9 a.m.

16. Officers should personally carry necessary utensils for messing as no mess-boxes will accompany the Battalion.

17. Further Orders will be issued later.

18. <u>ACKNOWLEDGE</u>.

(sd) R Boyle

Lieut.
Acting Adjutant,
2/[illegible]th Bn. The London Regt.

Copies issued to:-
1. Commanding Officer.
2. O.C. A. Coy.
3. O.C. B. Coy.
4. O.C. C. Coy.
5. O.C. D. Coy.
6. O.i/c H.Q. Details.
7. Quartermaster & Transport Officer.
8. 174 Infantry Brigade.
9/10. War Diary.
11. File.

SECRET. **MOVE from PROVEN to COULEMRY** 10

7th Bn. London Regt. 25.11.17.

APPENDIX 10

1. The Bn. will entrain at [illegible] at 12 noon for WIZERNES.

2. Reveille 6am. Breakfast 7am.

3. Companies will move to the Station in the following order:-

   H.Q. Coy
   A
   B
   C
   [illegible]

   Platoons at 100 yds. distance.

4. Starting Point will be the Entrance to the Camp. Leading Platoon will pass the starting point at 10.25 am.

5. Dress - Full marching order with one blanket rolled on top of valise.

6. Men will carry the unexpended portion of the day's rations.

7. The usual entraining states will be rendered by 9.30 am.

8. All water bottles must be filled, and [illegible] will be used to carry water for this purpose to the camp. As soon as they have been emptied, they must be stacked ready at the Camp Entrance to load on lorry on arrival. Arrangements have

already been made to provide carrying party to fill these sacks. The Sgt. Cook must see that as much dry wood as possible is also stacked on the lorry.

9. The Camp is to be left clean & tidy & all rubbish burned.

10. OC Companies & OC HQ Details will render a certificate to this Office by 9am that this has been carried out.

11. O/c ORDRS will obtain certificate from Camp Commandant to the effect that billets have been left clean & tidy.

12. ACKNOWLEDGE.

R[illegible]
Lt & A/Adjt.

Copies issued to:-
1. Commanding Officer
2. 2nd in Command.
3. OC A Coy
4. " B
5. " C
6. " D
7. " HQ Details.
8. Quartermaster.
9. 17th Infantry Bde.
10. } War Diary.
11. }
12. File.

MOVE from COULEMBY to QUESQUE

SECRET Order No. 34 Copy No. 11

7/4th [illegible] London Regt. 26/11/17

Ref:- HAZEBROUCK 5a.

APPENDIX 11

1. Reveille 7 am.
Rations to be drawn from QM 7.30 am
Breakfast 8.0 am

2. The Bn. will move tomorrow from COULOMBY to QUESQUE.

3. Companies will be formed up facing South in the following order:-
A Coy
B Coy
C Coy
D Coy
HQ

The right of A Coy will be in line with Bn. Orderly Room.

4. Dress - Full Marching Order.

5. Route - will be via VERNAL.

6. Blankets will be tightly rolled in bundles of 10, labelled and stored in the shed behind B Company's cookers by 9.30 am. Officers Kits

and Mess Boxes will be stored in the same place at the same time.

6. OC Companies + OC HQ Details will detail a fatigue party to draw rations from the QM Stores at 7.30 am.

7. The usual Marching Out States will be rendered by 8am sharp.

8. OC A Coy will detail 1 NCO + 8 Rfn to act as guard on the stores behind B Company's cooker from 8.30am onwards. This party will also act as loading party and when the stores have been cleared will accompany the Transport to QUESQUE.

9. Orders to Transport Officer have been issued seperately.

10. ACKNOWLEDGE.

1. CO
2. 2nd in Command
3. A Coy
4. B "
5. C "
6. D "
7. HQ Details
8. Brigade
9. Transport Officer
10 } War Diary
11 }

[signature]
Lt + A/Adjt
[illegible]/11/17

Instructions regarding War Diaries and Intelligence Summaries are contained in F. S. Regs., Part II. and the Staff Manual respectively. Title pages will be prepared in manuscript.

WAR DIARY
~~or~~
INTELLIGENCE ~~SUMMARY.~~
(*Erase heading not required.*)

2/6 London Regt

Vol 12

Army Form C. 2118.

Place	Date	Hour	Summary of Events and Information	Remarks and references to Appendices
QUESQUES.	1 Dec. 17	–	Lt Col BENSON returned from 18th CORPS course and assumed command.	RLS
	7		Training and refitting.	RLS
SENNINGHEM	7		Battn moved by march route to SENNINGHEM and APPRINGUES	Appendix I RLS
DIRTY BUCKET	8		Battn moved to DIRTY BUCKET CAMP by march route to WIZERNES thence by	Appendix II
CAMP	to		train to ELVERDINGHE, and thence by march route to DIRTY BUCKET CAMP	RLS
	11		Refitting in camp.	
TURCO HUTS	11		Battn moved to TURCO HUTS (HQ. A + B Coys) C+D Coys to HULLS FARM	Appendix III
	~~12~~		for work under 183rd TUNNELLING COY. Transport and QM Stores remained	RLS
	~~12~~ to		at DIRTY BUCKET CAMP.	
	13		Supplied working parties	RLS
	13		Camp shelled. Casualties 2nd Lt ALLDEN wounded at duty. 1 O.R. Killed 2 O.R.	RLS
	to		wounded (1 died of wounds following day)	
	16. to		Supplied working parties. Casualties 2 O.R. Killed (18th 40 O.R. from B Coy attached to 183rd Tun. Coy)	RLS
	20		QM STORES moved to RED CHATEAU (ELVERDINGHE) under Brigade arrangements	RLS
	21.		Supplied working parties. TRANSPORT moved to BRIDGE CAMP under Brigade arrangements	RLS
	22.		Supplied working parties. Casualty 1 O.R. wounded	RLS

T2134. Wt. W708–776. 500000. 4/15. Sir J. C. & S.

Instructions regarding War Diaries and Intelligence Summaries are contained in F. S. Regs., Part II. and the Staff Manual respectively. Title pages will be prepared in manuscript.

WAR DIARY
or
INTELLIGENCE SUMMARY.
(*Erase heading not required.*)

Army Form C. 2118.

Place	Date	Hour	Summary of Events and Information	Remarks and references to Appendices
TURCO HUTS	Dec 23 to 26		Supplied working parties	RLS
	27.		Supplied working parties. 1 Officer 33 O.R. of B COY attached to 183rd TUNNELLING COY.	RLS
	28.		Supplied working parties. Lt COL BENSON proceeded on course to BERTANGLES.	
	to		Major BROWNE assumed command.	RLS
	30		Supplied working parties	RLS
	31.		Supplied one working party. 25 O.R of A Coy proceeded to HULLS FARM (attached to 183rd TUNNELLING COY.	

[signature]

6th BATTN. CITY OF LONDON RIFLES.

MOVE from DIRTY BUCKET CAMP to TURCO [illegible] and HULLS FARM.

[illegible]

Reference [illegible]

Map Sheet [illegible]

[illegible]

A 3.

1\. The Bn. will move today as follows:-
Headquarters)
A. Coy.) to [illegible]
B. Coy.)

C. Coy.) except officers as detailed below,
D. Coy.) to BULL'S FARM.

2\. [illegible] Headquarters
A. Coy.
B. Coy.
C. & D. Coys. will proceed under Capt. [illegible] to BULL'S FARM.
Sapping [illegible] will parade as a [illegible] with Headquarters

3\. STARTING POINT. Entrance to camp. First platoon of Headquarters will pass the S.P. at 1-15 p.m.
The leading platoon of C.Coy. will pass the Starting Point 1/4 hour after the last platoon of B. Coy. has passed.
200 yards distance between platoons and Coys. will be maintained.

4\. [illegible] No special route is laid down.

5\. DRESS. Full marching order. Steel helmets to be worn.

6\. [illegible] will be ready at 12-45 p.m.

7\. [illegible] will be distributed amongst Coys. on arrival, under instructions of the [illegible] Officer.

8\. The following officers will proceed with C. & D. Coys:-
Capt. [illegible]
Lieut. [illegible]
2/Lieut. [illegible]
2/Lieut. [illegible]
This party will report to [illegible] Tunnelling Coy. at [illegible]
The remaining officers of C. Coy. will be attached to A. Coy. and those of D. Coy. to B. Coy.

9\. All other instructions have been issued separately.

10\. The camp will be left clean and tidy, and certificates will be rendered by O.C. Coys. by 12-30 p.m. that this has been done.

11\. ACKNOWLEDGE.

[signature]
Lieut.
Acting Adjutant.
[illegible] Bn. The London Regt.

Copies issued to:-
1. Commanding Officer.
2. O.C. A. Coy.
3. O.C. B. Coy.
4. O.C. C. Coy.
5. O.C. D. Coy.
6. O.i/c Headquarter Details.
7. [illegible] Inf. Bde.
8. Quartermaster & Transport Officer.
9/10. War Diary and File.

APPENDIX I

Reference
Map Sheet
CALAIS 13
HAZEBROUCK 5A
(1/100000)

ORDER NO. 3[illegible]
2/8th BN. THE LONDON REGT.

Copy No.....
6/12/17.

Move from QUEQUES to SENNINGHEM and AFFRINGUES

1. The Bn. will move tomorrow, the 7th inst. to SENINGHEM and AFFRINGUES.

2. ORDER OF MARCH

B. Coy.
C. COY.
D. Coy.
A. Coy.
Headquarters.

Portion of Transport going by rail will follow Headquarters.

BAND. The Band will march in front of B. Coy., falling back one Coy. at each halt.

3. PARADE.

The Bn. will be formed up with the right of B. Coy. at the first road-junction S.E. of QUESQUES, i-e. under first S. in QUESQUES, by 9-20 am. Markers report to RSM. at 9-40am.

4. DRESS.

Full marching order; one blanket per man to be carried. Steel helmets to be worn. Unexpended portion of the day's dry rations will be carried.

5. ROUTE. via COULOMBY.

6. BLANKETS.

One blanket per man of Coys. etc., billetted in QUESQUES will be rolled tightly in bundles of 10, labelled and stacked at Quartermaster's Stores by 7 a.m.

For those Coys. etc., ~~billetted~~ in LE VERVAL, outside Officers' Mess at gate by mainroad by 7-15 a.m. (C & D Coys. Officers' Mess).

Blankets badly rolled will be brought to the notice of the Commanding Officer.

7. COY. STORES & BOXES are to be ready at same times and places as blankets.

8. OFFICERS' KITS.

(a) QUESQUES. Stacked outside H.Q. Mess by 8 a.m.
(b) LE VERVAL. Outside C. Coy. Officers' Mess by 8-20 a.m.

9. BN. ORDERLY ROOM BOXES & MEDICAL STORES.

A limber will report to the Bn. Orderly Room at 7 a.m. to collect boxes and will then proceed to R.A.P. for medical stores.

10. OFFICERS' MESS BOXES will be collected by the Mess Cart. These are to be ready by 8-30 a.m.

Officers' Kits and Mess Boxes etc. are accompanying the Bn.

11. LOADING PARTIES. O.C. A. Coy. will detail 1 N.C.O. & 8 men to report to the Quartermaster at 7 a.m. to act as loading party for QUESQUES.

O.C. C. Coy. will detail a similar party to be at C.COY. Officers' Mess at 7-15 a.m. to act as loading party for LE VERVAL.

A relief must be provided for both these parties by the same Coys. so that these men may obtain breakfast.

12. RATIONS. Rations for consumption on the 8th will be issued in the new area.

13. BILLETS.etc. will be left clean and tidy. Os.C. Coys. & Oi/c H.Q. Details and N.C.O. i/c Transport Lines will render certificates to this office by 9 a.m. to this effect.

14. ACKNOWLEDGE.

[illegible] Lieut.
Acting Adjutant,
2/8th Bn. The London Regt.

War Diary

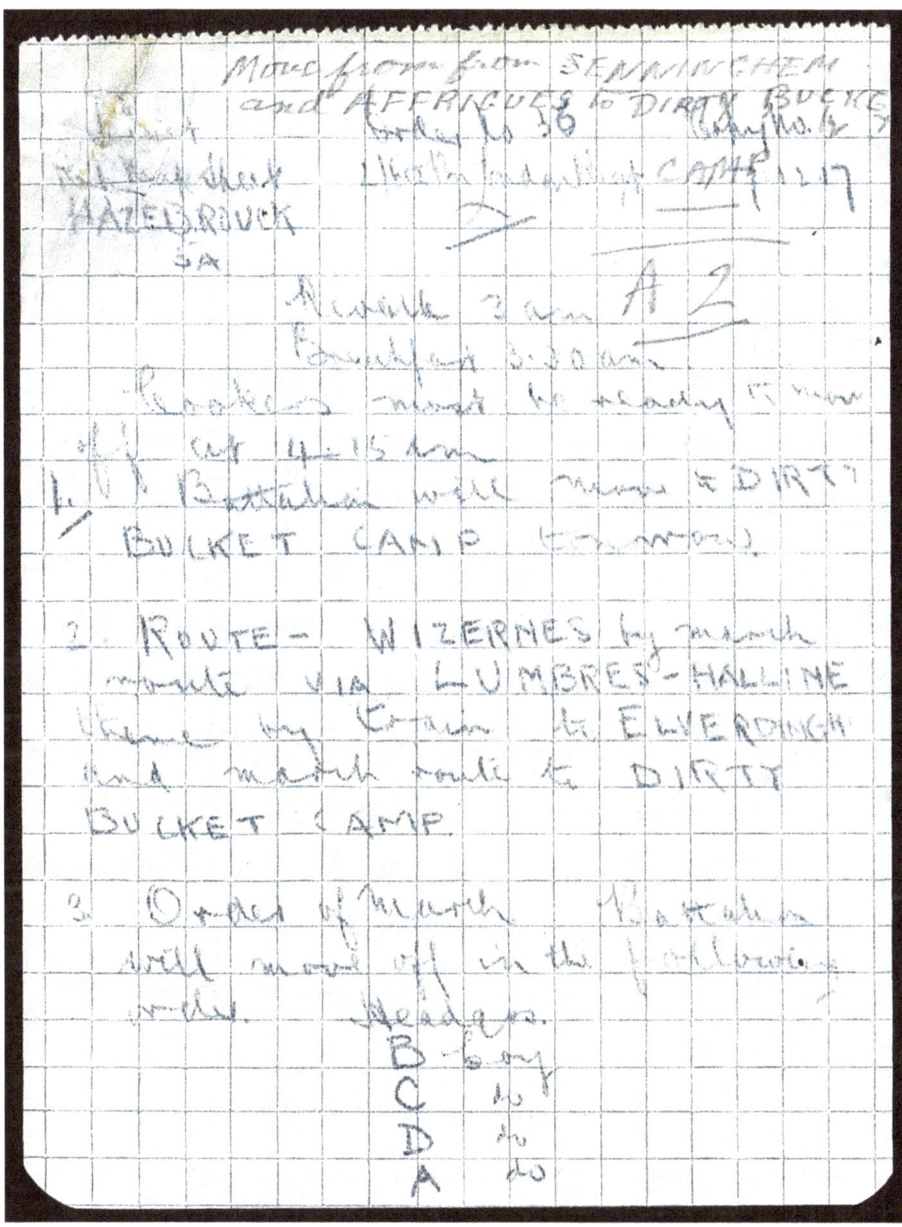

Move from from SENNINGHEM and AFFRINGUES to DIRTY BUCKET

[illegible] Order No. 36 Copy No. [illegible]
[illegible] HAZEBROUCK 5A [illegible] CAMP [illegible] 1.2.17

A 2

Reveille 3 am
Breakfast 3.30 am
Cookers must be ready to move off at 4.15 am

1. The Battalion will move to DIRTY BUCKET CAMP tomorrow.

2. ROUTE – WIZERNES by march route via LUMBRES-HALLINE thence by train to ELVERDINGHE and march route to DIRTY BUCKET CAMP.

3. Order of march Battalion will move off in the following order.

Headqrs.
B Coy
C do
D do
A do

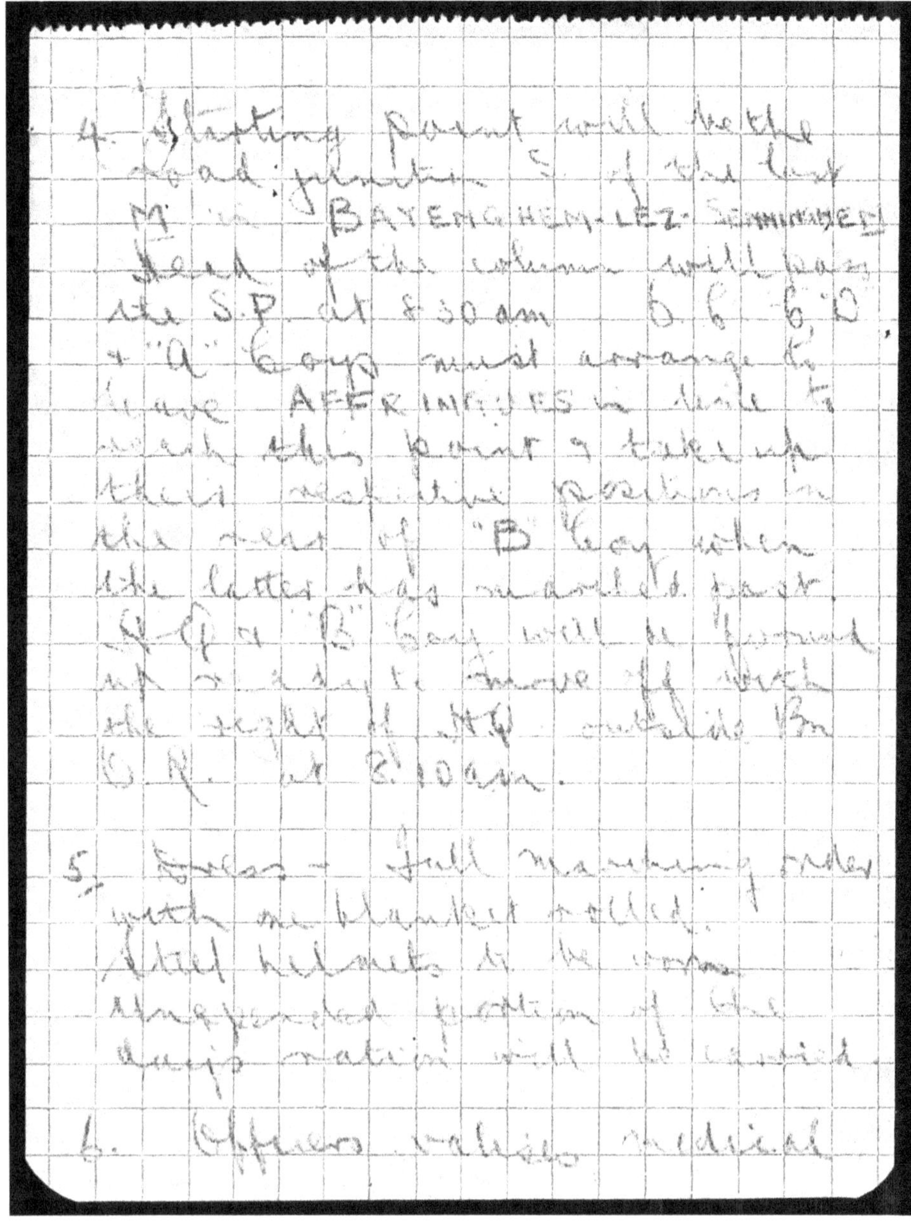

4. Starting point will be the road junction S. of the last M in BAYENGHEM-LEZ-SENINGHEM. Head of the column will pass the S.P. at 8.30 am. "C", "D" & "A" Coys must arrange to leave AFFRINGUES in time to reach this point & take up their respective positions in the rear of "B" Coy when the latter has marched past. H.Q. & "B" Coy will be formed up & ready to move off with the right of H.Q. outside Bn O.R. at 8.10 am.

5. Dress – Full marching order with one blanket rolled. Steel helmets to be worn. Unexpended portion of the day's ration will be carried.

6. Officers valises medical

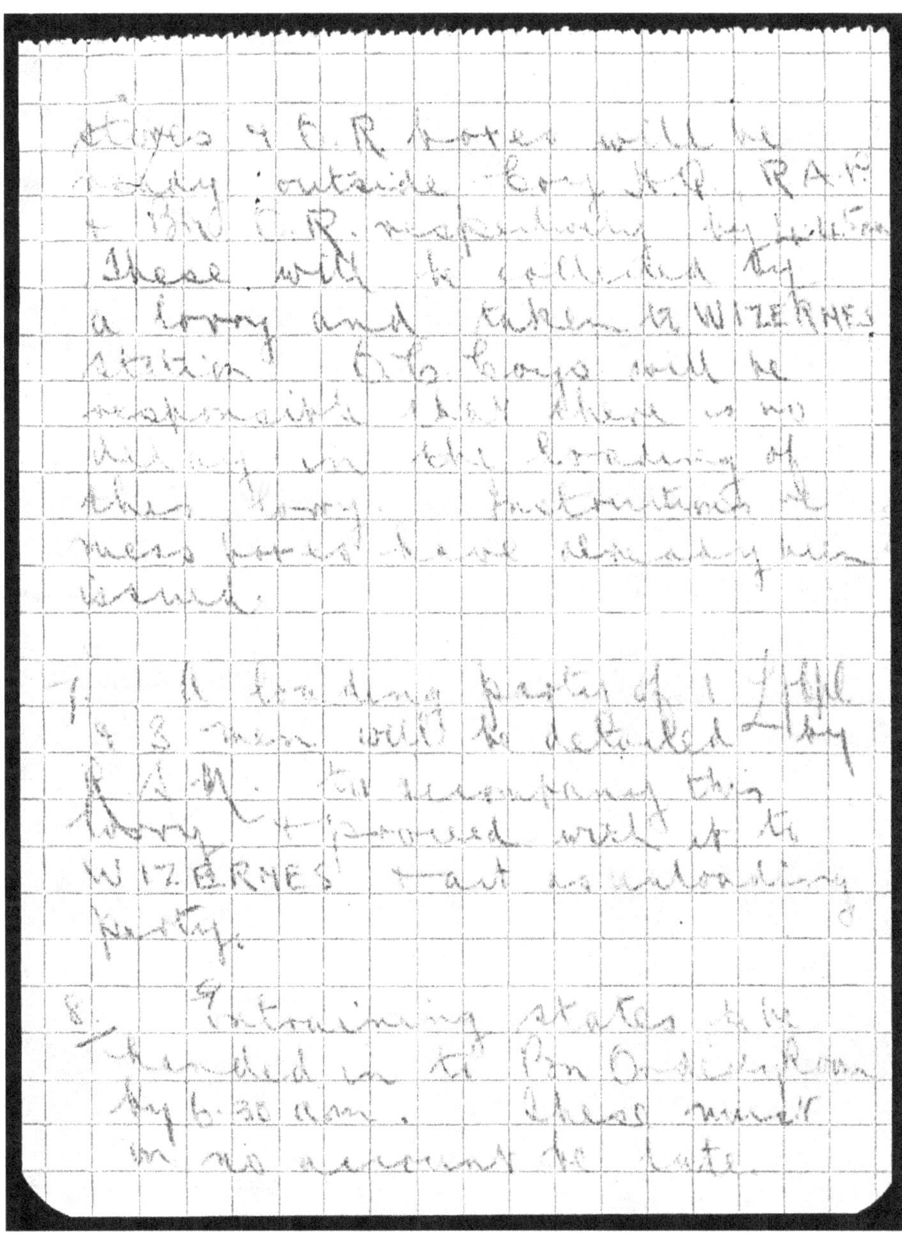

Stores & Q.R. boxes will be ready outside Coy H.Q. RAF & Bn Q.R. respectively by [illegible]. These will be collected by a lorry and taken to WIZERNES station. O.C. Coys will be responsible that there is no delay in the loading of this lorry. Instructions re mess boxes have already been issued.

7. A loading party of 1 L/Cpl & 3 men will be detailed by R.S.M. to accompany this lorry & proceed with it to the WIZERNES & act as unloading party.

8. Retaining states to be handed in to the Bn Orderly Room by 6.30 am. These must on no account be late.

Lieut: D.W. Vick will act as Entraining Officer & will report to Lieut Harrison Jones at WIZERNES Station at 9.45 am. He will collect Entraining States from Bn O.R. before leaving. This officer will wear a white armband while acting as Entraining Officer.

9. Detailed instructions have been issued to N.C.O. for Transport. Officers' chargers will not be available for the march tomorrow.

10. All billets will be left clean and tidy. O.C. Coys etc will render to this office a certificate to the effect that this has been done by 8 am.

11. After detraining the following distances will be observed:-

Between Coys 100 yds
do Bns 500 yds.

All movements E of the ELVERDINGHE-VLAMERTINGHE ROAD will be in file.

12. ACKNOWLEDGE.

(Sd) R Wylie Lieut & Adjt.
2/6 Bn. London Regt.

Instructions regarding War Diaries and Intelligence Summaries are contained in F. S. Regs., Part II. and the Staff Manual respectively. Title pages will be prepared in manuscript.

WAR DIARY
or
INTELLIGENCE SUMMARY.
(Erase heading not required.)

2/6 London Regt
Vol 13

Army Form C. 2118.

Place	Date	Hour	Summary of Events and Information	Remarks and references to Appendices
	1918			
TURCO HUTS	1.1.18 - 3		Supplied working parties.	Rlo
	4th		Lt Col BENSON assumed temporary command of Brigade. Major WHITEHEAD assumed command. Remainder of A Coy attached to 183 TUNNELLING COY at HULLS FARM.	Rlo
	5		Supplied working party	Rlo
	6 to 7		Cleaning up.	Rlo
	8		Battn present at TURCO HUTS moved to ROAD CAMP, PROVEN, by march route to BOESINGHE thence by train to PROVEN, and thence by march to destination. Completion reported 4.30 pm.	Appendix I Rlo
PROVEN AREA	9		cleaning up. Party attached to 183rd TUNNELLING COY rejoined Battn.	Rlo
	10		Cleaning up and refitting. Lt Col BENSON returned and assumed command.	Rlo
	11		Do Do	Rlo
	12		Medal presentation by G O C II CORPS 1 Coy of Battn paraded.	Rlo
	13-15		Training.	Rlo
	16-19		Training	Rlo
DEMUIN	19		Battn moved to DEMUIN by march route to PROVEN thence by train to VILLERS-BRETONNEUX thence by march route to destination. Arrival reported 5.30 am 20th.	Appendix II Rlo
			Lt Col BENSON D.S.O. proceeded on leave Major W.J. WHITEHEAD D.S.O. assumed command	Rlo

T2131. Wt. W708—776. 500000. 4/15. Sir J. C. & S.

Instructions regarding War Diaries and Intelligence Summaries are contained in F. S. Regs., Part II. and the Staff Manual respectively. Title pages will be prepared in manuscript.

WAR DIARY
or
INTELLIGENCE SUMMARY.
(Erase heading not required.)

Army Form C. 2118.

Place	Date	Hour	Summary of Events and Information	Remarks and references to Appendices
DEMUIN	20.1.1918		Cleaning up.	RLW.
	21 to 31.		Training. Strength of Battn on 31st Total Strength 37 Officers 714. O.R. Strength in Camp. 26 Officers 550. O R.	RLW.
			R Wolfe Capt & A/Adjutant.	

T2134. Wt. W708–776. 500000. 4/15. Sir J. C. & S.

APPENDIX 2

SECRET. Copy No. 12
18/1/18.

OPERATION ORDERS NO. 38
by
LIEUT-COLONEL C.B.BENSON,D.S.O.
COMDG 2/6TH BN LONDON REGIMENT.

Ref.:-
Map Sheet 27,
& AMIENS
Sheet 17.

1. The Battalion will move to MORISEL to-morrow 19th inst. by march route to PROVEN, thence by train to VILLERS-BRETONNEUX, thence by march route to MORISEL.

2. Starting Point :- Road opposite Battalion Orderly Room.

3. Route :- By main road to PROVEN.

4. Order of March :- "A", "B", H.Q. Details, "C", "D".
Distance :- 100yds between Companies.
The leading Company will pass the Starting Point at a time to be notified later.

5. Dress :- Full marching order with one blanket rolled on top of pack. Soft caps will be worn and helmets carried on back of pack.

6. Instructions re Officers' kits, Mess boxes, Orderly Room boxes, Spare Blankets etc. have already been detailed.

7. Os. C. Coys and O. i/c H.Q. Details will ensure that enou h string and labels are carried to enable the blankets carried by the men to be rolled in bundles of ten and stacked at Detraining Station if necessary.

8. Os. C. Coys and O. i/c H.Q, Details will render complete Entraining States to this office by 8.30 a.m. These will be collected by Entraining Officer at 9 a.m. Marching Out States will be rendered by 8.30 a.m. Marching In States will be rendered within one hour of arrival at destination.

9. The R.S.O. will detail one guide to report to Brigade Headquarters at 8.15 a.m. to conduct three lorries to Battalion Headquarters to-morrow morning. This guide will proceed in full marching order with lorries, when they are loaded, to PROVEN Station. He will obtain from the lorry drivers signed statement showing the time lorries were unloaded and this will be handed to the Adjutant when the Battalion arrives at the Station.

10. Os. C. Coys and O. i/c H.Q. Details will render a certificate that the Camp has been left clean and tidy to reach the Battalion Orderly Room by 8 a.m. The Orderly Officer will obtain a similar certificate from the Area Commandant to the same effect before leaving Camp.

11. ACKNOWLEDGE.

(Sd) R Wythe
Lieutenant & A/Adjutant,
2/6th Bn The London Regt.

APPENDIX 2

SECRET.

ADDENDA TO
OPERATION ORDERS NO. 36
by
LIEUT-COLONEL C.S.BENSON,D.S.O.
COMDG 2/6TH BN LONDON REGIMENT.

Copy No 12
18/1/18.

3. For para 3 - Route - read "via Transport Lines to PROVEN"

4. The leading Company will pass Starting Point at 9 a.m.

8. Dress :- Jerkins will be worn.

12. Loading Party :- Os.C. "C" and "D" Coys. will each detail 75 other ranks to act as unloading and loading party at PROVEN Station. O.C. "D" Coy will detail two officers and O.C. "C" Coy will detail Captain Lathbury to take charge of the party, which will parade outside Battalion Orderly Room and move off at 7 a.m. This party will report to Brigade Entraining Officer at 9.15 a.m., will unload the lorries and will load baggage on to the train.

13. Unloading Party :- Os.C. "A" and "B" Coys will each detail 1 officer and 50 other ranks to unload train on arrival at destination.

14. ACKNOWLEDGE.

(Sgd) R. [illegible]

Lieutenant & A/Adjutant,
2/6th Bn The London Regt.

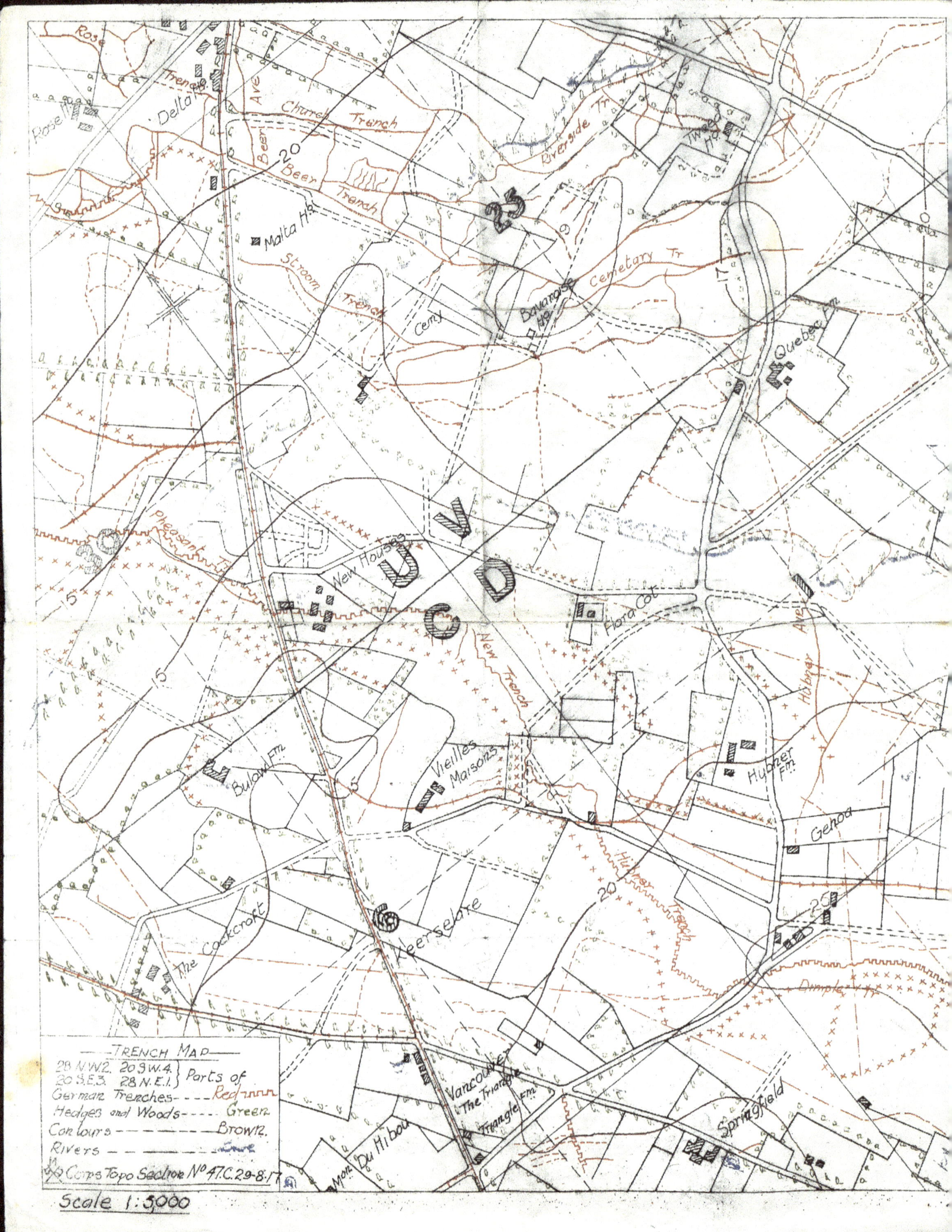

Rose
Trench
Delta
Rose
Beer
Ave
Church Trench
Beer Trench
Riverside Tr
Tweed Ho.
Malta Ho.
Stroom Trench
Cemetery Tr
Bavaroise Ho.
Cemy
Quebec Fm.
Pheasant Tr
New Houses
U
V
D
C
Flora Cot
New Trench
Hubner Ave
Vieilles Maisons
Bulow Fm.
Hubner Fm.
Genoa
Hubner Trench
The Cockcroft
Keerselare
Dimple Tr
Vancouver
The Triangle
Triangle Fm.
Du Hibou
Mon. Du Hibou
Springfield
TRENCH MAP
28 N.W.2. 20 S.W.4.
20 S.E.3. 28 N.E.1.
Parts of
German Trenches---- Red
Hedges and Woods---- Green
Contours ---- Brown.
Rivers ----
Corps Topo Section No 47.C. 29-8-17
Scale 1:5,000

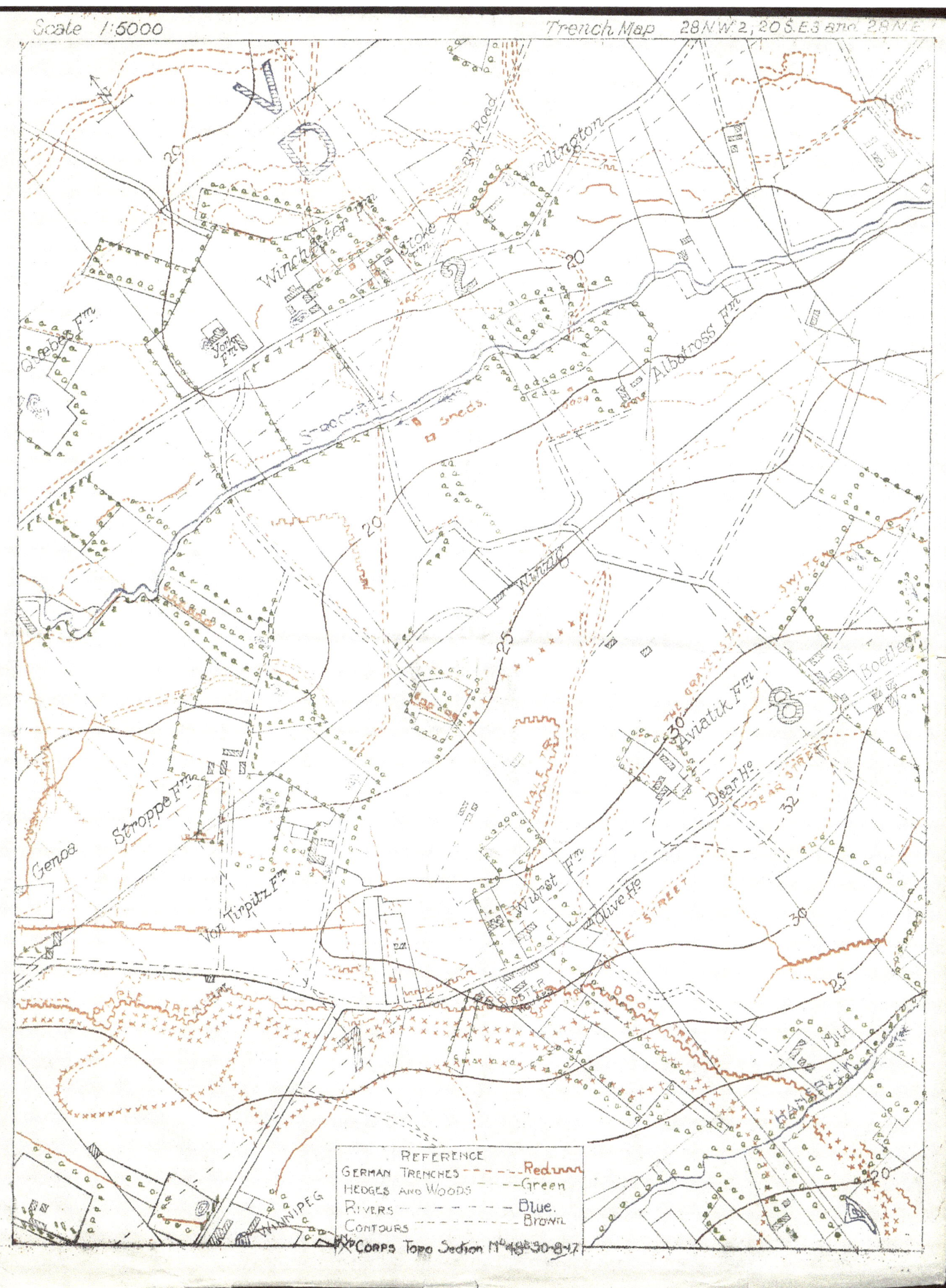
Scale 1:5000
Trench Map 28 N.W. 2, 20 S.E. 3 and 28 N.E.
Winchester Fm
Stoke Fm
Wellington
York Fm
Quebec Fm
Albatross Fm
Sheds
Winnipeg
Stroppe Fm
Genoa
Von Tirpitz Fm
Wurst Fm
Olive Ho
Aviatik Fm
Dear Ho
Boetleer
20
25
30
32
REFERENCE
German Trenches Red
Hedges and Woods Green
Rivers Blue.
Contours Brown
XIX Corps Topo Section No 48 30-8-17

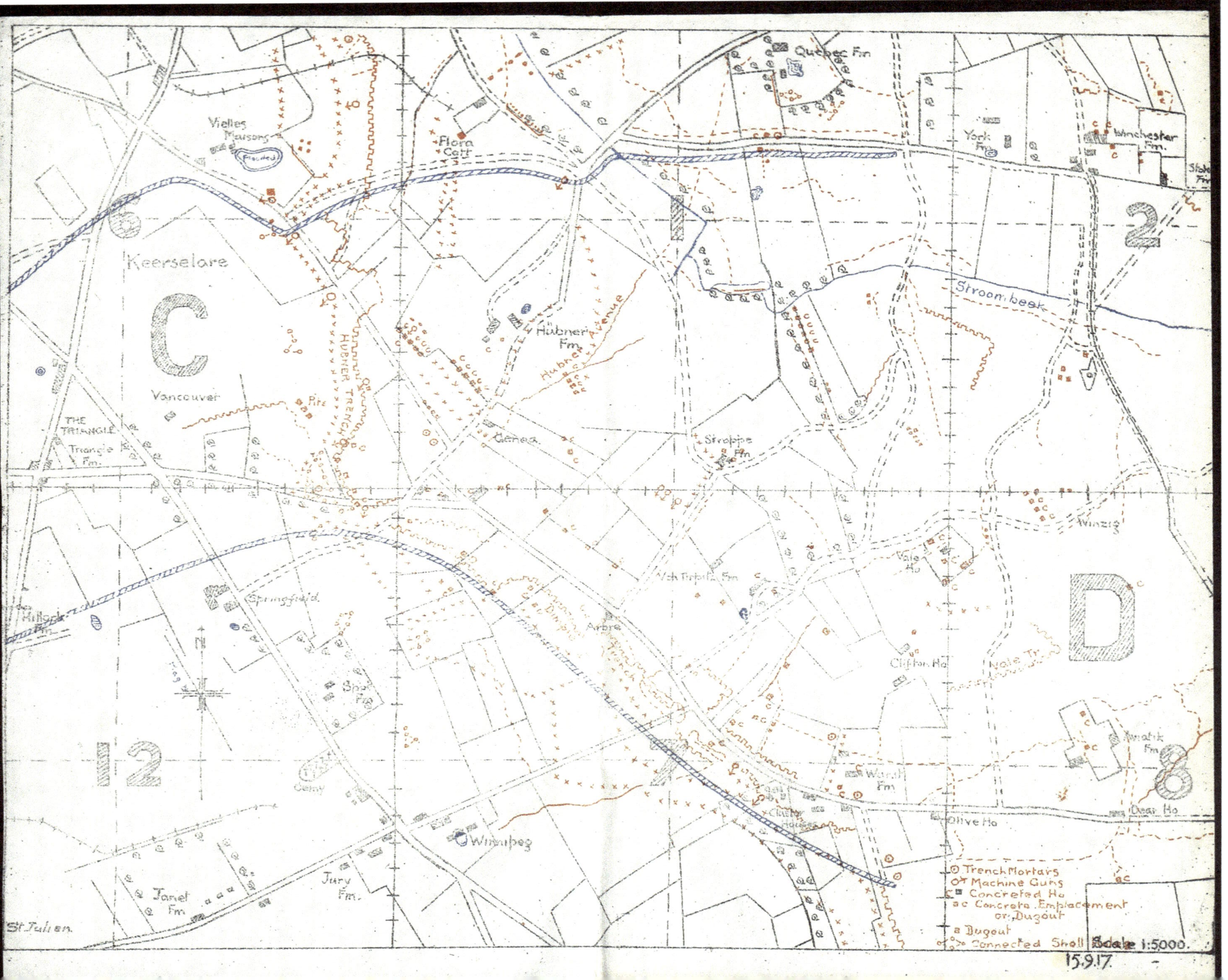
Quebec Fm
Vielles Maisons
Flooded
Flora Cott
York Fm
Winchester Fm
Stroombeek
Keerselare
C
Hubner Fm
Hubner Avenue
Vancouver
Pits
HUBNER TRENCH
THE TRIANGLE
Triangle Fm
Genea
Stroppe Fm
Winzig
Vale Ho
D
Springfield
Hillock Fm
Arbre
Clifton Ho
Vale Tr
Spot Fm
Kronprinz Fm
Wurst Fm
Olive Ho
Dear Ho
Cluster Houses
Winnipeg
Jury Fm
Janet Fm
12
2
8
N
St Julien
Trench Mortars
Machine Guns
Concreted Ho
Concrete Emplacement or Dugout
Dugout
Connected Shell
Scale 1:5000
15.9.17

Chinese House
Laudetbeek
Beek Villas
Lemnos House
Kangaroo Pond
Ferdan House
Huts
Brewery
Poelcappelle
Meunier House
Blue House
Red House
24
19
20
Louis Fm
Eagle House
Huts
Tracas
Retour Cross Roads
Gloster Fm
Double Cotts
White Mill
White Ho.
Rose House
Delta House
Beek Houses
Lekkerboterbeek
Redeemed Huts
Delta Huts
Pheasant Fm.
Malta Ho.
Oxford Houses
Terrier Fm
Dog Houses
Rat Ho
Cat House
Snipe House
Grouse Fm
30
25
26
County X Roads
Tweed Ho.
Bavaroise Ho.
Burns Ho
Cemy.
APPROX. LANGEMARCK - BRITISH - GHELUVELT LINE
U
V
New Houses
Cemetery
Haanixbeek Fm
Bulow
The Cockcroft
Vieilles Maisons
C
D
Winchester Fm.
Stoke Fm
Wellington
York Fm.
6
2
Keerselare
Stroombeek
Hubner Fm.
Mon du Hibou
The Triangle
Triangle Fm
Vancouver
Genoa
Stroppe Fm.
Albatross Fm.
PROTECTIVE BARRAGE
STANDING BARRAGE
Winzig
Hillock Fm.
Springfield
Vn. Bripitz Fm.
Spot Fm. POST
Clifton Ho.
Hugel Halles
Hugel Hollow
Gravenstafel Switch
12
Cemetery
Aviatik Fm.
8
Wurst Fm.
Dear Ho.
Boetleer
Olive Ho.
Hill 32
Dear Street
Dump
Winnipeg
Janet Fm
Jury Fm
St Julien
Jew Hill
Hanebeek
13.9.17
FRONT LINE
Schuler Fm
Nile
Hanebeek
Border Ho.
Riverside
Deuce House
Green Ho.
Fort Hill
Road House
Toronto
Corner Cot.
Canvas Hill
Can Fm
Fortuin
Cross Cotts.
Can Pond
Wine Pond
Pond Fm
Hindu Cott.
Kansas Ho.
Kansas Cross
Fokker Fm
18
13
14

Chinese House
Laudetbeek
Lemnos House
Kangaroo Pond
Ferdan House
Beek Villas
Huts
Brewery
Poelcappelle
Meunier House
Blue House
Red House
24
19
20
Louis Fm
Eagle House
Huts
Tracas
Retour Cross Roads
Gloster Fm
Double Cotts
White Mill
White Ho.
Rose House
Delta House
Beek Houses
Lekkerboterbeek
Redeemed Huts
Delta Huts
Pheasant Fm
Malta Ho
Oxford Houses
Terrier Fm
Dog Houses
Rat Ho.
30
25
County X Roads
26
Cat House
Snipe House
Grouse Fm
Bavaroise Ho.
Tweed Ho
Burns Ho
New Houses
Bulow Fm
Cemetery
Haanixbeek Fm
Quebec Fm.
The Cockcroft
Vieilles Maisons
York Fm.
Winchester Fm.
Stoke Fm
Wellington
6
Keerselare
2
Mon du Hibou
The Triangle
Triangle Fm
Vancouver
Albatross Fm.
BARRAGE
Winzig
Hillock Fm
Springfield
Spot Fm
POST
Clifton Ho
Hugel Halles
Hugel Hollow
12
Cemetery
Wurst Fm.
Olive Ho
Dear Ho.
Hill 32
8
Boetleer
Dump
Winnipeg
Janet Fm
Jury Fm
St Julien
Jew Hill
Hanebeek
Nile
Schuler Fm
Border Ho.
Green Ho
Riverside
Deuce House
Corner Cot.
Fort Hill
Canvas Hill
Cross Cotts
Road House
Toronto
Fortuin
Can Pond
Wine Pond
Hindu Cott
Kansas Ho.
Kansas Cross
Fokker Fm
13
14

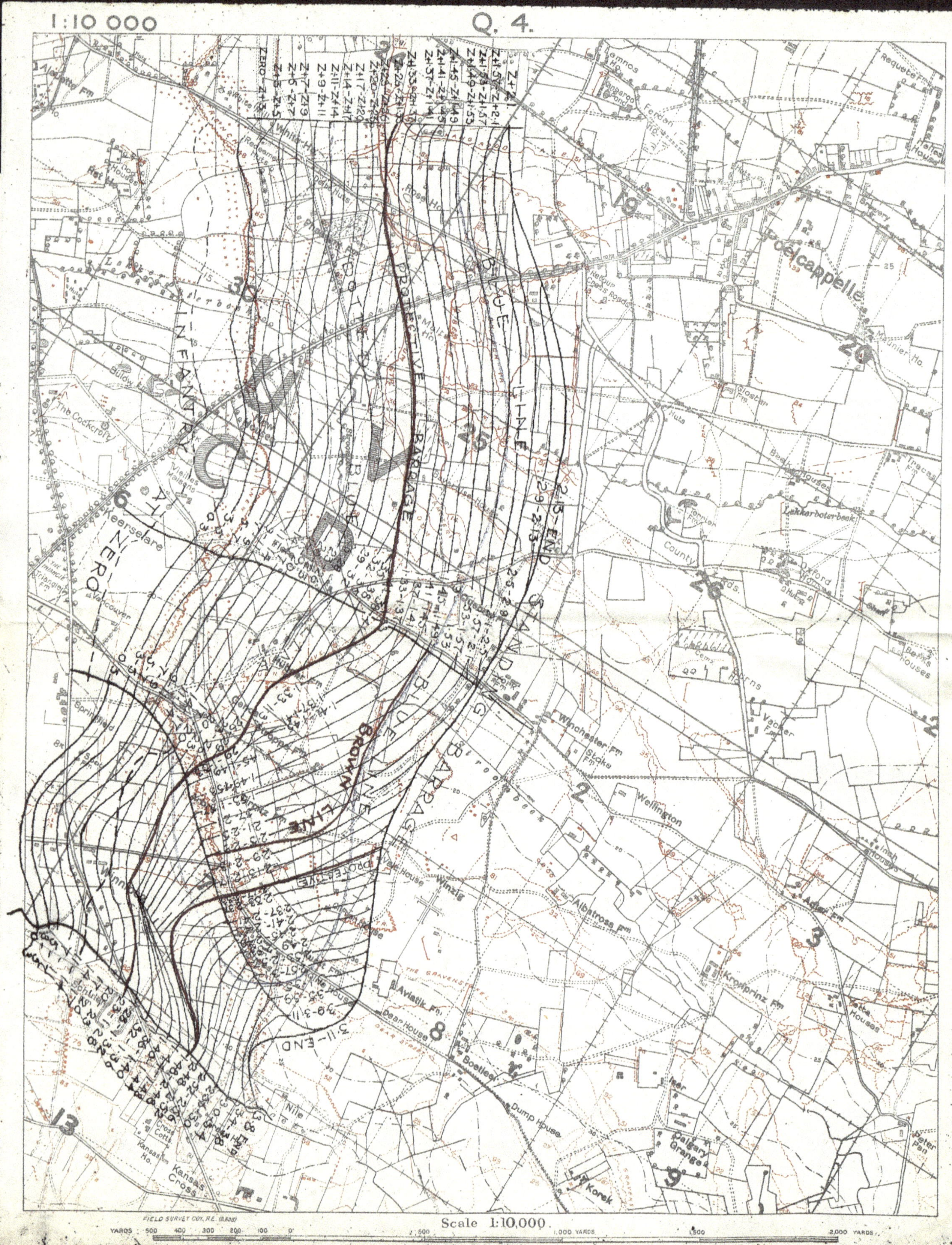
1:10 000
Q. 4.
Poelcappelle
Keerselare
Vancouver
The Cockcroft
Winchester Fm
Wellington
Albatross Fm
Kronprinz Fm
Aviatik Fm
Dean House
Boetleer
Dump House
Calgary Grange
Kansas Cross
Lekkerboterbeek
BROWN LINE
BLUE LINE
PROTECTIVE BARRAGE
Scale 1:10,000
FIELD SURVEY COY. R.E.
YARDS 500 400 300 200 100 0 500 1,000 YARDS 1,500 2,000 YARDS

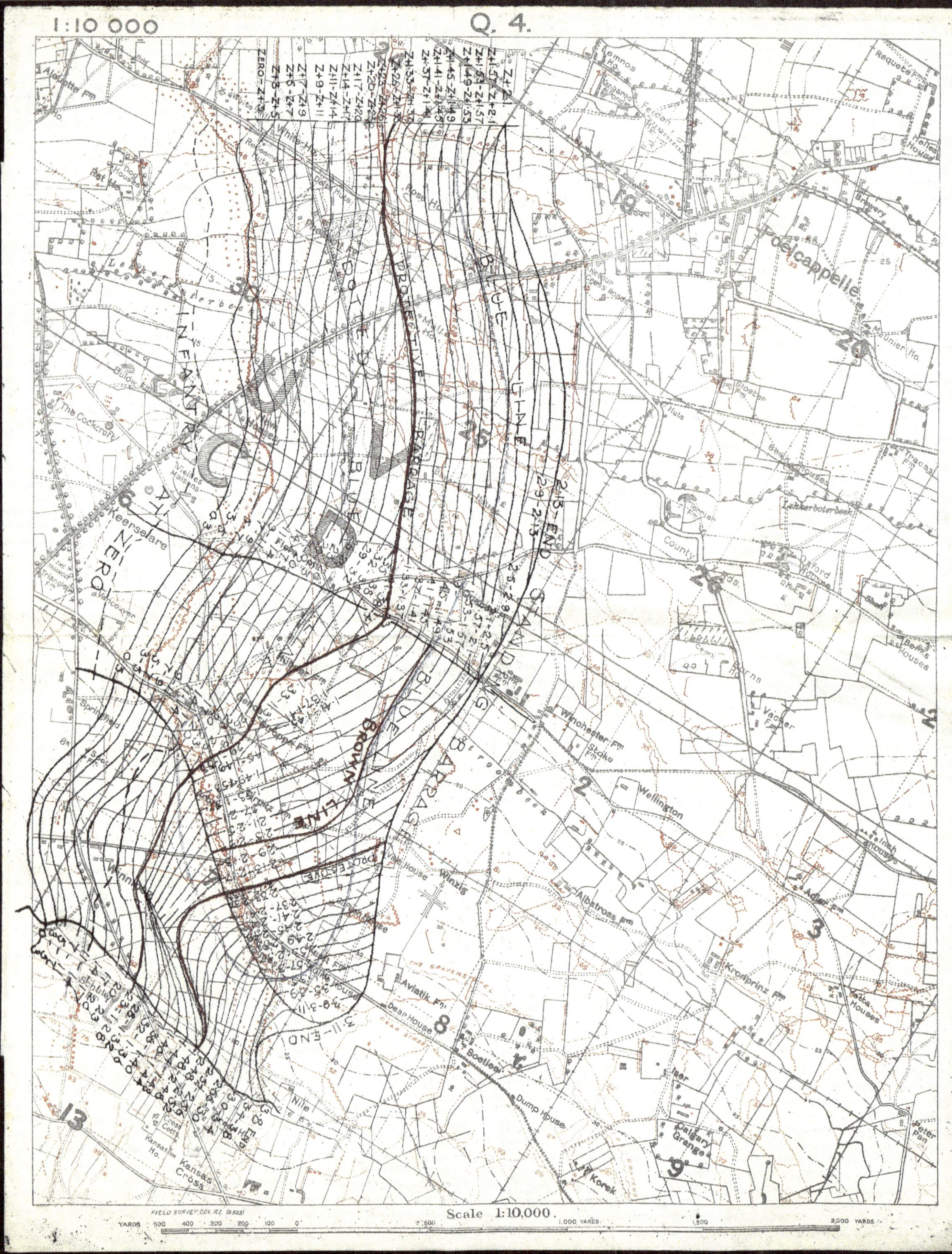

1:10 000
Q. 4.
Poelcappelle
Scale 1:10,000
FIELD SURVEY COY. R.E.

1:10 000
Q. 4.
Poelcappelle
Keerselare
Requete Fm
Lemnos Ho
Ferdan Ho
White Mill
White Ho
Redeemer Huts
Rose Ho
Pheasant Fm
Malta Ho
Meunier Ho
Gloster Fm
Bulow
The Cockcroft
New Houses
Vieilles Maisons
Flora Cott
Quebec Fm
Tweed Ho
County
Oxford Houses
Berks Houses
Barns
Vacher Fm
Hubner Fm
Springfield
Genoa
Winchester Fm
Stroppe Fm
Stroombeek
Wellington
Kirpitz Fm
Vancouver
Winnipeg
Winzig
Albatross Fm
Inch Houses
Adler Fm
Kronprinz Fm
Wurst Fm
Olive House
Aviatik Fm
Dear House
Boetleer
Dump House
Calgary Grange
Korek
Nile
Green Ho
Kansas Ho
Kansas Cross
Schuler Fm
Peter Pan
24
19
30
25
20
26
6
1
2
7
8
3
13
9
U
V
C
D
FIELD SURVEY COY. R.E.
Scale 1:10,000.
YARDS 500 400 300 200 100 0 500 1,000 YARDS 1,500 2,000 YARDS

www.ingramcontent.com/pod-product-compliance
Lightning Source LLC
Chambersburg PA
CBHW080839010526
44114CB00017B/2334
9781474531337